Britishness
Perspectives on the
Britishness Question

WILEY-
BLACKWELL

Britishness
Perspectives on the Britishness Question

Edited by
Andrew Gamble and Tony Wright

Wiley-Blackwell
In association with *The Political Quarterly*

Blackwell Publishing was acquired by John Wiley & Sons in February 2007. Blackwell's publishing programme has been merged with Wiley's global Scientific, Technical and Medical business to form Wiley-Blackwell.

Registered Office
John Wiley & Sons Ltd, The Atrium, Southern Gate, Chichester, West Sussex, PO19 8SQ, United Kingdom

Editorial Offices
350 Main Street, Malden, MA 02148-5020, USA
9600 Garsington Road, Oxford, OX4 2DQ, UK
The Atrium, Southern Gate, Chichester, West Sussex, PO19 8SQ, UK

For details of our global editorial offices, for customer services, and for information about how to apply for permission to reuse the copyright material in this book please see our website at www.wiley.com/wiley-blackwell.

Library of Congress Cataloging-in-Publication Data
Britishness : perspectives on the Britishness question / edited by Andrew Gamble and Tony Wright.
    p. cm.
  Includes bibliographical references and index.
  ISBN 978-1-4051-9269-9 (pbk.)
  1. National characteristics, British–History. 2. Group identity–Great Britain. 3. Nationalism–Great Britain–History. 4. Great Britain–Civilization. 5. Multiculturalism–Great Britain. 6. British–Ethnic identity. 7. Decentralization in government–Great Britain. I. Gamble, Andrew. II. Wright, Anthony, 1948- III. Political quarterly.

  DA118.B727 2009
  305.82'1–dc22   2009032798

A catalogue record for this book is available from the British Library.

Set in 10.5/12pt Palatino by Anne Joshua & Associates, Oxford

Printed in the UK by the Charlesworth Group

Contents

In memory of Bernard Crick,
who died while this book was in preparation

Notes on Contributors

Arthur Aughey is Professor of Politics at the University of Ulster.

Linda Colley is Shelby M. C. Davis 1958 Professor of History at Princeton University.

Bernard Crick was one of the longest serving editors of *The Political Quarterly*, holder of Chairs at Sheffield and Birkbeck, founder of the Orwell Prize, and Chair of the Advisory Group on the teaching of citizenship and democracy. His many books include *George Orwell: A Life*, and *In Defence of Politics*. He died in 2008.

Richard English is Professor of Politics at Queen's University, Belfast, and the author of *Armed Struggle: The History of the IRA* (2003) and *Irish Freedom: The History of Nationalism in Ireland* (2006).

Andrew Gamble is Professor of Politics, University of Cambridge, and joint editor of *The Political Quarterly*.

Gerry Hassan is a Demos Associate and Honorary Research Fellow at Glasgow Caledonian University. He was Head of the Demos Scotland 2020 and Glasgow 2020 programmes and is author and editor of numerous books on UK and Scottish politics.

Richard Hayton is a Research Associate and Tutor in the Department of Politics at the University of Sheffield, where he recently successfully completed his PhD thesis on contemporary Conservative politics.

Robert Hazell is Professor of Government and the Constitution and Director of the Constitution Unit at University College London.

Peter Hennessy is Attlee Professor of Contemporary British History at Queen Mary, University of London and author of *Never Again: Britain 1945-51* and *Having It So Good: Britain in the Fifties*.

Charlie Jeffery is Professor of Politics and Head of the School of Social and Political Science at the University of Edinburgh.

Peter Kellner is a recovering journalist and President of YouGov.

Michael Kenny is a Professor of Politics at the University of Sheffield and Visiting Research Fellow at the ippr.

Iain McLean is Professor of Politics, University of Oxford, Official Fellow Nuffield College.

David Marquand is former Principal and honorary fellow of Mansfield College Oxford.

Bhikhu Parekh is Emeritus Professor of Political Philosophy at the Universities of Westminster and Hull.

Jean Seaton is Professor of Media History at the University of Westminster.

Varun Uberoi is Post-Doctoral Fellow at the Department of Politics and International Relations, University of Oxford.

David Willetts is the Shadow Secretary of State for Universities and Skills with special responsibility for Family Policy. He has been the Member of Parliament for Havant since 1992.

Tony Wright is the Labour MP for Cannock Chase and chair of the Public Administration Select Committee. Before entering Parliament in 1992 he was Reader in Politics at the University of Birmingham where he is now an Honorary Professor.

Introduction: The Britishness Question

ANDREW GAMBLE and TONY WRIGHT

THESE are difficult times to be British. Maybe it was even harder at the time of Hadrian, when the Romans used to refer to the inhabitants of the islands they had conquered as Britunculi, loosely translated as 'wretched little Britons'. But for the last three centuries the Britons have not been subjects of a foreign empire but the creators of their own, and much effort was put into making the identity of Britishness an identity of which all the component nations of Great Britain and later the United Kingdom could be proud. The union of Scotland and England in 1707 made necessary a new nomenclature for the state, to accommodate the Scots, which was later extended to the nations the English had conquered, the Irish and the Welsh. The term 'Briton' began to be used indiscriminately to mean anyone who was a citizen of the United Kingdom. For a short time this allowed for the Irish to be promoted to the status of being West Britons, just as the Scots were North Britons. But while there was some historical warrant for applying the terms 'Britain' and 'British' to the island of Britain, it was hard to treat the island of Ireland as part of Britain, or to call the groups of islands the British Isles, since that implied that the larger island was the only one that mattered. The issue is complicated by the fact that some of the keenest adherents of Britishness and a British identity are today to be found in Northern Ireland. But this merely reminds us that it is in the end cultures and communities that are important for identity, rather than particular territories.

Being British is less easy than it was, because the state which underpinned the British identity is no longer the confident structure of earlier times. Many British people have become much more aware of their separate identity as Scottish, or English or Welsh, and for an increasing number of them this other national identity has come to be regarded as a primary identity, and the British identity only a secondary identity, or even an identity they no longer want. Nationalists draw the conclusion that the primary national identity should determine the boundaries of the state, and press for the break-up of the United Kingdom into its component nations. On this view, the British state and the British national identity was always a sham, a political creation which suited the interests of those groups in all nations which favoured the Union and wished to create a new supranational focus for loyalty and allegiance.

The United Kingdom certainly has some peculiarities. From the start it was a multinational state, dominated by the largest nation, the English. Yet there were only sporadic attempts to obliterate the national cultures and national allegiances of the four component nations, and create a new national culture in their place. English became the common language, but the other languages survived, and eventually revived—very strongly in the case of Wales. The

Published by Blackwell Publishing Ltd, 9600 Garsington Road, Oxford OX4 2DQ, UK and 350 Main Street, Malden, MA 02148, USA

kind of nation-building that was practised in many other countries, aimed at rooting out older allegiances and identities, and constructing a single nation and a single national identity, did not succeed and was only partially attempted in the United Kingdom. Part of the explanation is that there was no need. Apart from the Irish, the other nations of the United Kingdom were full and willing participants, and accepted the British identity alongside their other national identity, seeing them as complementary rather than conflicting.

The Union suffered its first major blow with the separation of Ireland from the United Kingdom in 1922, but although extremely serious for the British state and its Empire, its effects within the rest of the Union were muted because so many of the Irish, apart from the Unionists in the North, had always been ambivalent about accepting that they were British, and an increasing minority had been violently opposed. In the rest of the United Kingdom the allegiance to the British state was still exceptionally strong, and the roots of Britishness went deep. The establishment of democracy in the twentieth century increased rather than diminished ideas of Britishness, both through the creation of many new British institutions, such as the BBC and the welfare state, and also through the experience of war, and the enormous sacrifices made in defence of the British state and the British Empire. Universal welfare and universal military service gave Britishness a solid basis in everyone's experience.

The weakening of the attachment to Britishness has been associated with the weakening of the two enterprises that defined a large part of what Britishness meant in the twentieth century: empire and welfare. States do not need an overriding purpose, and are often better without one as Arthur Aughey has argued, but in a multinational state like the United Kingdom, the common enterprises were very important in sustaining support for the British state in the four nations. Take the common enterprises and purposes away and there are still many common institutions, including Parliament, the monarchy, the armed forces and the BBC, but there are also factors which emphasise difference rather than unity. Sport, for example, is often organised in terms of the four nations rather than the United Kingdom. Team GB in the Olympics is a notable exception, but there is never likely to be a Team GB in the World Cup. The use of separate national anthems rather than the British national anthem in several sports has grown.

Membership of the European Union makes small European nations viable, and makes multinational states like the United Kingdom appear overcentralised and anachronistic. The relationship of Ireland with Britain has improved considerably since Ireland joined the EU, and it is an example noted by Nationalists in Scotland and Wales. Unionists argue that it is better to be part of one of the large states in the EU to exert greater influence over decision making, but nationalists counter that many specific regional interests, like Scottish fishing, are ignored or traded away by the metropolitan power. The continued existence of the United Kingdom is something of a historical anomaly in contemporary world politics. Most of the other large

2

multinational states in Europe have long since collapsed. The principle of national self-determination has achieved an ascendancy unthinkable one hundred years ago. The Union was undertaken in very different circumstances, and its rationale in a world of nation-states and larger supranational frameworks like the European Union has come under scrutiny. Small nations can belong to the EU and participate in its institutions without needing to be part of larger multinational units.

None of this means that Britishness or the Union are doomed to dwindle away. The break-up of the United Kingdom has been confidently predicted many times, but it continues to survive. Great multinational states which foundered in the past, and with which the United Kingdom is sometimes compared, such as the Ottoman Empire or Austria–Hungary, are not very good precedents, since they were not democracies. Ireland separated from the United Kingdom before the United Kingdom became a democracy. The experience of established democracies shows that it is very rare for such states to break up. The way democracies work, however imperfectly, means that concessions are offered to minorities that demand them, and this granting of autonomy decreases the attractiveness of leaving the union altogether. States tend to break up because of intransigence and coercion. It is much harder for it to happen when the centre shows flexibility and tries to accommodate the demands of its regions.

Present fears for the Union and the survival of Britishness stem in part from the implications of the devolution measures introduced by the Blair government, which saw the establishment of a Welsh Assembly and the reestablishment of a Scottish Parliament. At first the impact of devolution was muted because both Scotland and Wales elected Labour dominated administrations, which worked fairly closely with the Labour government at Westminster. All changed in 2007, when the Scottish Nationalists took control of the Scottish executive, and Plaid Cymru entered into coalition with Labour in Cardiff.

Such a test for the Union and for the idea of Britishness was bound to happen sooner or later, once devolution had been decided on. But support for the nationalist parties is not yet matched by support for independence, and there are numerous hurdles before Scotland or Wales could actually separate from the UK. But the erosion of support for Unionist parties, particularly in Scotland, is palpable, and it helps to explain why Gordon Brown has set out to revive the idea of Britishness. In itself this is nothing new. A discourse on Britishness and how to promote it has always been a necessary part of any Unionist project in a multinational state like the United Kingdom. Recognising the distinctiveness of the four nations has been accompanied by an emphasis upon the unitary character of the association. This is pre-eminently the domain of Britishness. To be British is to feel a part of the whole United Kingdom, not just one of its component nationalities.

The high tide of Britishness in the 1940s was supported by the still strong enterprise of empire and the new enterprise of social justice. The bonds of Britishness were intensified by the championing of these common enterprises by the two main Unionist parties, Labour and Conservative, which had representation throughout the United Kingdom. A large part of their identities came to be bound up with these common enterprises, and the strength of these parties contributed to the strength of the Union. The weakening of the Union in the last few decades has come about in part through the weakening of the common enterprises, so that the purpose of the Union and therefore of Britishness has seemed less obvious. At the same time, the strength of nationalism has grown, so that the political spaces of the United Kingdom are no longer contested simply between the Unionist parties. In Scotland in particular the SNP openly questions the need for the common enterprises that have come to define Britishness.

Brown has argued that Britain should not retreat into the 'nineteenth century conceptions of blood, race, and territory'. He wants a refreshed British identity, once again celebrating something that is bigger than the sum of its parts. But it is sometimes hard to discern exactly what this new British identity could be. Brown argues that Britain used to be defined by certain achievements, in particular its empire, its military victories, its tradition of liberty, and its vibrant civil society. But he acknowledges that many of these achievements lie in a receding past. Britain is no longer able to celebrate its empire in the way that it did one hundred years ago; it no longer has daily proof of its own greatness. Brown's new idea of Britishness, at least until the credit crunch cast its long shadow, was that it should express Britain's economic success in the previous ten years, which he used to proclaim in his budget speeches. He argued that this economic success allowed the development of a new sense of national purpose. The new enterprise was to continue to strive to be one of the most successful economies in the new global economy, able to weather its storms and meet its challenges. It all looked rather different after the great crash of 2008.

Brown's concept of Britishness is built on a number of key values—liberty for all, responsibility by all, fairness to all—and a number of key qualities— creativity, innovation, enterprise, and internationalism. Many critics have argued that talking of Britishness in terms of values rather than policies or institutions is rather nebulous and hard to pin down. Brown's concrete proposals for encouraging a sense of Britishness are distinctly meagre. There have been suggestions for a British national day, for encouragement to Britons to fly the flag in their gardens, making the teaching of citizenship involve instruction in British history, for the creation of an Institute of Britishness, and a national conversation on Britishness, charged with drawing up a list of the values everyone can agree on as constituting part of Britishness.

This will be hard to deliver, especially at a time when financial crisis has shattered the basis of the common economic enterprise Brown seeks to promote. Brown's belief that the Union can be held together if only everyone will acknowledge their shared British heritage and shared British values ignores the fact that many of the values are so general that they are not specific to Britain or British culture; and too great an emphasis on common values mistakes the real strength of Britishness. People in different parts of the UK do not have to accept exactly the same values and sense of purpose in order to support remaining British and part of the Union. They can do so on entirely pragmatic grounds and on grounds of mutual interest, while being quite diverse in their choice of values and lifestyles. The future of Britishness may depend on sustaining those institutions which already embody it, and which allow citizens to feel part of the same community. Allegiance and commitment are often strongest when they do not need to be put into words.

This does not mean that a contemporary conversation about Britishness is not needed, or worth having. There is a long history of such conversation; and other periods (such as the generation following the Second World War) when it largely falls quiet and unspoken. As circumstances change, so does the nature of the conversation. It is not difficult to identify those contemporary circumstances which have given a new urgency to the conversation about Britishness. There is the impact of immigration and multiculturalism. There is the assault from Islamic fundamentalism. Then there is the new political assertiveness from the constituent nations of the multinational kingdom. Yet even this familiar list does not exhaust the environment of change. Old solidarities have eroded. Shared British enterprises (notably empire and war) have disappeared from view. Globalisation has removed traditional anchors. Europe as a political association has challenged national sovereignty. International mobility has quickened, making loyalties more contingent.

All this is shorthand, but it is more than enough to prompt a revived conversation about Britishness. Nor is it surprising that a British government concerned with social cohesion and the future integrity of the United Kingdom should want to promote such a conversation. Indeed, without any official intervention, the debate is already taking place, and with some popular vigour. It surfaces every time the cultural or religious demands of a minority group to behave differently rub up against law or majority norms. It is heard from nationalists in Scotland who demand political independence, and from those in England who think the Scots are already getting a better deal than the English. It does not require any official intervention to get a conversation about Britishness going, although it may help to structure it.

It may also, unless it is careful and honest, help to stifle or distort it. Any attempt at imposition would be doomed, and (in a British way) lampooned. Histories are always more complex and ambiguous than official lists of 'British values' are apt to allow for, just as values are always more contested. Nor is it clear whether the 'British values' that the Brown government wants to see articulated are intended to be descriptive or aspirational. If the former, they will have to include some decidedly unlovely characteristics of con-temporary Britain (such as the fact, reported here by Peter Kellner, that for those under 35, Britain's top-scoring attribute is 'drunken', just beating 'democratic'). If the latter, then more intellectual rigour (as well as political boldness) will be required.

There is also the matter of whether values are intended to be substantive or procedural. The former are notoriously tricky, especially if they are intended to distinguish 'British' values from those held by other people or wider traditions. A more urgent, and useful, task might be to give attention to key procedural values, such as tolerance towards the views of others, the manner of resolving differences, living together and reaching agreement. Instead of trying to find a version of Britishness that identifies it with social cohesion or political union, it may be better to concentrate on those procedural values which enable difference and disagreement to be negotiated in a tolerably civilised way. This would not be a celebratory exercise, but one of advocacy, argument and persuasion.

It would find assistance from what has often been claimed as a British attribute, which is a disposition to muddle through and not push matters to their logical extreme in pursuit of abstract principle. On this view, 'asymmetric' devolution is not an affront to constitutional reason but a sensible way of accommodating political change. Living with anomalies can be a recognition that some solutions are worse than the problems. Similarly, negotiating cultural differences in a way that seeks to find some common ground can be more productive of social cohesion than the rigid application of abstract principles. This also recognises that, whatever else it is, Britishness is a cluster of attributes and tendencies, the balance between them always contested and constantly being reshaped. It is the product and expression of common experience, but of an experience that is forever on the move.

What now seems to be on the move is Britain itself. Underlying much of the contemporary discussion of Britishness is the question of whether Britain is in the process of breaking up. Nationalism in Scotland finds its echo in a quickening of Englishness, both demanding political expression. There is talk of a world 'after Britain'. Devolution was intended to keep Scotland in the union, but if Scotland does vote for independence it is clear that Westminster will not stand in the way. As the dominant partner in the union, England seems remarkably relaxed about Scotland going its own way if that is what it wants, but much less relaxed about perceived inequalities within the devolved union. This makes it unlikely that an official mobilisation of Britishness as a way of saving the union will succeed.

This does not mean that the union is doomed; only that its future is a matter of political choice. Already its shape has radically changed, a union state but not a uniform state, and will inevitably change further. This is why the distinction between Britishness as identity and Britishness as political association is so important. Most people carry with them a collection of identities and loyalties, in an often disorderly mixture, and this is perfectly compatible with membership of the same civic association. Survey evidence seems to suggest that this is still the case for most people in Britain, who see themselves (but do not describe themselves) as, in varying degrees, Scottish–British or Welsh–British or English–British (and many other hybrids too).

The point is not that Britishness is just about membership of a political association and identity or culture is about something else, but that the distinction is important. Britishness is about both, but they are not the same. An independent Scotland will have made a decision about political association, but it will still carry the historical and cultural baggage of Britishness. A Scotland that rejects political independence will not have diminished its Scottishness. The very capaciousness of 'Britishness', a mansion of many rooms, enables multiple identities and loyalties to flourish within it, which is a strong argument for not trying to pin it down in a way that excludes.

There is great merit in something so slippery and elusive, perhaps even something 'very British'. Those in search of firmer ground prefer to confine Britishness to a set of institutions and bundle of interests, buttressing attachment to a multinational state. There is attraction in this, and it recognises that issues of identity need to be disentangled from issues about constitutional arrangements. However, it surely goes too far to suggest that Britishness is only about institutions and interests, notwithstanding the key role of these in underpinning the British state. As contributors to this volume point out, central 'British' institutions (such as the National Health Service) are anyway being denationalised (or renationalised) in a variety of ways as devolution develops. Whether this is a threat to Britishness, or simply an opportunity to combine commonality and diversity, remains to be seen.

From a number of directions, then, there is an attempt to engage with Britishness in a way that goes beyond the conditions of formal citizenship. In particular the impetus comes from a much more culturally variegated society, and the need to establish the nature of the common civic space. From another direction come the fissiparous pressures from a disuniting kingdom, and the need to consider the future of the union. There are competing versions of Britishness, as there always have been, with different consequences. It remains to be seen if Britishness becomes a comfortable accommodation with plurality and diversity, and whether its political expression remains a multinational union. This is a matter for political choice. But it is also a matter for statecraft—for negotiating change, accommodating and adjusting, not pushing to extremes—which the British political tradition likes to think it has been rather good at.

These are all themes that are explored by contributors to this book. There is no orthodoxy here, or common line. There are different approaches, lively disagreements, and disputed conclusions. The contributors were asked to engage with the question of Britishness in whatever way they wanted to. This means that the chapters range widely, but together provide a rich exploration of Britishness with direct relevance to contemporary debate.

There is a reminder by Marquand that there has always been a conversation about Britishness, but that it needs now to be an honest conversation—'a dishonest conversation would do more harm than good'—that confronts myth with reality. Colley revisits the themes of her landmark *Britons: Forging the Nation: 1707–1837* and makes suggestions to remedy 'the negligence that politicians here seem often to demonstrate in regard to issues of national identity and culture'. The need for careful distinctions is argued by Parekh, but a proper wariness about 'Britishness' should nevertheless acknowledge that it 'relates to what binds us together, makes us this community rather than some other'. He further argues that Britain 'badly needs a coherent and inspirational conception of its identity'. Whether there is a justification for the state involving itself in such matters is examined by Uberoi and McLean, who argue that the need for mutual trust and common sacrifice means that 'a justifiable role for those who run the state is to use it to clarify what British people share'.

For Willetts, Britishness has 'a marvellous openness' but its weak cultural identity (unlike Englishness, or Scottishness) means that is should be regarded as a political identity represented by a set of political institutions. Kellner trawls survey evidence to show that Britishness 'means different things to different people'. Yet values and traditions score consistently higher than institutions as attributes of Britishness. While arguing that Britishness 'can only be a co-production', not an imposition, Seaton identifies the role of key institutions and in particular the BBC in 'metabolising the nation's sense of self'. Hassan critically dissects the evolution of Gordon Brown's political thinking, and presents his preoccupation with Britishness as 'part of his eternal quest to see the world in terms of moral missions and crusades'. Hazell is also interested in how Brown refers to Britishness (in what is 'always essentially the same speech'), but argues that he 'misses something . . . in omitting the *interests* and *institutions* which bind the British together, as well as their values'.

What devolution means for Britishness (and vice versa) is a recurrent theme. Jeffery argues that while there may be shared values, there are increasingly different institutional structures and policy outcomes. In his view the United Kingdom has so far 'failed to identify how 'Britishness'—in this sense some conception of the interests shared by all citizens, across all UK-level, English and devolved jurisdictions—can be understood, debated and delivered by the post-devolution political system'. How the increased political salience of Englishness fits with Britishness is considered by Richard English et al., who reject the notion of a zero-sum game and want to consider 'how a positive vision of Englishness can complement, rather than threaten, a rejuvenated civic Britishness'. In similar vein Aughey contests 'the chipper certainties of the narrative of disintegration' and explores the grounds upon which 'a refurbished common citizenship can be sustained within the United Kingdom'.

Someone who has done more than anyone else to advance both the theory and practice of citizenship in Britain is Bernard Crick, who sadly died at the turn of the year. His contribution to this volume will have been one of the last pieces he wrote, and we dedicate the book to him. He is scathing about attempts to define, or press into political service, a conception of Britishness: it is 'political folly for politicians, or anyone else, to attempt to *define* or redefine such a protean concept'. In particular, 'Britishness does not explain why the United Kingdom has held together, nor does it validate the recent and topical belief that by lack of clarity about Britishness the UK may fall apart'. Finally, Hennessy reminds us of someone who did, memorably, put 'the shared compost that has made us' into incomparable language. This is Churchill's Dover speech of 1946, at the high tide of Britishness, invoking 'our own English and British way of life' with its 'tolerances and decencies'. It all seemed so much more straightforward then.

'Bursting with Skeletons': Britishness after Empire

DAVID MARQUAND

The condition of Britain Question

PARTICULARLY at a time when tormenting Gordon Brown has become a favourite national sport, it is all too easy to mock his attempt to stimulate a national debate on Britishness. One frequent tactic, beloved of cocksure academics, is to say, with a knowing smirk, that talking about Britishness is itself un-British. Another is to insist that other nations do not discuss their national identities, and that it is therefore indecent for the British to do so. Yet the truth could hardly be more different. Russians have been arguing about Russianness since the nineteenth century, when Westernisers and Slavophiles anxiously debated the nature and destiny of their extraordinary country. The same is true of the United States. Books about America's God-given role as the 'city on a hill', as the last best hope of suffering humanity, have been pouring from the presses since the American Revolution. And a fierce, sometimes bloody dispute about Frenchness has been a central theme of French intellectual and political history since 1789.

Exactly the same has been true of Britain. After the Act of Union, which set up a new, and at first highly insecure British state in place of the pre-existing English and Scottish states, immense quantities of emotional energy and rhetorical skill were devoted to forging a 'British' nation and a 'British' identity, subsuming the several nations and identities of the British archipelago. *Rule Britannia* and *The British Grenadiers* are two particularly evocative examples; *God Save the Queen* is a rather less evocative one. Meanwhile, a favourite trope of Whig rhetoric (and the Whigs ruled Britain for most of the eighteenth century) was that the Glorious Revolution and Hanoverian Succession had made Britain an exemplar of ordered freedom and peaceful evolution, unique in the world. Edmund Burke castigated George III's 'King's Friends' for trying to subvert that constitution; defended the rebellious American colonists on the grounds that they breathed the spirit of British liberty; and fulminated against the French revolutionaries on the grounds that they were too blinded by specious theorising to follow the trail that Britain had blazed. In his reply to Burke, Tom Paine did his best to de-mystify the hallowed Whig constitution, based on precedent and prescription, and persuade his readers to campaign for a better one, embodying fundamental human rights. But though Paine appealed to natural, God-given human rights, Burke's argument turned on the assumption that the freedoms that the ancient British constitution guaranteed were rooted in the specificities of

Published by Blackwell Publishing Ltd, 9600 Garsington Road, Oxford OX4 2DQ, UK and 350 Main Street, Malden, MA 02148, USA

Britain's history and culture. The debate was, in other words, an inescapably British one.

So was the century-long debate over the relationship between Ireland and Great Britain. The fierce debates over Catholic Emancipation in the 1820s and over Irish Home Rule in the 1880s and 1910s went to the heart of Britain's identity and self understanding; that was why they were so fierce. Gladstone and his fellow home rulers sought to reconstruct the British state and re-model the British constitution on generous and pluralistic lines; in doing so they were also seeking to redefine Britain's identity and self-understanding. Their Unionist opponents fought to preserve that identity and self-understanding in their existing, essentially monist forms. Each party to the conflict held up a mirror to the British in which they would supposedly recognise their true selves— fuzzily generous in the case of the Liberal mirror, and hard and intransigent in the case of the Unionist one. Much the same was true of the battle between Stanley Baldwin and Winston Churchill over Dominion status for India. Baldwin fought for a vision of Britain as India's tutor in the values and practices of self-government, and of the British empire as a collaborative commonwealth of moral equals. Churchill fought for an empire of power and glory, rooted in enduring British superiority to Britain's non-white subjects.

Politicians were not alone in debating Britishness. The 'condition of England Question' that preoccupied Victorian intellectuals as diverse as Thomas Carlyle, George Eliot, Matthew Arnold, John Ruskin and Edward Carpenter was, in reality, a 'condition of Britain' question. The great Whig historians, T. B. Macaulay and (later) G. M. Trevelyan were not just historians; they were the hymnodists of a particular vision of Britain and Britishness as the home of a unique combination of ordered freedom, peaceful evolution and responsive government. J. R. Seeley's *The Expansion of England* would have been more appropriately entitled *The Expansion of Britain*; when Kipling asked 'What do they know of England who only England know?' he could equally well have asked the question about Britain. The same is true of George Orwell's quirky, occasionally curmudgeonly and wonderfully eloquent wartime depiction of 'England' as a unique and special place, whose people were gentler than other peoples, whose grass was greener, whose coins were heavier and whose culture was uniquely shaped by 'solid breakfasts and gloomy Sundays'. Famously, Orwell saw his England of the imagination as 'a rather stuffy Victorian family . . . with all its cupboards bursting with skeletons', and with 'the wrong members in control'.[1] But when he talked of England, he meant Britain.

A providential nation

Naturally, the wide-ranging, long-drawn-out, and often acrimonious national conversation about Britain and Britishness reached no conclusions. Different traditions, different visions and different narratives jostled with each other in confused and confusing ways. Orwell's Britain was not G. M. Trevelyan's; Carlyle's bore little resemblance to Matthew Arnold's. All the same, certain themes cropped up again and again. For virtually all the protagonists, Britain was an exceptional nation, and the British an exceptional people. They were uniquely freedom-loving, and at the same time uniquely oceanic and uniquely imperial; and their imperial, oceanic vocation was inextricably connected with their love of freedom. When the then colonial secretary, Viscount Goderich, declared in 1833 that the purpose of Britain's imperial policy was to embed 'the spirit of civil liberty' in 'distant regions',[2] he used a rhetorical trope, which was to be heard again and again for well over a century—and to which Tony Blair was to give his own special gloss at the start of the twenty-first century.

It was, of course, profoundly misleading, as well as blatantly condescending. The British Raj in India, by common consent the brightest jewel in the British Crown, was based ultimately on force, as was Britain's rule over her vast colonial empire in Africa. And the notion that distant regions would benefit from the British spirit of civil liberty presupposed British superiority to other peoples. But this did not detract from its persuasive power. The trope encapsulated a Myth with a capital 'M'—not only in the sense that it distorted reality, but in the deeper sense that it gave its votaries a vocation and an identity in which they could take pride.

It told the British, not just that they were a uniquely freedom-loving and oceanic people, but that they had *become* a people when they decided to turn their backs on continental absolutism and 'plant the flag of liberty beyond the ocean'.[3] For the half-American Winston Churchill, it also told them something even more uplifting: that, by virtue of their uniquely oceanic and freedom-loving character the British were part of a world-wide family of freedom-loving 'English-speaking peoples'.[4] George V's speech on the occasion of the Royal Jubilee in 1935 (drafted by G. M. Trevelyan) belonged to the same genre. Britain's balanced constitution, he enthused, sprang from 'the impulse towards liberty, justice and social improvement *inherent* in our people down the ages'. (My italics.) His audience, he added, should give thanks that 'under our flag of freedom, so many millions eat their daily bread, in far distant lands and climates, with none to make them afraid.'[5] (What Irish Republicans and Indian nationalists made of that is not recorded.)

In moments of exaltation and danger, Britishness had an even grander dimension. The British were not only uniquely oceanic and freedom loving; they were a *providential* people, summoned by a higher power to fight for freedom against slavery, and for good against evil. That dimension was particularly evident in the glorious, terrible summer of 1940, when Britain glowered in lonely and powerless defiance at a Nazi-dominated continent. It suffused Churchill's great speech after Dunkirk, promising that, even if the home island were 'subjugated and starving' the 'Empire beyond the seas, armed and guarded by the British Fleet' would fight on 'until, in God's good time' the new world came to the rescue of the old.[6] The same note had sounded in the Younger Pitt's defiant boast that 'England' had saved herself by her exertions and would save Europe by her example. In a rather more mystical fashion it had also echoed through Blake's haunting lines evoking a vision of the 'Holy Lamb of God' walking on England's pleasant pastures, and of Jerusalem miraculously resurrected 'in England's green and pleasant land'. Milton's vision of revolutionary London as the 'mansion house of liberty', and his boast that God had revealed himself 'as His manner is, first to his Englishmen',[7] struck essentially the same note.

There was more than one version of the Myth of imperial, oceanic, freedom-loving and, at a pinch, providential Britishness. Socialists and Radicals, like George Orwell and Michael Foot, played down, and sometimes even dissented from, its imperial dimension. But, as Foot showed in his remarkably bellicose speech in the Commons debate on the eve of the Falklands war, his dissent did not go very far. In his own special way, he was imbued as strongly with oceanic patriotism as was that inveterate champion of Britain's world role, Ernest Bevin. And Orwell's contempt for the Bloomsbury intellectual 'with his mechanical snigger' exceeded even his loathing for the selfish and stupid British ruling class. A. J. P. Taylor once mischievously said that the unilateralists who joined the Campaign for Nuclear Disarmament in the 1950s and 1960s were 'the last imperialists'; and there was something in it. The campaign counterposed a patriotism of morality to the patriotism of power. It was premised on the assumption that if Britain gave up her nuclear weapons, others would follow; that although she was no longer a great power in a military sense, she still possessed a special kind of moral authority that gave her the right and duty to teach other nations how to live.

As always, that shadowy figure, the man (or woman) in the street is harder to read. In a famous study, Robert Roberts wrote that the Salford slum-dwellers among whom he grew up before the First World War were 'staunchly patriotic. "They didn't know", it was said, "whether trade was good for the Empire or the Empire was good for trade, but they knew the Empire was theirs and they were going to support it." '[8] Roberts may have been untypical; the historian of empire, Bernard Porter, has argued forcefully that most working-class people were indifferent to it, while some were hostile.[9] But the indifferent and hostile had no counter-Myth to tell the British who they were and what their national vocation was. A few anti-imperialists may have flirted with the notion that the ruling class had forced the British working class into imperial aggrandisement against their will. J. A. Hobson, the precursor of Keynesian economics, saw imperialism as the product of a search for markets on the part of profit-hungry capitalists. But it was hard to construct a counter-Myth out of such uninspiring materials, and occasional attempts to do so were signally unsuccessful.

Not surprisingly. In sober truth, the British state was inescapably an imperial state. It came into being in the first place because the ruling elites in England and Scotland believed, albeit for different reasons, that Union would make it easier for them to hold their own in the endless struggle for wealth and power that shaped Europe's state system. Once it had come into existence it became the most successful imperial predator in modern European history. It beat the bigger and more populous French state in the race for empire—a victory only partly tarnished by the loss of the American colonies. By the end of her reign, the dominions of the Queen Empress Victoria covered a quarter of the earth's surface. The Royal Navy policed the world's sea lanes and the City of London dominated its capital markets. The myths and symbols of empire were everywhere. Regimental battle honours from half-forgotten colonial wars, Rudyard Kipling's Indian tales, G. A. Henty's schoolboy adventure stories, the ties of ethnicity that bound the 'mother country' to the self-governing white Dominions, and innumerable globes spattered with red all told the same story. For at least 200 years, empire—whether of power, or morality or both—was of Britain's essence. Anti-imperialists were shaped by it as much as imperialists, liberals and socialists as much as conservatives.

After Empire

Gordon Brown's rather down-beat attempt to encourage a national conversation on 'Britishness' comes into the story at this point. Naturally, his motives are mixed. As a Scot representing a Scottish constituency in the Westminster parliament, he is bound to see the spectre of Scottish secession from the Union not just as a political threat, but as an existential one. For him, far more than for any other Prime Minister since the end of the First World War, the end of the Union would spell political death. (Ramsay MacDonald, the only other Scottish Prime Minister since 1918, sat for a Welsh constituency when he first entered Number Ten, and later for an English one.) To overcome the threat of Scottish secession, Brown has to play the British card; and he hopes that a Britain-wide debate on Britishness will help him to do so.

But I doubt if this is his sole motive. I suspect he realises, more clearly than all but a handful of his Labour followers, that the existing British state, which mainstream British social democrats have traditionally seen as the chief agency for promoting social justice, is now broken-backed: that whatever may be true of 'the State' as a philosophical abstraction, the real-world British state is no longer the focus for the unquestioned loyalties of the society over which its presides; that it is no longer sustained by what Abraham Lincoln called 'the mystic chords of memory'. That realisation has been fundamental to the whole New Labour project. The vast middle class that holds the key to electoral success now views the state in essentially instrumental, hedonistic terms—as a consumerist machine for delivering higher living standards and even socially provided goods like better health care, to atomistic *individuals*, rather than as an agency for realising *collective* choices. In a society shot through with individualistic consumerism, redistribution is bound to be a sin that dares not speak its name. It is still feasible—just. But the open use of state power to improve the position of the poor minority at the expense of the vast middle class is a doomed enterprise. The only way to realise the traditional social-democratic commitment to redistribution is to pretend that it is not taking place. And that sets narrow limits on the policies of any social-democratic government.

This is the social-democratic case for a national conversation on Britishness, and it is a strong one. The content of the conversation is another matter. Brown's own contributions to it have been distinctly Whiggish—no bad thing in some ways, since the Whig tradition that goes back to Burke and Locke has a lot to be said for it. Ordered freedom and evolutionary progress *have* been among the hallmarks of modern British history, and they *should* command respect and even admiration. The British tradition of Whiggish gradualism and Whiggish tolerance helped us to escape the horrors of Fascism and Communism, and to liquidate our Empire with much less pain than the equivalent process caused in France or even Belgium.

The limits of Whiggery

But Whiggery is not enough. Brown was right to extol the 'British tradition of liberty' in his speech on the subject last autumn.[10] It is part of our heritage, and it is something to be proud of. But it is not the only part. There is an ugly side to Britishness as well; and even the sides of which we can be proud are more complex—and sometimes more ambivalent—than Brown saw fit to mention. British troops died fighting Nazism in the Second World War, but ninety years before, British troops had suppressed what used to be called the Indian Mutiny with ruthless savagery. The British empire was built, in part, on the slave trade; British settlers in Australia subjected the indigenous population to an appalling genocide. Milton deserved the praise Brown gave him in his speech on liberty; but the regime Milton served as Secretary for Foreign Tongues was responsible for the Drogheda massacre, in which defenceless women and children who had taken refuge in one of the town's churches were burned alive. Even in the Second World War Britain's record was not as spotless as we like to think. There was no military justification for the bombing of Dresden, which killed far more innocent people than any al-Qaeda atrocity has done, and which, by any reasonable reckoning, should rank as a war crime.

A conversation on Britishness that ignored the dark side of empire would be a travesty. The last thing we need is a national apology for crimes committed by our ancestors; by definition, that could do nothing for the victims and would only bolster the politics of inherited victimhood that reinforces the already dangerous tendency of our multicultural society to fragment into warring tribal enclaves. But we cannot converse honestly about Britishness without coming to terms with the shameful episodes in our history. And a dishonest conversation would do more harm than good.

So would a conversation that ignored the two most vexed questions that currently face the multinational British state—its relationships with continental

Europe on the one hand, and with the particular nations of the British archipelago on the other. The first has been a running sore ever since the Second World War. Immediately after the war, the then Foreign Secretary, Ernest Bevin, dreamed of a 'middle kingdom', led by Britain and consisting of the British Commonwealth and the war-devastated nations of western Europe, strong enough to hold the balance between capitalist America and totalitarian Russia.[11] But the dream turned out to be chimera; and, as everyone knows, when the six heartland countries of western Europe eventually came together in the Coal and Steel Community, Britain stood aloof. She took part in the European project in the end, but in a curiously resentful and suspicious way. The notion that the British are 'bad Europeans', unable or unwilling to play the Union game by the Union rules is baseless. The legion of British officials who take part in the endless horse-trading and power-sharing of the Union process fit rather well into the club: clubbability is something that British bureaucrats instinctively understand. The same applies to British members of the European parliament. But the people in whose name they act do not take Britain's European vocation for granted as even Eurosceptics mostly do in other European countries.

The Myth of Britain and Britishness that I tried to dissect a moment ago bears a large part of the blame. Deep down in the British psyche the vision of Britain as an exceptional, even providential nation still lurks. *We* are oceanic and freedom-loving. *They* are landlocked, and torn between anarchy and despotism. *We* belong to the world-wide family of English-speaking peoples and therefore enjoy a special relationship with the United States. *They* are incorrigibly inward-looking. Above all, *we* are moral, while *they* are cynical. It goes without saying that the gap between Myth and reality is enormous. Britain is exceptional only in the sense that all European nations (and indeed the pre-modern provinces whose bones can still be detected beneath the skins of the nation states of modern Europe) are exceptional. Europe is not a homogeneous monolith and never has been. French exceptionalism is at least as deep-seated as British; though few Germans still accept the notion of a unique German *Sonderweg*, or special path, it had a good run for its money and captured a substantial part of Germany's cultural and political history. Nor, for that matter, is Britain uniquely freedom-loving: it was in Paris, not London, that the revolutionary slogan of 'liberty, equality and fraternity' first burst on to the world. In the great revolutionary wars of the late-eighteenth and early-nineteenth centuries, the British fought for monarchical repression and the French for the Rights of Man. But national Myths rarely conform to reality, and no one should be surprised that ours does not.

The real point is that our Myth *distorts* reality and that, in doing so, it prevents us from understanding our history and knowing who we are. The truth is that British history has been part of European history since the Romans, and arguably for much longer. In medieval times, the Kings, Queens and great noblemen of England spoke French; and some of them had vast estates in France. Simon de Montfort, who is often credited with inventing the

English parliament, was a *French* nobleman as well as an English one. English churchmen belonged to a Europe-wide Church, whose head was bishop of Rome. The French wars, which helped to generate a specifically English national consciousness were not wars of England against France; they were wars of parts of what is now France against other parts.

After the great rupture of the Reformation, English Protestants saw themselves as part of a European family of Protestants, at war with popery. When the English landed class decided that they had to get rid of the Stuarts to safeguard their property and their religion, they turned to the Dutchman, William of Orange, for salvation. The debate between Arminians and orthodox Calvinists that figured so largely in the English civil wars was a European debate as well as an English one. Most of the apostles of British freedom lauded by Brown were protagonists in European debates extending far beyond the English Channel. One of Milton's most famous poems is a lament for a massacre of Alpine Calvinists perpetrated by Italian Catholics. John Stuart Mill was a passionate francophile, heavily influenced by Alexis de Tocqueville, and was buried in France. That *echt* Englishman, George Orwell, fought in the Spanish Civil War alongside Spanish anarchists and assorted Trotskyites. The world wars of the last century, which killed hundreds of thousands of British men and women, bankrupted the British state, and dealt a fatal blow to the British empire, were triggered by ethnic conflicts in East/Central Europe.

I don't suggest that a national conversation about Britishness should be deliberately designed to counter the Myth of sea-girt, freedom-loving British exceptionalism. Worthwhile conversations can't be designed. Nor can they produce clear, straightforward conclusions. Alternative voices have to be heard; and the talk has to be open-ended. The Russian conversation between Westernisers and Slavophiles is no nearer a resolution now than it was a century ago. The post-revolutionary French conversation about the meaning of Frenchness is as vigorous and indeterminate at the start of the twenty-first century as it was in Tocqueville's day. What I do suggest is that the conversation must focus, among other things, on the dilemmas, uncertainties and perversities of Britain's relationship with the rest of the European continent; and that what I have called the Myth (and what others will doubtless call a sober depiction of reality) must be open to searching scrutiny, instead of being taken for granted. Such a debate would be as unwelcome to the present Labour government as to the Conservative opposition. No heavy-weight British politician in either major party wants the issues I have been discussing to be brought out into the open. This is one of the strongest arguments for doing just that.

The worm in the British bud

Still less do Westminster politicians want a searching debate on the vexed relationship between the multinational British state and the nationalities it subsumes. The reconstruction of the British state to take account of non-English national aspirations was a crucial part of the New Labour project; and it was both its most successful element and its most original. Asymmetric devolution to elected assemblies in Edinburgh, Belfast and Cardiff, combined with the continuing supremacy of the Westminster parliament which was also the English parliament, was intended to draw the sting out of the varied nationalisms of the British periphery. The price was a transfer of competence and authority from Westminster to the non-English nations of the Union, but that was a price worth paying for peace in Northern Ireland and contentment in Scotland and Wales. In England, meanwhile, the Anglo-British state arrogated ever-more power to itself, and bore down ever-more fiercely on the civil liberties which had lain at the heart of the Myth of sea-girt freedom. That was the deal. From Westminster's point of view—or, to put it more precisely, from the point of view of New Labour parliamentarians at Westminster—it was a good one. Labour's Scottish and Welsh fiefdoms continued to send MPs to Westminster, where they helped to sustain a majority Labour government. And Labour dominated the internal politics of Scotland and Wales.

But the deal is manifestly unravelling in the three nations of Great Britain—though not, it seems, in Northern Ireland. Scotland now has an SNP government, headed by one of the most skilful and charismatic politicians in the United Kingdom. The Welsh government is a coalition of Labour and Plaid Cymru. English complaints about the funding formula that enables the Scottish administration to spend more public money per head than the Westminster government spent in England, are becoming more scratchy and vociferous. The 'English Question', from which Blair and his colleagues resolutely averted their eyes, hovers menacingly on the edge of the political agenda. Devolution to Scotland and Wales has provoked a remarkable growth of national feeling in England. In 1992 only 31 per cent of people living in England had described themselves as 'English' rather 'British'. In 2007 the authoritative British Social Attitudes survey reported that the proportion had risen to 40 per cent.[12] (In 2003 the proportion of Scots who thought of themselves as Scottish rather than British was 65 per cent, but the figure had hardly changed since 1992.)[13] By 2007 some polls showed 60 per cent support for an English parliament, compared with only 17 per cent between 1999 and 2003.[14] The Conservatives are considering a plan to ensure that English bills will be debated only by English MPs. There is not much doubt that the ground is shifting beneath the halfway house of asymmetric devolution. For the first time since the Act of Union, England's constitutional future is coming into contention, and with it the fundamental assumptions underpinning the multinational British state.

Consultation is a double-edged weapon. It usually starts from the top, with a troubled elite hoping to a halt a drain of legitimacy, but, once it starts, the consulted may take control away from those who do the consulting. I suspect that this is happening now. New Labour saw that the British state was losing

legitimacy. The devolution settlements in the British periphery were supposed to halt the drain. Unfortunately, they did not do so; Brown's talk of
Britishness is his response to that failure. But the conversation is already
bursting the bounds that he and his colleagues hoped to set. Contentment no
longer reigns in Edinburgh and Cardiff. The SNP administration is committed
to a referendum on Scottish independence. The Labour–Plaid Cymru coalition in Wales speaks of 'clear red water' between itself and the New Labour
regime in England. The blogosphere is full of English attacks on the British
state and demands for an English parliament. Albeit without saying so in so
many words, the Conservative party has abandoned the tradition of unques-
tioning unionism which has traditionally been one of its most obvious
hallmarks. If things go on as they are, Brown and his colleagues will soon
be the only full-hearted unionists left in British politics—the political
equivalents of the boy who stood on the burning deck whence all but he
had fled.

The implications are extraordinarily complex. I shall pick two. The first is
that the turbulence which now envelops the half-way house of asymmetric
devolution within Britain is closely related to the confusions and ambiguities
of her relationship with the rest of Europe. When the European project was
launched sixty years ago, the founding fathers took it for granted that their
union would be made up of more-or-less homogeneous nation states. What in
fact happened was that integration on the supranational level was accompanied by fragmentation on the national level. In the familiar nation-states of the
nineteenth and twentieth centuries—in Belgium most obviously, but even in
centralised France—older identities emerged from the deep freeze into which
'modernising' regimes had forced them. In this perspective, it is not in the
least surprising that Scottish, Welsh and English nationalism have become
forces to be reckoned with. Increasingly, the postmodern Europe of the
twenty-first century looks more like medieval Europe, with its hodgepodge
of fissiparous kingdoms, principalities, bishoprics and self-governing cities,
than like the modern Europe of the recent past. Flickering on the horizon is
the vision of a Europe of the Regions in place of the present Europe of the
Nations. If we are to conduct a worthwhile conversation about Britishness
that must be a central theme.

The second implication is more uncomfortable, at least for liberals and
social democrats. The English Question may not yet be on the table, but it is
undoubtedly getting close. However, there is an ominous difference between
it and the Scottish and Welsh Questions that preceded it. Whatever may
have been true of Scottish and Welsh nationalism in the past, they are now
broadly social-democratic in rhetoric and outlook. English nationalism
appears—I say 'appears' because I am not sure—to be a nationalism of the
right. There are lots of reasons. One is that the English have been the top
dogs in the United Kingdom, though they have been too modest and polite
to draw attention to the fact, and that their position in the pecking order of
Britannic nationalisms is now in question. Postdevolution nationalism in

England is faintly reminiscent of post-Soviet nationalism in Russia. It is a nationalism of relative decline: a nationalism of resentment. Another reason is that British liberals and social democrats have been uncomfortable with ethnicity—and particularly with English ethnicity. The most forthright champions of English nationhood and English national aspirations have been on the right: Lord Salisbury, Enoch Powell and Margaret Thatcher come to mind. Yet there is no reason to believe that the English hegemony of the right is divinely ordained. Not the last of the arguments for a searching conversation about Britishness is that it might open a space for a left vision of England.

Notes

1 George Orwell, 'The lion and the unicorn: Socialism and the English genius', in Sonia Orwell and Ian Angus eds., *The Collected Essays, Journalism and Letters of George Orwell*, vol. II, *My Country Right or Left*, Harmondsworth, Penguin Books, 1970, pp. 74–134.
2 Quoted in P. J. Cain and A. G. Hopkins, *British Imperialism, 1688–2000*, London, Longman, 2002, p. 98.
3 G. M. Trevelyan, quoted in David Cannadine, *G. M. Trevelyan, A Life in History*, London, Harper Collins, 1992, p. 112.
4 Winston S. Churchill, *A History of the English-speaking Peoples*, 4 volumes, London, Cassell and Co., 1956-58.
5 Quoted in Cannadine, *G. M. Trevelyan*, p. 123.
6 Quoted in Martin Gilbert, *Finest Hour, Winston S. Churchill 1939–1941*, London, Minerva, 1989, p. 468.
7 John Milton, 'Areopagitica', *Milton's Prose Writings*, London and New York, Everyman's Library, 1958, p. 177.
8 Robert Roberts, *The Classic Slum, Salford Life in the First Quarter of the Century*, Harmondsworth, Penguin Books, 1973, pp. 143–4.
9 Bernard Porter, *The Absent-Minded Imperialists, Empire, Society and Culture in Britain*, Oxford, Oxford University Press, 2004.
10 www.number10.gov.uk/output/Page13630.asp
11 Michael J. Hogan, *The Marshall Plan: America, Britain and the Reconstruction of Europe*, Cambridge, Cambridge University Press, 1995.
12 www.natcen.ac.uk/natcen/pages/news_and_media_docs/BSA_%20press_release_Jan07.pdf
13 Christopher G. A. Bryant, *The Nations of Britain*, Oxford, Oxford University Press, 2006, p. 5.
14 Guy Lodge and Katie Schmuecker, 'The end of the Union?' in *IPPR Public Policy Research*, June–August 2007, p. 93.

Does Britishness Still Matter in the Twenty-First Century—and How Much and How Well Do the Politicians Care?

LINDA COLLEY

It is arguable that the perception of 'Britain' has never been more than part of Westminster's perception of its relation to the world.[1]

THIS essay draws on history in order to explore what can appear a persistent paradox and peculiarity.[2]

In 1992, I published *Britons: Forging the Nation 1707–1837*. As the title suggests, this was primarily a scholarly text about the past. But *Britons* was also written in the hope it might broaden and deepen awareness of a set of circumstances possessing continuing relevance. The first of these was that, while England or Scotland, say, can be described as 'old' countries, Great Britain, and still more the United Kingdom, were comparatively recent constructs patched together at different stages and in different ways. Although successive Anglo–Norman monarchs certainly strove to leave an imprint on Wales and Scotland and, after 1170, on Ireland, Parliamentary union between England and Wales—very much on London's terms—only took place in the 1530s and '40s.[3] Dynastic union between these countries and Scotland, by contrast, was effected by a Scot, by James VI of Scotland inheriting the thrones of England and also of Ireland in 1603. The making of England, Wales and Scotland into 'one united kingdom by the name of Great Britain', with (until recently) a single Parliament at Westminster, was only achieved through the Treaty of Union of 1707. The Act of Union of 1801 effected a further change of name and political organisation by establishing the United Kingdom of Great Britain and Ireland. After the Irish Revolution of 1916, and subsequent struggles, the title of this conglomerate became instead the United Kingdom of Great Britain and Northern Ireland.[4]

This is a highly simplified account, which leaves out this polity's ultimately massive overseas empire and its connections at different times with parts of Continental Europe: important strands in the story to which I will return. The crucial thing to hold onto at this stage is that the territories now making up the UK have been subject over the centuries to many contingencies, and to a great deal of organisational flux. My second general point in *Britons* followed on from this. Although Britishness, as an idea and a set of loyalties, can be seen as emerging markedly from at least the eighteenth century, it was superimposed over, and had to co-exist with other identities, in a partial and sometimes untidy fashion. Thus, while most Victorian Scots were Unionists, willing to define themselves as British as well as Scottish, this

© 2009 The Author. Editorial organisation © 2009 The Political Quarterly Publishing Co. Ltd
Published by Blackwell Publishing Ltd, 9600 Garsington Road, Oxford OX4 2DQ, UK and 350 Main Street, Malden, MA 02148, USA

same era—the nineteenth century—also witnessed growing enthusiasm north of the border for the cult of William Wallace as the champion of Scottish freedom from English conquest and invasion.[5] People's identities in these islands have frequently been plural and shifting. Men and women have been fiercely Scottish in some contexts, British in others; immersed in their locality for the most part, say, but able in certain circumstances to identify with the UK, and so on.

That Britishness proved able in the past to coexist with other loyalties in this fashion, and that many (never all) of the inhabitants of these islands could view first Britain and ultimately the UK as a nation of sorts—by which I mean, in Manuel Castells's words, a communal entity 'constructed in people's minds and collective memory by the sharing of history and political projects'—was owing to a variety of forces.[6]

The ideological, governmental, economic and coercive input of London played a part of course. So did internal trade and migration and intermarriage between people from the four countries of the UK. In the eighteenth, nine-teenth, and early twentieth centuries there were other important influences. It mattered enormously that different forms of Protestantism constituted the majority religion in England, Wales, Scotland and the north of Ireland, though not of course in the south. Modes of church government and precise theo-logical doctrines might vary, but the wide spread of Protestantism allowed for commonalities of culture and language as well as belief. It mattered, too, that a succession of wars, or threats of war with other European powers—be it Spain, France, Germany, and ultimately the Soviet Union—placed a premium over the centuries on arguments for British-wide national cohesion and action. It mattered that the scope of Britain's imperial and commercial reach, plus its pioneering industrialisation, made allegiance to this polity for a long time attractive to the ambitious, greedy and restless. It mattered that, unlike dynasties in many other parts of the world, Britain's monarchy was not extinguished by war or revolution, but persisted as a focus for allegiance. Belief in the superiority of British political, institutional and legal freedoms was also important. This idea of superior British liberty was in part a selective myth. As late as 1914, and despite three Reform Acts, the UK possessed one of the narrowest electoral franchises in Western Europe. But such inconvenient realities did not prevent confidence in British freedoms possessing, for a substantial period, cross-class, cross-country and in some contexts multi-ethnic appeal.

As will be easily apparent, and this was the final general argument of *Britons*, many of these one-time cements have ceased to function or become much weaker. Except perhaps in parts of Northern Ireland, Protestantism has lost much of its broad embrace and cohesive power, and so even has Christianity. The royal family, too, has lost much of its former capacity to focus loyalty and a sense of British national unity.[7] For all of politicians' references to 'a war on terror', which can anyway have a divisive effect, there is no longer a widely accepted foreign enemy, a clearly perceived 'other', against which Britannic solidarities can be rallied to the degree that proved possible at intervals in the past. In addition, devolution and the Irish peace process bear witness to how much relations between the component parts of the UK are in flux, and likely to continue being so. Moreover, while this remains a rich polity and disproportionately powerful for its size, it is considerably weaker than in the eighteenth, nineteenth, and early twentieth centuries, and is felt to be so. This has implications for 'Britishness' as for so much else. Decisions made in Washington now impact on the UK to a degree that would have been unthinkable before the Second World War; so do decisions taken in Brussels.

There has been another substantial post-1945 change. Because these islands are open to multiple seas, they have also always been open to contact with different peoples, by way of trade, navigation, military invasion, migration and varieties of empire. Ethnic and religious diversity here is emphatically not a new phenomenon. It remains the case, however, that—unless they were involved in overseas activities of some sort, or lived in London or other major ports—most Britons before 1945 went through life rarely seeing or having contact with individuals who were not white and/or not Christian. Since the war, however, the scale and the diversity of inward migration have expanded substantially, though not to a uniform degree across the UK. The 2001 census revealed that about 10% of the population was made up of ethnic minorities; it also showed that almost 45% of Asian and black Britons lived in London.

I begin with this summary of past conditions in part so as to develop a specific point about political arguments and actions (and also inaction) in the UK now. Official statements and initiatives to do with 'Britishness' have magnified since 9/11 and 7/7, especially under the current Prime Minister, Gordon Brown. Yet, as I have outlined, the reasons why Britishness seems now so much in question are in fact various and profoundly historical. This is not an issue that has arisen simply because of a particular alienated minority grouping, anymore than it is only to do with current partisan alignments in Scotland. The scale of division and debate over identity happening in the UK today is not a consequence merely of developments taking place in recent years.

This being so, it is not so much the volume of political noise about Britishness and its frailties that merits attention and explanation, but rather the extent to which those in politics and government have so often demonstrated only limited and shallow interest in these matters.

Consider, for instance, the realms of education and public culture. The Department for Culture, Media and Sport (DCMS) has recently asked museums in the UK to investigate what contributions they can make to current debates about British identity. This initiative is partly a response to proposals by senior figures in the Conservative party for a new Museum of British History.[8] This almost certainly impractical project has also excited some Labour support and media comment. Yet even were such a museum realisable, it would likely function only as a small, decorative and expensive cart, as opposed to what must be the obvious workhorse in this context: namely, politicians providing for better and more synchronised history teaching throughout the UK.

Some of my fellow professional historians disapprove of such a prospect, because they reject any idea of British history functioning as crude state propaganda. So do I. But if the UK is to persist as some kind of coherent entity, its population ideally requires better education about this polity's evolution over time and about its component parts and peoples. At present, history teaching in many UK schools is patchy and random; and, as children get older, history provision often gets worse. After the age of 14, only three out of ten children in *English* secondary schools study history at all. Of those who do continue the subject, an overwhelming majority study Nazi Germany; by contrast, the history of postwar Europe (which might provide children with some wider context for their own experience) gets short shrift. And though the Key Stage 3 history syllabus provides an option, for instance, to study eighteenth-century Britain, few schools take this up. Consequently, hardly any English children have an opportunity to learn anything about the 1707 Treaty of Union.[9] Simultaneously, not only is Scottish history flourishing in schools and universities in Scotland (as it should), but so are versions of that country's past representing its southern neighbour as straightforwardly distinct, just one more foreign country among others.[10] If the Union is to survive in some form, all this surely merits more attention and reaction from unionist politicians at Westminster.

It is comparatively straightforward for ministers to urge initiatives in support of 'Britishness' on cultural organisations like museums that are dependent on state funding. Tackling the role of history in education throughout the UK would require by contrast a very different level of political effort and risk. There would be the fundamental challenge that England, Wales, Scotland and Northern Ireland have separate educational jurisdictions; and the practical problems posed by an already crowded school curriculum. And there would be the abiding, intransigent question of just what kind of UK history was to be involved. Whose history?

Recently, a report was produced by the History Practitioners' Advisory Team, a group set up by the Conservative Shadow Minister for Schools to advise on the reform of the history curriculum. It was a good, thoughtful report that argued strongly for British history being made compulsory for all children between 11 and 16. But of the eleven teachers and academics involved in producing it, no fewer than nine worked in London, Oxford, or in or near Cambridge.[11] This was very much a southern English document: at once a conscientious attempt to address some of these issues, and an illustration of how hard it is to get them right. But the biggest obstacle to providing for some sort of synchronised history teaching in all UK schools is that this seems never in fact to have been rigorously attempted. Not until 1870, much later than most of its European rivals, did the rulers of the British state make education for children of any secular variety compulsory. Even after this, politicians demonstrated only limited concern by European and American standards for providing systematic school instruction in real or mythic national history. 'As late as the First World War', Peter Mandler remarks:

Few classrooms had the flags or maps that are supposed to provide the foundation for the 'banal nationalism' of the modern citizen; they had instead bibles and religious tracts . . . Accordingly many early-twentieth century schoolchildren recalled in their memoirs that they had long thought 'their country' was the Holy Land.[12]

Those in charge of the British state have also often displayed casualness in regard to the national uses of public culture more broadly. Traditionally, they have been far less interventionist in this regard than politicians in France, who tend still to be aggressive about sponsoring the country's film industry, and about defending trade-mark cultural sites and enterprises such as the Paris fashion industry, or that city's small, uneconomic, but totally distinctive food stores. The more relaxed British official attitude is often put down to a commitment to economic liberalism, yet more is involved than this. Manifestly, the USA also possesses an unabashed cult of the free market. But, in addition to making provision for an elaborate calendar of patriotic celebrations, and (inefficiently) for the teaching of a certain version of American history in its schools, US governments also require their major newspaper owners to be citizens. No comparable laws operate in the UK, though it is hardly coincidental that *its* foreign media owners tend to come disproportionately from one-time regions of the empire.[13]

The anthropologist Benedict Anderson famously observed that it was important for people to be able to imagine their nation. The inhabitants 'of even the smallest nation' he wrote, 'will never know most of their members . . . yet in the minds of each [member] lives the image of their communion'.[14] It is the BBC (like many other Britannic institutions, substantially the creation of a Scot) that has most consistently and actively provided for a cultural image of Britain, and which stands as a conspicuous exception to this pattern of considerable official *laissez-faire* in regard to public culture. The BBC is sporadically criticised for being London-centric and insufficiently representative of minorities, for partisan bias, for failing to live up to its public service brief, and for being out of step with the pace of technological and media change.[15] But it remains a rare, globally-recognised, *explicitly British* institution, and it is probably still the most reliable medium existing for generating some image of communion across the UK. The BBC's multi-episode series *Coast*, for instance, which showed how the different islands, beaches and seas of the UK were linked historically, geographically and ecologically, was probably more potent than any ministerial speech about Britishness. True to form, however, it is unclear how far present-day British politicians have fully thought out the potential of the BBC, or how far they still support it. Demands at Westminster for reforms of different kinds jostle at present with calls for the licence fee to be dropped so that other, mainly foreign-owned TV companies can have a larger slice of the broadcasting pie.

Why have UK politicians, most of whom are still nominally unionist, not been more consistently concerned with issues of British identity? Why have they not sought to advance a coherent UK-wide vision as much or as imaginatively as they might? One answer is that politicians can be as confused and uninformed about these matters as many voters. But partisan and electoral self-interest are also a factor, as is the asymmetry of the territories making up the United Kingdom. Manifestly, England is much larger, wealthier and possesses far more population—and consequently many more voters—than Wales, Scotland or Northern Ireland, and this asymmetry has always posed ideological and policy challenges.

As far as Labour is concerned, it has for instance compromised the progress of devolution. In Wales, Scotland, and Northern Ireland, devolution could attract support in the 1990s because it promised greater autonomy and self-definition. But Labour's plans for regional assemblies in England could seem to offer only new fractures, an affront to Englishness, not a fresh expression of it, which is one reason why devolution schemes here have thus far foundered. As Charlie Jeffery and Daniel Wincott have documented, outside of London, England is now something of a centralised black hole in an otherwise more devolved United Kingdom.[16] There is another, deeper sense in which the implementation of devolution in the 1990s failed to allot sufficient attention to the UK as a whole. A comparison with Spain—a composite state-nation and one-time empire possessing many resemblances to the UK—is instructive here. Since 1978, Spain's governments have granted enhanced autonomy to all of that country's small nationalities and regions. But this was only done after a new Constitution was passed proclaiming the indissoluble unity of the Spanish nation, and stipulating for instance that Basques, Catalans, Galicians or whoever must fly the Spanish flag alongside their own separate flags. The whole of Spain was thus given thought to, in advance of devolving power to its component parts—unlike the more piecemeal alterations occurring in the UK.[17]

The Conservatives too sometimes fail to act as though they possessed a macro-perspective on the UK, in part again because of the disproportionate size and population of England, where most of their support is concentrated. David Cameron, has come out strongly in support of the Union. But, on the basis of media statements and speeches, other Conservatives seem drawn to viewing theirs' as quintessentially the party of English nationalism; and some appear willfully (or perhaps unconsciously) insensitive to the fact that England is not the same country as Great Britain or the UK—errors that are of course widespread. I think of those Tory journalists who sought to argue it was somehow improper for a Scot to become British Prime Minister; or of the distinguished Tory cultural commentator who argued in print that Scotland was bound to become independent because Edinburgh's architecture was so unlike London's (as though there was somehow a single prevailing mode of British architecture necessarily determined by southern English styles); or of the Tory MP I encountered who claimed not to understand the fuss about declining levels of Britishness, since he was always careful during major international sporting events to affix a small flag of St George on his car.

As has been argued, one way of correcting for such partisan blinkers would be to implement electoral reform: replacing the current first-past-the-post system in elections to Westminster—which rewards parties whose support is geographically concentrated—with proportional representation.[18] This would moderate the close connection both Labour and the Conservatives possess with particular parts of the UK, and so make it easier for each party to claim to represent all of the UK. Had proportional representation been in operation in 1997, it is unlikely that the Conservatives would have been wiped out in Wales and Scotland, and thus made to appear, including in their own eyes, so much an *English* party. There are other corrective measures that the political parties might conceivably implement. Is it necessary for instance for Labour, Conservatives and the Liberal Democrats to hold their prime annual party conferences so invariably in English seaside towns and major postindustrial cities? Since these are UK political parties, could not their main annual conferences be held just occasionally in Swansea, or Glasgow, or Belfast?

There are few signs of such changes being seriously contemplated, anymore than at present there seems much evidence of Conservative, Labour and Liberal Democrat politicians in the Edinburgh Parliament effectively muting their tribal antagonisms, so as to offer a more creative and coherent alternative to the SNP's separatist agenda. Such failures in initiative are interesting and suggestive. It may be true, as David Goodhart argues, that 'a renewed sense of civic British nationalism cannot simply be commanded by well-meaning politicians', but many of the issues central to the Britishness debate *are* to do with levels of political will and with political leadership.[19] This is manifestly true of electoral reform, no less than it is of constitutional reform. There are some reforms and remedies that only professional politicians can plausibly attempt.

One can still encounter the argument that a written constitution would be alien to the 'pragmatic spirit' of these islands, and that such texts are suitable only for newer, postcolonial nations, or republics founded by revolutions. Yet, as a major exhibition in the British Library is about to demonstrate, these islands have generated scores of influential constitutional documents over the centuries, some of which pertain just to one of the home countries, while others address the whole of Great Britain or the UK.[20] Since the 1640s and '50s, however, there has been no attempt at a single written constitution extending over these islands. As a result, and as Lord Scarman observed, the UK's working constitution is not so much unwritten as dispersed among a vast miscellany of texts and legal decisions, 'hidden and difficult to find'.[21] It is partly on account of this that British citizenship has remained unevenly developed as a language and concept. The absence of a written constitution, which might conceivably serve as valuable cement in a fast-changing UK, also reflects the fact that this polity has remained a monarchy, and that for a long time it was the centre of a worldwide empire.

Almost by definition, monarchical empires do not favour written constitutions. Nor do they normally favour precise statements as to who their component populations are, and of the quality of these peoples' rights and allegiance. Those in charge of empires are concerned to exercise often widely different levels of authority over different peoples in geographically dispersed territories, and accordingly tend to make use of baggy and capacious political language that is focused on the person or the ruler. It is in large part because Britain was for so long a monarchical empire, that the language of a discrete national citizenship—of individual citizens in a bounded terrain with well defined rights—has never taken deep and unproblematic root here, only the more elastic language of subjecthood. A century ago, there were still millions of people in Asia, Africa, Australasia and North America who—alongside the peoples of the UK—were all encouraged to view themselves as subjects of the British Crown, with certain rights to protection and a collective duty of allegiance.[22] Now, however, the British empire has gone, and while the monarchy's capacity to act as a charismatic centre is not yet negligible, it has diminished. Yet the limited and limiting language of subjecthood lingers on.

It is this background that supplies one of the strongest arguments for some kind of re-worked and written British constitution and for a new Bill of Rights. The ending of empires usually involves the imperial metropolis, and not just its one-time colonies, in making political adjustments. As far as the UK is concerned, some of these postimperial adjustments have long since been underway, but there remains unfinished business. Since the UK is no longer an imperial monarchy, the elastic, indeterminate language of subjecthood is out of date. A stronger language of citizenship is necessary (and not just better welcoming ceremonies for new citizens) and achieving this will require new constitutional statements and initiatives on the part of Westminster.

The empire fits into this argument about Britishness and the politicians in another respect. It has frequently been suggested in recent years that 'the building of the British state was fundamentally an English expansionist project', and consequently that the end of the empire overseas is *bound* to be followed by this domestic expansionism's unravelling, and by the 'break-up of Britain'.[23] This is certainly possible, but claims that the end of empire *must* also and desirably result in the disintegration of the UK, are driven at once by selective history and teleology. The degree to which the rulers first of England, then Great Britain, and finally the UK were implicated in dynastic connections with parts of Continental Europe, and increasingly from 1600 in colonisation outside Europe does however help to account for the negligence that politicians here seem often to demonstrate in regard to issues of national identity and national culture. Quite simply, and for a very long time, there have been geographically much more extensive games for them to play. In wartime, and especially when invasion has threatened, British governments and civil servants have, to be sure, displayed singular ingenuity and energy in seeking to foster mass unity at home.[24] But, at times of reduced danger from without, official interest in investing in 'Britishness' has often come a poor second to preoccupation with the idea that, as Winston Churchill put it: 'we belong to no single continent, but to all'. [25]

For much of the twentieth century the transcontinental quality of British official thinking and policy-making—the abiding lure for Westminster politicians of the global and international stage—was offset by an enormous expansion in the reach and machinery of the British state. First the warrior state, and then the creation of the welfare state permitted British politicians a practical UK-wide reach and embrace without their needing to think over-much about defining the nation. There was a sense in which an expanding state stood in for the nation.[26] It may be, then, that along with the *longue durée* changes I outlined at the outset, the end of empire, and more recent emergencies, a contributory factor to the current anxieties about 'Britishness' has been the advance of privatisation since the 1970s. Perceived changes in the nanny state may have fostered as well a public sense of a slackening nation state.

All of these developments place unionist politicians in the UK under a distinctive set of pressures. Like their counterparts elsewhere, they have to respond to modern globalisation's assaults on territorial, economic and attitudinal boundaries. But they also face more specific and domestic challenges. Crucially, just what is the United Kingdom for in the twenty-first century exactly? In the wake of devolution, and with so many customary landmarks and systems gone or eroding, is it feasible—or even advantageous—to seek to maintain this political construct? Does the United Kingdom still cater to its varied inhabitants' needs and aspirations more effectively than alternative political configurations might do? And could it be re-invented and relaunched so as to function better and in a more pluralistic fashion? It is not simply that these are major and possibly intractable issues. Even fully acknowledging their seriousness and determinedly seeking out adequate responses is likely to require change in governing style, a discarding of traditional casualness, and a shift in customary focus on the part of UK politicians.

Notes

1 J. G. A. Pocock, 'The limits and divisions of British history: In search of the unknown subject', *American Historical Review*, 87, 1982, p. 331.
2 This is a revised version of a lecture delivered for the Smith Institute in London on 24 January 2008. I am most grateful to the Institute and to its Director, Wilf Stevenson, for their support and enthusiasm.
3 Though the term 'Great Britain' appeared earlier. See Ralph Griffiths, 'The island of England in the fifteenth century: perceptions of the peoples of the British Isles', *Journal of Medieval History*, 29, 2003, pp. 177–200; and R. R. Davies, *Domination and Conquest: The Experience of Ireland, Scotland and Wales 1100–1300*, Cambridge, Cambridge University Press, 1990.
4 A new edition of *Britons* with a revised preface will be published in July 2009 by Yale University Press.

5 T. M. Devine, 'In bed with an elephant: almost three hundred years of the Anglo-Scottish Union', *Scottish Affairs*, 57, 2006, pp. 1–18.

6 Manuel Castells, *The Power of Identity*, Oxford, Blackwell, 1997, p. 51.

7 Though the monarchy's importance in Northern Ireland remains considerable, and the significance of Elizabeth II's extraordinarily long reign merits far more investigation.

8 Museums, Libraries and Archives Council seminars on 'Identity, Britishness, Collections, and Museums', held in London and Edinburgh June 2008. Lord Baker has been the foremost but not the only Conservative advocate of a bricks and mortar Museum of British History.

9 See the online version of the Royal Society of Arts debate in London on 7 February 2007: 'Teaching History: Narrative and the Challenge of Britishness'.

10 Richard J. Finlay, 'New Britain, New Scotland, New History? The impact of devolution on the development of Scottish historiography', *Journal of Contemporary History*, 36, 2001, pp. 383–93.

11 *Ex informatio* Seán Lang, Chair, History Practitioners' Advisory Team (HPAT).

12 Peter Mandler, 'Nation and power in the liberal state: Britain c.1800–c.1914', in Len Scales and Oliver Zimmer, eds., *Power and the Nation in European History*, Cambridge, Cambridge University Press, 2005, p. 360.

13 The considerable grip that press barons from one-time colonial regions, mainly present-day Canada, Australia, and the USA, have long had on the British media is an aspect of the empire striking back that merits more discussion.

14 Benedict Anderson, *Imagined Communities: Reflections on the Origin and Spread of Nationalism*, London, Verso, 1991.

15 See the online report of the 'Broadcasting Britishness?', conference, Said Business School, Oxford University, 17 June 2008.

16 In 'Devolution in the United Kingdom: statehood and citizenship in transition', *Publius: The Journal of Federalism*, 36, 2006, pp. 3–18. Like so much else in Britishness debates, this is an issue with a past. In the 1880s, the leading Conservative, Joseph Chamberlain, argued in regard to a possible federal structure for the UK that: 'England undivided would dominate any federation, but England divided was neither desired by nor acceptable to English nationalists': John Kendle, *Federal Britain: A History*, London, Routledge, 1997, p. 71.

17 See http://countrystudies.us/spain/78.htp under 'Regional Government'.

18 See, for instance, Robert Hazell, 'The continuing dynamism of constitutional reform', *Parliamentary Affairs*, 60, 2007, pp. 3–25.

19 David Goodhart, *Progressive Nationalism: Citizenship and the Left*, London, Demos, 2006.

20 'Taking Liberties': an exhibition scheduled to open in the British Library in London in November 2008.

21 Lord Scarman, *Why Britain Needs a Written Constitution*, London, Charter 88, 1992, p. 4.

22 Hannah Weiss is currently at work in Princeton University on a doctoral dissertation on subjecthood and the varieties of British empire.

23 Mary Hickman, 'A new England through Irish eyes?' in Selina Chen and Tony Wright, eds., *The English Question*, London, Fabian Society, 2000, p. 101; and for a classic statement of this thesis: Tom Nairn, *The Break-Up of Britain: Crisis and Neo-Nationalism*, London, NLB, 1981.

24 See, for instance, chapters 4, 5 and 7 of *Britons*; and Brian Foss, *War Paint: Art, War, State and Identity in Britain, 1939–1945*, London, Yale University Press, 2007.
25 Quoted in David Reynolds, 'Britain and the New Europe: the search for identity since 1940', *Historical Journal*, 31, 1988, p. 225.
26 See James E. Cronin, *The Politics of State Expansion: War, State and Society in Twentieth Century Britain*, London, Routledge, 1991.

Being British

BHIKHU PAREKH

I always said and believed that the British character is quite different from the character of people on the continent—quite different. There is a great sense of fairness and equity in the British people, a great sense of individuality and initiative. They don't like being pushed around. How else did these really rather small people, from the times of Elizabeth on, go out in the larger world and have such an influence upon it?

I set out to destroy socialism. I feel it was at odds with the character of the people. We were the first country in the world to roll back the frontiers of socialism, then roll forward the frontiers of freedom. We reclaimed our heritage.

Margaret Thatcher[1]

We have a great deal to be ashamed of in our history. We promoted and profited by the slave trade; we plundered India and Africa . . . we forced the opium trade on China, attempted to suppress the American, French and Russian revolutions, and were guilty of centuries of oppression of the Irish people. I do not want a school history which boasts about our victories over lesser breeds—Spaniards, Frenchmen, Germans, Russians, Argentinians—nor over helpless colonial peoples.

Christopher Hill[2]

IN RESPONSE to the widespread anxiety about the increasing diversity and fragmentation of British society, it is widely argued that we should find ways of fostering Britishness, a term used to refer to what binds and distinguishes the British people and forms the basis of their unity and identity.[3] Although the term is not new, the frequency of its usage and the weight put upon it are. The term is used in two different senses, the essentialist and the empirical, both of which are suspect. In the first sense, popular among some groups of Conservatives including Enoch Powell and Margaret Thatcher, it refers to an ahistorical essence, a kind of *Volkgeist*, that British people share in common and by virtue of which they are all British. There is and there can be no such essence. As self-determining agents the British people freely decide what kind of country they wish to be. Although they cannot do so unconstrained by their past and must take full account of it, the past does not determine them. It is never homogeneous and monolithic either. It is a cluster of trends and tendencies, and the country needs to decide which ones to build on to meet its current challenges. Being British is a political project, not the actualisation of some primordial and unchanging essence.

Second, 'Britishness' is sometimes used as an empirical generalisation of the qualities all or most British people are supposed to share in common, a usage popular among some empirically minded liberals. Britishness here is seen as a set of attributes or features that all Britons individually possess or should possess, in broadly the same way that all yellow or red objects share yellowness or redness in common. It is taken to consist either in such qualities of temperament as stubbornness, stoic self-discipline, emotional self-restraint, understatement and uncomplaining nature, or in such habits and practices as the love of animals, gardening, personal hobbies and of sports, keeping one's distance from others, and the tendency to mind one's own business.

The empirical view of Britishness is open to objection. The qualities and practices involved are not shared by all or even most Britons. They largely apply to the English, though by no means all of them, and here too they vary with regions, class, gender and generation. If they are taken to define Britishness, many legitimate Britons would have to be classified as not British or even un-British. Besides, these qualities and practices are ethno-cultural not public and political in nature, and at best define the British as a people, not Britain as a political community. Being British is not a matter of sharing certain individually possessed contingent attributes but rather a form of relationship, a way of relating to the country and its people and seeing it as one's country and them as one's fellow members.

Although the term 'Britishness' is misleading, and is best avoided or used with great caution and in full awareness of its ambiguity, it highlights an important question. The question relates to what binds us together, makes us this community rather than some other. To say that one is British is to say that Britain means something to one, that one's membership of it is a significant element in one's identity and says something important about oneself, that one is shaped by it, has some degree of attachment to it, and feels at home in it. Mere residence does not make one British. Even the formal status of being its citizen is not enough. An individual might enjoy all the rights of citizenship and discharge his obligations conscientiously, but take a wholly instrumental or detached view of his relationship with the country. It means nothing to him, he has no personal bond with it, he feels no wrench or sense of loss when he leaves the country, and might just as well live elsewhere. British citizenship makes it easier to be British but the two are not the same.

Being British, seeing Britain as a more or less valued part of one's personal identity, implies identification with Britain.[4] Identification is necessarily a matter of degree. Some feel passionately committed to the country, are profoundly shaped by it, and identify with its way of life. For them it is their home and an object of intense love. At the other end, some identify with some aspects of its way of life and feel alienated from others, and only feel at home in it just enough to want to continue to live in it. Most people's identification with Britain falls somewhere between these extremes. If one has no sense of identification with it, sees nothing of oneself in it and of it in oneself, it is difficult to see in what sense one is British.

Identification with the country is a highly complex process. It is not entirely a matter of conscious personal choice or decision, and develops at its own pace. Several factors of varying degrees of importance contribute to it, such as shared historical experiences, common struggles for liberation from alien rule or defence against foreign invasion, and imaginative literature which interprets different individuals and groups to each other and creates among them a shared collective identity. The way a country treats its members plays a particularly important role. They are more likely to identify with the country if they are accepted as its full and legitimate members and treated with respect, enjoy equality with the rest, are free to express their other cherished identities, and have the opportunity to lead a minimally decent life. Conversely they are unlikely to feel at home in the country and see it as theirs if their very presence is resented, if they are subjected to discriminatory treatment, mocked and ridiculed with impunity, or if they are required to sacrifice their other identities as a precondition of their membership of or proof of their commitment to the country.

The way a country defines itself is the basis of its unity and identity. It unites its members around a shared view of who they are as a political community and why they belong together, and it also distinguishes them from others and tells them why they are part of this community and not any other. Every country needs and as a rule tends to develop a shared self-definition. In a well-ordered and stable society, such a self-definition is often inarticulate, taken for granted, woven into its way of life, and shapes the lives and choices of its members without their becoming self-conscious of it or needing a clearly formulated view of it. The situation changes when a society passes through rapid and extensive changes or faces an internal or external threat to its way of life or very existence, forcing it to ask itself what it stands for, what holds it together, what unites and distinguishes it.

Although the Act of Union 1707 brought Britain or rather Great Britain into existence, the resulting union was loose, and neither united the English and Scottish peoples nor required strong bonds of unity and identity between them. Great Britain was largely taken to refer to the state, a legal entity, and being British consisted in loyalty to the Crown, the Parliament and the laws. Things changed radically in the aftermath of the French Revolution and the Napoleonic wars that threatened Britain's very existence as an independent nation and its North American empire. The country needed a strong sense of unity and identity, both of which it forged against the background of the hostile other. Britain now defined itself as radically different from France in things that were deemed to go to the very heart of its way of life. It was Protestant, France Catholic; it was a constitutional monarchy, France despotic; it was individualist, France statist; it had nothing but neighbourly goodwill to other European countries whereas France, like Spain before, had hegemonic ambitions. Although this oppositional or contrastive view of its identity involved considerable exaggeration and simplification, it had some basis in facts, and hence a degree of plausibility.[5] It gave the British people a clear and unambiguous sense of what their country stood for, and became the basis of their unity. Although views of national identity rarely go uncontested and usually take time to take root, the Napoleonic wars and the way they were conducted and conceptualised expedited the popularisation and consolidation of the new view of British identity, and the ensuing victory conferred a historical and even providential legitimacy on it.

From around the second half of the nineteenth century onwards, Britain began to undergo important changes and faced new challenges to which the earlier self-definition was inadequate. It had extended its empire to large parts of Asia and Africa, and it needed to justify it in its own and their eyes. Thanks to the industrial revolution, to which the empire was closely linked, the economy came to play a decisive role in national life, and Britain's relations with the rest of the world changed radically. The rising middle and working classes demanded the vote and Britain embarked upon a democratic journey. Class conflict began to take acute forms, and the country needed to unite its major classes around a shared self-understanding. Not surprisingly, Britain began to define itself as the industrial workshop of the world, a constitutional democracy, and a country made up of an enterprising and superior people charged with the historical task of civilising the 'inferior races'. The Second World War deepened its civilisational identity and sense of superiority, and it came to see itself as a custodian of western values and a protector of its ineffective European neighbours.

During the past few decades almost all the earlier markers of national identity have either disappeared or are in the process of disappearing. The empire is gone, though its psychological legacy in the form of a sense of national superiority survives among some sections of the population. Immigration has brought people from ex-colonies, and deepened the cultural diversity of the country. Religion plays a limited role in the life of the British people, and does not even persist as a major cultural force. Britain is no longer at the cutting edge of the new industrial revolution, and its manufacturing base has declined considerably. Scotland, Wales and Northern Ireland assert their national identities and demand greater autonomy. Europe plays a far greater role in British life than it did before. British individualism is widely perceived to have gone too far and to have become too defiant, and the traditional social and moral constraints that had hitherto checked its excesses are proving ineffective.

In the light of all this Britain badly needs a coherent and inspirational conception of its identity. The Thatcherite view did not measure up to the challenge. It was deeply rooted in imperial consciousness, relied heavily on religion, fed the aggressive individualist impulse, felt deeply uncomfortable with Britain's cultural diversity, was too English in its orientation to understand the desire for autonomy of the three nations, and too heavily Atlantic to appreciate Britain's European roots. Blair's view of British identity was an improvement on Thatcher's, but it too was inadequate. He was more sympathetic than her to the pressure for devolution and the demands of cultural diversity, but had no coherent framework to accommodate them. He talked of social responsibility and social justice, but did little to check unrestrained individualism. He remained ambiguous about the empire, and never assessed and came to terms with its legacy. He stressed Britain's European and Atlantic ties, but failed to reconcile the two, and ended up alienating the bulk of his countrymen by siding with the US on many important issues including the disastrous war on Iraq. Thanks to his failure to offer a coherent view of British identity, there is a widespread sense of disorientation and a lack of direction and purpose in national life.

As I argued earlier, Britain has faced the question of self-definition several times in the past, and the present situation is by no means new. A national self-definition cannot be imposed from above or prescribed by politicians. It must grow out of a public debate, and what I propose below is intended as a small contribution to it. Since the subject is large and complex, I shall do no more than highlight some of the important components of British identity.

Britain is made up of four ethno-cultural communities or nations. It is not just a formal political union superimposed upon these nations and lacking a substantive content of its own, as some have argued. Rather it is a distinct political community with a recognisable identity. Over the centuries its constituent nations have 'interacted so as to modify the condition of one another's existence' and created a common political culture.[6] The latter includes English language and literature, its most important medium of expression. The English language and literature are unimaginable without the contributions of Walter Scott, Thomas Carlyle, Samuel Smiles, Chaucer, Shakespeare, Wordsworth, Shelley, Oscar Wilde, W. B. Yeats, James Joyce, George Bernard Shaw, and others, all drawn from different British nations. This is equally true of British social and political thought to which David Hume, Adam Smith, John Stuart Mill, Edmund Burke, Hobbes, Locke and others contributed, all again drawn from and bringing with them the historical experiences and aspirations of the four nations. British political and legal institutions too bear their collective imprint, and British liberalism and democracy are their joint creations. The industrial revolution was their collective product and gave rise to a nationally integrated economy and pan-British middle and working classes. The British Empire was created and run by the four nations together, and the smaller of them embraced it with great enthusiasm as a global stage on which to affirm their patriotism and acquire a sense of pride and importance.[7]

Britain thus exists at two levels. At one level there are four nations, each with a thick and comprehensive culture including its rituals, customs, social practices, folk memories, regional basis, its brand of Protestantism, heroes, literature, food, sense of humour, way of structuring the self, and so on. At another level, they share a common British identity which is political in nature and based on a common *public* lecture. The public culture is not comprehensive and all-encompassing, and does not include shared myths, folk memories, social rituals, etc. Rather it is limited to the civil and public sphere of life and is articulated in terms of certain institutions, values and practices. This common culture is the collective product of the four nations, and provides a framework within which they interact and which both shapes and is in turn shaped by them. British identity thus is multicultural, in the sense that it both includes four vibrant and territorially concentrated cultural communities and is itself a product of and includes strands of thought deposited by them. Hugh Kearney was right to have originally wanted to give his fine book *The British Isles: A History of Four Nations*, the different title of *The British Isles: A Multicultural Approach*.

Britain has been a great and largely successful multicultural experiment. Not that it was always tolerant of its national communities. Apart from Scotland whose identity was enshrined in the Act of Union, it tried to suppress the Welsh and Irish identities. But these identities persisted partly because of their vitality, partly because their suppression was not as brutal and systematic as in some other countries, and partly because the empire concentrated the country's attention overseas and allowed these identities a global stage for self-expression. Since the wider British identity and the narrower national identities do not compete in the same political space, and since each generally respects the other, every Briton feels comfortable with his or her dual identity. They can be British without ceasing to be Scottish, Welsh or Irish. This duality is a necessary part of being British, and an integral feature of the kind of country Britain has become.

Britain's past and present immigrant communities easily fit into this framework. Just as it has learned to respect the diversity of its four nations, it should respect the diversity of its immigrants. And just as its common public culture is a product of the constructive interchanges between the four nations, it can readily accept such creative contributions as its various immigrant communities are able to make. Since Scots and Welsh can be British without ceasing to be Scottish or Welsh, the Indians, the Afro-Caribbeans and others too can be British without abandoning the valuable components of their cultural identity. And the same creative process by which the English, the Scottish, the Irish and the Welsh identities both shape and are in turn shaped by the wider British identity can be extended to the immigrants. While shaping the wider British culture, they are also shaped by it, reinterpret and revise their cultures accordingly, and develop areas of growing convergence between the two.

Britain, I have argued, represents a political community based on shared public culture growing out of and co-existing with the comprehensive cultures of its constituent communities. This public culture includes a set of institutions, practices, values, and a particular orientation to the world, which collectively define its identity. I shall highlight four of its many important constituents that deserve particular attention in the current context. First, a set of democratic institutions and practices in terms of which the British people conduct their common affairs and to which they feel loyal. They fought for these, indeed in some respects they were the first to do so, shed their blood, and have rightly come to see these as their great historical achievement and an integral part of their identity.

Second, a set of basic public values which collectively define Britain as a liberal society. It is true that each of its four constituent nations represents a different *Sittlichkeit* or moral and cultural ethos, which is why the predominantly English Thatcherite vision of Britain, for example, found little support in Scotland and Wales. Despite these differences, however, they all subscribe to certain common public values. These include such values as individual liberty, equality of respect and rights, tolerance, mutual respect, a sense of fair play and the spirit of moderation.

It is sometimes argued, wrongly in my view, that since these values are also shared by other societies, they are not uniquely British. They are uniquely British in two related senses. They are products of the struggles of the British people and are embedded in and draw their vitality from their unique historical experiences. The British arrived at and internalised them in their own way, and rightly see them as their collective achievement. Furthermore the British define, relate and prioritise these values differently from the way other societies do. Although the French and Germans too value liberty, they see it as the creation of the state, whereas the British define it as whatever the state does not ban, and relate it to the law very differently. Again, the US too values free speech, but it takes a more or less absolutist view of it and protects even hate speech except when there is a danger of imminent violence. The British impose greater restraints on free speech in the interest of social harmony and a climate of mutual respect. In other words the concept of shared values is ambiguous and complex. Values need to be interpreted, related and prioritised. While sharing common values with other societies, we might define and prioritise them quite differently, and it is this that distinguishes us as a moral community.

Thirdly, Britain is a multicultural polity built on and forged out of its constituent nations. It does not merely tolerate but values and respects their diversity and provides them a secure space for self-expression. The same multicultural spirit should be and is generally extended to the immigration-generated diversity provided that the latter does not violate the basic values of the British public culture. Different cultural communities in Britain are not ghettoised but expected and encouraged to interact with each other as well as with the shared public culture in a spirit of open-minded dialogue. The common public culture would not have come into existence without such an interaction, and bears witness to the spirit of dialogue that lies at the heart of the kind of multiculturalism to which Britain has historically been committed.

Fourthly, Britain's orientation to the world is complex and layered. Thanks to its geography, it has for centuries been deeply involved in European affairs and shares a common European heritage. For obvious historical reasons, it also has close ties with the US whose political culture reflects its own in many respects. And thanks to its empire, large parts of the world too are an integral part of its history and continue to shape its political consciousness, not least in the shape of the post-war immigrants and the Commonwealth of over fifty countries. Britain's global identity is not only a precipitate of its history but also a necessity in an increasingly globalising world. A country with its kind of economy and worldwide interests cannot define itself in isolation from the rest of the world. Britain is thus at once European, Atlantic and global, and none of these alone fully captures its identity. It is a bridge, if we must use that tired and rather mechanical metaphor, between all three and not just the first two.

Democracy, liberal values, cultural diversity, and the European, Atlantic and global orientation then are some of the important ingredients of British identity. To be British is to cherish them as part of one's historical inheritance and to build on them. This does not mean that all Britons agree on what each of these four means and involves and how to resolve their conflicts. While some are happy with the current state of its democracy, others wish to deepen and widen it by devolving more powers to the four nations and their local bodies, introducing proportional representation, electing the House of Lords, and so on. They also disagree about the relative weight of liberal values. Some want free speech to be restricted if it leads to racial or religious hatred, threatens civil disorder or causes distress; others see no need for such restrictions. Some privilege equality over liberty, others propose the opposite. Views also vary about the limits of cultural diversity, and whether to give greater importance to the European, Atlantic or global dimension of its identity. These and other inescapable differences are the stuff of politics, and represent different ways of understanding and building on the country's inherited identity. Although different groups interpret, relate and extend the four basic components of British identity differently, they all value these and resolve their differences within their framework. If any of them were to reject democracy, liberal values or cultural diversity or insist that Britain turn inwards, they would be going against the flow of its history and the logic of its identity. Britain, to put the point differently, is constantly in the making, and is not a fixed entity. It is an ongoing political project, and to be British is to participate in this project in a spirit of commitment and critical sympathy.

As newcomers seek to become part of British society, they and the wider society enter into an implicit moral covenant. The former should undertake to respect its democracy and liberal values, and participate in the ongoing conversation on the kind of country it should be. For its part the wider society should accept them as its legitimate and equal members, and remove obstacles in the path of their full participation in its collective life. It should also respect their legitimate differences because this shows respect for their bearers, and because the differences have the potential to enrich its shared public culture. We should ask both parties to discharge their respective obligations, and require nothing more as the assimilationists demand and nothing less as the isolationist immigrant groups do. As they fulfil their part of the moral covenant, they develop a sense of mutual identification and forge bonds of unity based on a shared political identity.[8]

Notes

1 *Newsweek*, April 1992.
2 'History of patriotism' in Raphael Samuel, ed., *Patriotism: The making and unmaking of British National identity*, Vol. 1, London, Routledge, 1989, p. 203.
3 The term 'Englishness' seems to have been first used by William Taylor of Norwich in 1805 in conscious imitation of the term *Deutschtum* of the early German Romantics. It was widely criticised because it is 'not sanctioned or not current in our language', and also because of its holistic and essentialist implications. See Paul Langford, *Englishness identified: Manners and Character 1650–1850*, Oxford, Oxford University Press, 2000. The term 'Britishness' entered the vocabulary a little later. It is striking that while it has analogues in some countries, it is remarkably absent in others. Few talk of Americanness, Australianness, Brazilianness or South African-ness.
4 For a further discussion, see chapter 4 in my *A New Politics of Identity*, Basingstoke, Palgrave Macmillan, 2008. I briefly distinguish between national character, which pertains to a people, and national identity which pertains to a political community, at p. 284. In British discussion, the political character of the country and the ethno-cultural qualities of its people are systematically confused.
5 For an excellent discussion, See Linda Colley, *Britons: Forging the Nation 1707–1837*, Princeton, Princeton University Press, 1992.
6 John Pocock, 'The limits and divisions of British history: In search of the unknown subject', *American Historical Review*, vol. 87 2, 1982, p. 317.
7 For a most helpful discussion, see Krishan Kumar, *The Making of English National Identity*, Cambridge, Cambridge University Press, 2003.
8 For a fuller discussion, see chapter 5 in my *A New Politics of Identity*. For a long time that lasted well into the 1990s, it was common to talk of people of 'British stock' and to refer to those in Australia, New Zealand and elsewhere as our 'kith and kin'. Today that manner of speaking appears odd, and is rarely used. The term 'British' is now de-ethnicised and used in a largely political sense. No one legislated this change, which is largely a result of a profound transformation in British self-understanding brought about by the presence of ethnic minorities. It is also striking that many ethnic minority members tend to call themselves and are called by foreigners 'British' or 'Britishers' rather than 'Britons', which still retains some of its original ethnic sense.

Britishness: a Role for the State?

VARUN UBEROI and IAIN McLEAN

IN RECENT years the UK government has adopted a broad but ill-defined role in relation to Britishness. It compels those who want to become citizens to participate in citizenship ceremonies which 'reflect our national character'.[1] It provides new immigrants with a description of what it means to be British.[2] Cabinet ministers Jack Straw and John Denham both argue that an 'inclusive British history' needs to be taught to schoolchildren to cultivate a sense of Britishness, and of course Gordon Brown has made numerous speeches on this subject also.[3] At times Conservatives seem more sceptical about any role for government in this area. Hence David Cameron criticises Gordon Brown's 'top down approach to patriotism'[4] and his willingness to 'institutionalise Britishness'.[5] This seeming difference between the government and the Conservatives illustrates that those who run the state can adopt different roles when it comes to Britishness. They can be 'hands off' or act as its custodian, they can try to change the British identity or they can encourage people to remain true to it. But any acceptable role would be one that seemed justified, and in this article we explain why, when it comes to Britishness, a justifiable role for those who run the state is to use the latter to clarify what British people share.[6]

We show why this role is justified in three stages. First, we explain what we mean by Britishness, being British and the British identity (all of which we use interchangeably). Second, we explain why if those who run the state use it to clarify what British people share, they are justified to do so. Third, we show why the objections against such a role are unconvincing, after which we conclude.

What is Britishness?

Politicians, journalists and academics often emphasise the importance of Britishness but it is seldom clear what they are emphasising. Hence Bhikhu Parekh says:

I do not quite know what the word [Britishness] means. It is also rather striking that we seem to be one of the few countries in the world to use that expression. No one talks about 'Americanness', 'Canadianness', 'Frenchness', 'Indianness' or 'Germanness'.[7]

The confusion over Britishness is made worse by some thinking that it is a 'state identity'.[8] They argue that Britain is not a nation but a state, a collection of legal and political structures which control what some, perhaps following Max Weber, call 'the legitimate powers of coercion' in the United Kingdom.

Published by Blackwell Publishing Ltd, 9600 Garsington Road, Oxford OX4 2DQ, UK and 350 Main Street, Malden, MA 02148, USA 41

And if Britain is a state, then it seems to follow that Britishness is a state identity. But this seems incorrect because Britain is not just a state. Historians agree that by the twentieth century those living in Britain shared a ruling class, an empire, an economy, a labour movement, a language and a scientific, intellectual and literary culture.[9] Some of these things have disappeared; but not all of them—in which case Britain is not just a state and Britishness not a state identity, but what then is Britishness?

We take Britishness to denote a national identity but saying so settles little, because what precisely is a national identity? This is not an easy question to answer but we can start by noting that a national identity is a type of identity, and like any identity it summarises something about what its bearer is. Indeed, by the bearer of an identity we mean only the person or group who we usually think of as having an identity which summarises something about them because it distils something more complex about what they are. Hence a person's identity as a father summarises the fact that he has children and a range of parental responsibilities, or a person's identity as a Catholic summarises the fact that she has faith in pre-Reformation Christianity. But by summarising something about what its bearer is, an identity also helps to differentiate them from others. Hence a person's identity as a father summarises the fact that he has children and a range of parental responsibilities, but it also helps to differentiate him from those who have no children or any parental responsibilities. And a person's identity as a Catholic summarises the fact that she has faith in pre-Reformation Christianity, but it also helps to differentiate her from those who believe in other faiths and those who believe in none.[10] An identity then summarises something about what its bearer is; in doing so it helps to differentiate them from others and as this is true of all identities it is also true of national ones.

But who might the bearer of a national identity be? Some might say 'a nation' but this seems misleading. After all, the bearers of a national identity are *members of a nation*, not a nation per se, as it is they who feel and describe themselves as British, French, American and so on. However, if the bearers of a national identity are members of a nation, this means that a national identity must summarise something about what each of them is and the question then is what? As a national identity summarises something about what each member of the nation is, it must summarise something that each of them shares, but what might this be? Anthony Smith gives us a clue when he describes a nation as 'a named human community occupying a homeland, and having common myths and a shared history, a common public culture, a single economy and common rights and duties for all members'.[11] Members of a nation thus share a homeland and a history, they believe in similar myths, possess common rights and duties, adhere to the same public culture and so on. And as they share such things, their national identity must summarise this fact. For each member of a nation, then, their national identity summarises what history, homeland, public culture, rights, duties and so on they share, and in doing so it helps to differentiate them from others. To illustrate the point consider those who say such everyday things like, 'As an American I . . .' or 'I am French, therefore . . .' or 'We the British are . . .' In each case a national identity is being used to summarise what members of a nation share and in doing so it helps to differentiate them from others.

But how do the members of a nation know what they share? After all, each member of the nation may share an understanding of the good life, an ethnicity, a hobby or an occupation with a number of others. But these people are few in number and this does not explain what homeland, history, public culture, rights, duties and so on members of their nation share. Indeed, this knowledge comes from politicians, officials and intellectuals. The latter write books and articles in which they attempt to describe the nation's history, explain why the national homeland is to be revered, suggest how it is meant to be governed and so on. From time to time politicians will also write such books and articles, hence Winston Churchill wrote his *History of the English Speaking Peoples* and James Madison, John Jay and Alexander Hamilton wrote the *Federalist Papers*. But on the whole, politicians and officials suggest what members of the nation share using the state's 'legitimate powers of coercion'. Thus the education system is used to suggest the history that members of the nation share and the law is used to suggest the common rules under which all members of the nation live. Indeed, whilst it can be unclear to politicians and officials that they are using the state to suggest what members of the nation share, there are times when they will be explicit about doing so. Hence, in his address 'To the Italians' in 1871, the great Italian nationalist Giuseppe Mazzini spoke of using the state to develop 'a national conception of life'.[12] In our own day the British government is proposing a 'Statement of Values' and a 'Bill of Rights and Duties', and both are supposed to help clarify what it means to be British.[13]

Some may assert that this is a very 'top down' conception of national identity and resist its application to Britishness. They would reject the reliance that we claim all national identities, including the British one, has on the state. This is because the state only appeared in the modern era and if Britishness is reliant on it, then an identity that many think is authentic and old seems fabricated and new. But any resistance here seems to be part of the 'socio-logical self-deception' that Ernest Gellner once claimed was part of nation-hood.[14] This is because those who form a nation sometimes forget its relatively recent provenance, and this sometimes occurs in Britain as people forget that it did not exist prior to the Anglo-Scottish Union of 1707. For sure, the English, Scots and Welsh identities pre-date the British one. But it was only after the Union that being English and being British became conflated and many of those who regarded themselves as Scottish (and Welsh) began to associate themselves with, and indeed were encouraged to associate them-selves with, being British.[15] So like all national identities, Britishness emerged in the modern era, summarises for each member of the nation what they share and partly does so because the state is used by politicians and officials to suggest what they share.

A role for those who run the state

British politicians and officials thus use the state to suggest to all those living in Britain that they share certain things, and this seems unavoidable. Thus even if the frontiers of the state were 'rolled back', the British government (like any other) would use the state to create a minimal set of laws which would affect all its citizens, enforce these laws in a uniform way, devise common methods to settle disputes and so on. The government of the day cannot avoid using the state to suggest that British people share certain things. But the clarity with which people understand what they share is contingent upon the way that the state is used. So, for example, the fact that the law is used to uphold the same rights for all British citizens and to compel them to perform the same duties will always indicate that they share certain rights and duties. But unless the state is also used to clarify exactly which rights and duties these are, this information will remain somewhat unclear. Or the fact that those who run the state uphold certain traditions like the opening of Parliament or commemorate certain historical moments like the Queen's Golden Jubilee will always indicate to citizens that the polity in which they live has a history. But unless the state's various education systems are used to explain precisely what this history is, it will remain unclear.

Politicians and officials cannot then avoid using the state to indicate that those who live in Britain share certain things. But unless they also use the state to specify what precisely these things are, the understanding that these people have of what they share will remain vague. Those who live in the United Kingdom will perceive that they share certain things but be unsure of precisely what they are. And if their sense of what they share seems unclear, so too will their summary of what they share, so too will their national identity. Hence if the British identity is to be clear, politicians and officials must use the state to clarify what British people share.

But why does the British identity have to be clear? In order to answer this question we must note that those who share national identities are also usually members of the same polity and are thus expected to *trust* one another not to be free riders, to obey the law and bear their fair share of the burdens of collective life. They are also expected to make *sacrifices* for one another, hence they pay taxes which provide services that they may not use, delay their demands so that the more urgent ones of others can be met and they may even be asked to die for one another in times of war.[16] Much is expected of those who share a polity and while the law could be used to compel them to perform such activities, if coercion is to be kept to a minimum it is important that they willingly perform them. But why would the people who share a polity do so? After all, they are largely unknown to one another and we do not usually trust and make sacrifices for strangers. Throughout the modern era national identities have helped those who share a polity to meet this need. This is because, as we have seen, those who share a national identity also believe that they share a history, a homeland, a public culture and so on. Despite their countless differences, in occupation, education, class, sexuality and so on, those who share a national identity feel that they share something significant, something that makes them a group. And like all those who feel that they share something significant, the members of these groups feel attached to one another. Benedict Anderson called this attachment a 'deep horizontal comradeship'; in the modern era those who share it became more willing to trust and make sacrifices for one another and it is easy to understand why, as we are usually willing to trust and make sacrifices for those who we feel attached to. A national identity thus cultivates an attachment between those who share it and helps them to trust and make sacrifices for one another.

But if it is unclear to its bearers, a national identity is less able to perform this function. This is because when a national identity is unclear to its bearers then their summaries of what they share are unclear, thus so too is any reason that they have for thinking that they share anything significant. And if their reason for thinking that they share anything significant is diminished, so too is their attachment to one another and thus their willingness to trust and make sacrifices for one another also. The British identity must be clear to its bearers if it is to cultivate an attachment between them which helps them to trust and make sacrifices for one another. And as we have seen, if the British identity is to be clear, British politicians and officials have to use the state to clarify what British people share.[17]

Arguments against clarifying what British people share

A critic, however, might object to this in one of four ways, and in the first instance he might say that the state should not be used to promote Britishness because doing so is un-British. Indeed, this is precisely how Conservatives have criticised the government's actions in relation to Britishness. Hence, David Cameron refers to the 'understated nature' of the 'British character' and the fact that 'so many of Britain's virtues aren't really for parade'.[18] Now, we accept that using the state to clarify what British people share involves promoting Britishness. After all, if the government were to introduce a programme that clarified what British people share they would have to explain why they want to do so. This would be very difficult without saying that such a programme would also help to clarify the British identity and this is important because it will help British citizens to trust and make sacrifices for one another. As explaining why there is a need to clarify what British people share entails explaining why the British identity is important, the latter is being promoted and there is no escaping this. But it seems strange to suggest that such promotion is un-British.

After all, this notion assumes that the British people share a culture of understatement which, at best, seems more applicable to the English than to the British. Equally, this objection is not, at least logically, a reason for those who run the state to eschew promoting Britishness. Instead it is an observation in which the promotion of Britishness is thought of as inconsistent with a culture of understatement and as far as observations go, it is unclear why it is important. Further, any remaining force that this argument has is removed once we note that historically the state has been used to promote Britishness: thus doing so is actually very British. Consider how politicians and officials have promoted the monarchy as a national symbol. Such promotion occurred with the visit of George IV to Edinburgh in 1822, and gathered pace with the Jubilees of Queen Victoria in 1887 and 1897.[19] And by the coronation of George V, David Cannadine claims *'the departments of state* and the Royal household which had been woefully ignorant of precedent and ceremonial in 1887, had become expert'.[20] Indeed, Cannadine goes on to show how the state was used throughout the twentieth century to make and preserve the monarchy as a national symbol. Given that the state has been used for this purpose and for so long, it is difficult to argue that promoting Britishness is now in some way un-British.

But the critic might offer another objection by noting what could happen if the state is used to clarify what British people share. Politicians and officials will inevitably decide to emphasise certain things, be they historical episodes, myths, symbols or traditions, and in doing so they may decide to exclude or assimilate minorities. After all, politicians and officials could use the state to emphasise that British people share an ancestry and a race neither of which minorities can acquire. Equally, they could use the state to emphasise that British people share a public culture based on a particular religion which religious minorities cannot share unless they convert. By using the state to clarify what British people share, the state can also be used to exclude or assimilate minorities.

We agree that this could happen and historically has done so. But note that this is not a reason for the state to eschew clarifying what British people share and instead it is a warning that those who run the state should be careful about how they do so. After all, the state need not suggest that British people share a race. Instead the state could be used to clarify that British people share many different ancestries and yet they still call Britain their home. Such practices occur in America, Australia and Canada and of course some might claim that these are 'immigrant nations', but this does not explain why such practices should not occur in Britain. The people of Britain share English, Scots, Welsh, Pakistani, Indian, West Indian, Polish and various other ancestries and still call Britain their home.

Nor need the state be used to clarify that British people share a public culture based on a particular religion. Indeed, by a public culture we mean only a body of beliefs and practices that regulates the shared life that members of the polity possess, and the state can be used to suggest that this public culture is thin and capacious.[21] This is because the beliefs and practices that comprise it can be, as much as possible, about procedural issues and preventing certain morally repugnant practices, thus there is plenty of room for other beliefs and practices also. Indeed, Americans are often thought to possess such a thin public culture which, as Michael Walzer claims, leaves 'room for thickness elsewhere' so that people can be 'African American', 'Italian American' and so on.[22] The beliefs and practices that comprise this thin public culture will still contain some bias and they may periodically need to be rethought. But this thin public culture can even be one in which diversity is valued and akin to the public culture that the Canadian federal government has used its policy of multiculturalism over thirty-five years to create.[23] Indeed, in recent years the UK government has used the state to encourage just such a public culture and, of course, some commentators have attacked the government for doing so.[24] But such attacks need not prevent the state from being used to emphasise that British people share a thin public culture in which cultural diversity is valued. And if this occurs minorities are not excluded from, nor do they have to assimilate into, a public culture.

But the critic might deploy a third objection because, as Table 1 shows, Britishness seems to have declined in salience for British citizens whilst their English, Scots and Welsh identities have increased in salience.[25] The data in the table is generated by forcing respondents to choose a national identity which describes them best. And when they are asked this 'forced choice question', clearly there has been a decrease in the number of respondents in England, Scotland and Wales who are prepared to say that their British identity describes them best. This may lead some to claim that clarifying what British people share in order to clarify the British identity is useless because the latter's time has passed.[26]

But this seems unconvincing because a decrease in the salience of the British identity and an increase in the salience of the English, Scottish and Welsh ones may make clarifying what British people share and thus their summary of what they share (their British identity) more urgent. Equally, the data in Table 1 is derived from a forced choice question which as most scholars admit is 'relatively crude'.[27] And we can see why as it asks people to choose the one national identity which describes them best, but the fact that this is their English, Scottish or Welsh identity need not mean that their British identity is unimportant to them. Just as a woman might feel that her identity as a mother describes her best, but her identities as a lover, a lawyer, a sister and a daughter all in different ways say something important about her, so too those who say that their English, Scots or Welsh identity describes them best may still feel that their British identity says something important about them. Indeed, this seems plausible when we ask the more sophisticated 'Moreno' question, which is: 'Which of these statements on this card best describes how you see yourself? Scottish not British, More Scottish than British, Equally Scottish and British, More British than Scottish, British not Scottish'.[28] A similar question is asked to English and Welsh respondents and by doing so the figures shown in Table 2 are generated.[29]

Clearly, an increasing number of people in England, Scotland and Wales do not feel British at all. But at most this is only 17 per cent of the English, 36 per

Table 1: Trends in 'forced choice' national identity—England, Scotland and Wales 1979–2006

	Column percentages							
	1979	1992	1997	1999	2001	2003	2005	2006
England								
English identity	n/a	32	33	44	43	39	40	47
British identity	n/a	63	56	44	45	48	48	39
Other/none	n/a	5	11	12	12	13	12	14
Base		2424	2490	2684	2768	3708	3643	3666
Scotland								
Scottish identity	56	72	73	77	77	72	79	78
British identity	38	25	20	17	16	20	14	14
Other/none	6	3	7	6	7	8	7	8
Base	658	956	874	1481	1605	1508	1549	1594
Wales								
Welsh identity	58	n/a	63	57	57	60	n/a	n/a
British identity	34	n/a	26	30	31	27	n/a	n/a
Other/none	8	n/a	11	13	12	13	n/a	n/a
Base	858		686	794	1085	988		

Sources: British Election Studies 1992–1997; British Social Attitudes Surveys 1999–2006; Scottish Election Surveys 1979–1997; Scottish Social Attitudes Surveys 1999–2006; Welsh Election Survey 1979; Welsh Referendum Survey 1997; Welsh Assembly Election Survey 1999; Welsh Life and Times Surveys 2001 and 2003.

cent of the Scottish and 24 per cent of the Welsh respondents in 2003, 2001 and 2007 respectively. Equally, the vast majority of respondents in England, and a majority in Wales and Scotland, say that they feel British at least to some extent. Little wonder then that Anthony Heath et al. say that 'a sense of British identity . . . remains widespread in all three territories, the majority of British residents . . . have dual identities, as both British and Scottish, British and Welsh or British and English'.[30] Indeed when the majority feel British and Scottish, British and Welsh and British and English, the time of Britishness cannot have passed and clarifying what British people share and thus the British identity is not useless.[31]

Finally, the critic might still cast doubt on whether the state should be used to clarify what British people share by pointing to the difficulties of doing so. After all, under the devolution settlement of 1997–9 many educational and cultural functions are administered in Scotland and Wales, both of which (along with Northern Ireland) have nationalists in government who will be unwilling to use their powers to clarify what British people share, so how is this to occur?

We agree that nationalist governments in Scotland and Wales are unlikely to use their 'legitimate powers of coercion' to clarify what British people

Table 2: Moreno question

England			Column percentages			
		1997	1999	2001	2003	2005
English not British		8	17	17	17	14
More English		17	15	13	20	12
Equally		45	37	42	31	45
More British		14	11	9	13	8
British not English		9	14	11	10	10
Other/none		7	7	8	9	10
Base		2488	2721	2786	1916	2367
Scotland	1992	1997	1999	2001	2003	2005
Scottish not British	19	23	32	36	32	32
More Scottish	40	38	34	30	33	32
Equally	33	27	23	24	22	22
More British	3	4	3	3	4	5
British not Scottish	3	4	4	3	4	5
Other/none	1	4	4	4	5	5
Base	951	876	1481	1605	1508	1549
Wales		1997	1999	2001	2003	2007
Welsh not British		13	18	24	21	24
More Welsh		29	20	23	25	20
Equally		26	35	28	30	32
More British		10	7	11	9	9
British not Welsh		15	14	11	9	9
Other/none		6	6	4	6	5
Base		182	795	1085	988	883

Sources: England—British Election Surveys 1997 and 2005; British Social Attitudes Surveys 1999, 2001 and 2003. Scotland—Scottish Election Studies 1992 and 1997; Scottish Social Attitudes Surveys 1999, 2001, 2003, 2005. Wales—British Elections Survey 1997, Welsh Assembly Election Survey 1999 and Welsh Life and Times Survey 2003, 2007.

share. But as the history of the Parti Québécois shows, such governments come and go and this seems particularly true when they are a minority government as in Scotland, or members of a coalition as in Wales. Those who do not want secession can also then hold power and, in certain situations, could willingly use their 'legitimate powers of coercion' to clarify what British people share. This could occur in two ways. The first is if they were given resources to clarify what British people share, and the Canadian federal government have shown how this could be done. This is because education is a provincial responsibility in Canada. Yet the Canadian federal government has long given, *inter alia*, the provinces financial incentives to deliver citizenship education which helps to clarify what Canadians share, and the UK government could do something similar.[32] Second, the Scottish and Welsh governments could, if they wished, use their 'legitimate powers of coercion' to clarify that Britain is 'a nation of nations'.[33] Again Canada is instructive because a long line of Quebec nationalists from Henri Bourassa to André Laurendeau as well as Anglophone Prime Ministers like Lester Pearson thought that Quebecers belonged to the Quebec nation *and the Canadian nation* and have tried to use the state to affirm this.[34] Similarly, those who control Scotland's and Wales's respective education systems could use them to teach Scottish and Welsh children that they share a homeland that is comprised of three nations as well as several other communities and a history that is intertwined with the history of these other nations and communities also. Indeed, doing so not only has the virtue of truth, it also does not 'crowd out' Scottish and Welsh identities; it *affirms them* whilst also cohering with the thin public culture in which diversity is valued that we pointed to earlier.

Of course, all too often the powers of the state have not been used in this pluralistic way. Instead they have been used to usurp other identities, be they minority national or minority ethnic. But those who run the state need not behave in this way and the UK government could take the lead with the children of England. They could be the first to be taught that they share a homeland comprised of three nations as well as a number of other communities and a history intertwined with these other nations and communities. If this occurred, then those who once used the state to usurp other identities would show that they are now serious about affirming the English, Scottish and Welsh ones, but by clarifying what British people share and thus the British identity also.

Conclusion

In this chapter we have taken Britishness to denote a national identity that summarises for each member of the nation what they share and in doing so helps them to trust and make sacrifices for one another. But its ability to do so is hampered if it is unclear. Thus to make sure that Britishness is clear, those who run the state could use it to clarify what British people share and, as the objections against doing so are unconvincing, when it comes to Britishness, a justifiable role for those who run the state is to use it to clarify what British people share.

Indeed, solely in terms of clarifying what British people share, the UK government's proposed Bill of Rights and Responsibilities seems justified, as it would aid such clarification. If the government were clear about what the values are, this also seems to be true of the government's proposed Statement of Values. But proposals like 'a Britishness day'[35] or flying the union flag from every government building seem more difficult to justify.[36] This is because they seem only to promote Britishness, and while we have recognised that using the state to clarify what British people share entails such promotion, the latter should occur for a reason. Or people inevitably question why Britishness is being promoted, wonder what is to be achieved by doing so and suspect ulterior motives. Proposals then that promote Britishness for the sake of promoting it seem unjustified, but it should now be clear that this is not true of proposals that clarify what British people share.

Notes

1 Home Office press release, 'Citizenship ceremonies welcomed', 9 December 2003. See Section 1 of the Immigration, Nationality and Asylum Act 2002.
2 Home Office, *Life in the United Kingdom*, London, 2006, p. 15.
3 Jack Straw, Cyril Foster Lecture, 25 January 2007, p, 4; J. Denham, 'Who do you want to be?', *Fabian Review*, Winter 2005, p. 7.
4 Conservative party press release, 27 January 2006.
5 D. Cameron, 'Politicians should never try to claim Patriotism for one party', speech, 26 January 2006.
6 By a justifiable role we mean only that there is a clear reason for those who run the state to adopt the role and in doing so, anything seemingly problematic about this role is on reflection unproblematic, or outweighed by the reason for adopting it.
7 Hansard, 28 February 2008.
8 F. Bechhofer and D. McCrone, 'Being British: a crisis of identity?', *The Political Quarterly*, vol. 78, no. 2, 2007, p. 253.
9 K. Kumar, *The Making of the English National Identity*, Cambridge, Cambridge University Press, 2000, p. 173.
10 For fuller discussion see V. Uberoi, 'Do policies of multiculturalism change national identities?', *The Political Quarterly*, vol. 79, no. 3, 2008.
11 A. D. Smith, *Nationalism*, Cambridge, Polity, 2000, pp. 13–15.
12 G. Mazzini, 'To the Italians', in V. Pecora ed., *Nations and Identities*, Oxford, Blackwell Publishing, 2001.
13 Ministry of Justice, *The Governance of Britain*, London, 2007.
14 E. Gellner, *Nations and Nationalism*, Oxford, Blackwell Publishing, 1983, p. 57.
15 For an example of such encouragement see I. McLean and A. McMillan, *The State of the Union*, Oxford, Oxford University Press, 2005, p. 98; see also E. Hobsbawm, *Nations and Nationalism since 1780*, Cambridge, Cambridge University Press, 1991, p. 35.
16 We are grateful to Bhikhu Parekh for the examples used to make this point. B. Parekh, 'Common belonging', *Cohesion, Community and Citizenship, Proceedings of the Runnymede Conference*, 2002, p. 4.
17 A critic might say that surely there are potential alternatives to using the state to clarify what British people share. Hence John Rawls might suggest that a political conception of justice can foster an attachment amongst the citizens of a polity and Jürgen Habermas might suggest that a 'Constitutional Patriotism' can do so also. We accept that these potential alternatives exist, but we don't have the space to consider them here, yet nor do we need to. After all, these potential alternatives need only be entertained if something is seriously wrong with the state being used to clarify what people share, and in the penultimate section of this article we show why the potential criticisms against doing so are implausible. See J. Rawls, *Political*

Liberalism, New York, Columbia University Press, 1996, p. 133–68; J. Habermas, *Between Facts and Norms*, Cambridge, Polity, 1998, pp. 498–517.

18 D. Cameron, speech, ibid.

19 McLean and McMillan, *State of the Union*, p. 98; L. Colley, *Britons*, London, Vintage Books, 1996; D. Cannadine, 'The context, performance and meaning of ritual: the British monarchy and invention of tradition, 1820–1977', in E. Hobsbawm and T. Ranger eds., *The Invention of Tradition*, Cambridge, Cambridge University Press, 1983.

20 Ibid., p. 134; emphasis added.

21 W. Kymlicka, 'Misunderstanding nationalism', in Ronald Beiner ed., *Theorizing Nationalism*, New York, State University of New York Press, 1999, p. 133.

22 M. Walzer, 'Nation states and immigrant societies', in W. Kymlicka and M. Opalski, *Can Liberal Pluralism Be Exported?*, Oxford, Oxford University Press, 2001, p. 151.

23 See V. Uberoi, 'Do policies of multiculturalism change national identities?', and V. Uberoi 'The Canadian constitution and policy of multiculturalism, *Political Studies*, forthcoming.

24 To see how such a public culture is being encouraged see Home Office, *Improving Opportunity, Strengthening Society: The Government's Strategy to Increase Race Equality and Community Cohesion*, 2005, and to find someone who opposes it see M. Phillips, *Londonistan*, London, Gibson Square, 2006.

25 A. F. Heath and J. Roberts, *British Identity: Its Sources and Possible Implications for Civic Attitudes and Behaviour*, research report for Lord Goldsmith's Citizenship Review, 2008, p. 6; www.justice.gov.uk/docs/british-identity.

26 Lucy Stone and Rick Muir from the Institute of Public Policy Research seem to suggest just this when they say that the implications 'for policy makers keen to promote a renewal of Britishness is that they have to reverse a current trend': L. Stone and R. Muir, 'Who are we?', London, IPPR, 2007, p. 10.

27 Ibid.

28 So called because first suggested by the Spanish political scientist Luis Moreno: L. Moreno, 'Scotland and Catalonia: the path to home rule', in D. McCrone and A. Brown eds., *The Scottish Government Yearbook 1988*, Edinburgh: Unit for the Study of Government in Scotland, 1988, pp. 166–82.

29 Heath and Roberts, *British Identity*, p. 7.

30 Ibid., p. 2. Even Bechhofer and McCrone, who have been integral to arguing that there has been a shift away from it and towards minority nationalist identities, argue that 'for most people, it is still a question of being both English (or Scottish) and British'; See F. Bechhofer and D. McCrone, 'Talking the talk: national identity in England and Scotland', in *British Social Attitudes: The 24th Report*, London, Sage, 2008, p. 100.

31 We should be very careful, because the fact that in recent years the British identity has decreased in salience when compared to the English, Scots and Welsh identities need not signify anything out of the ordinary. Obviously, we have no polling data from the eighteenth and nineteenth centuries and the first three quarters of the twentieth century. But it is reasonable to assume that there were other periods when the salience of the British identity rose and fell in comparison to the English, Scottish and Welsh identities. So, for example, after the Second World War the British identity may well have been very salient to the people of

England, but less so when England won the World Cup in 1966. What we are witnessing, then, may be just the usual rise and fall of the British identity.

32 A. Sears, 'Instruments of policy: how the national state influences citizenship education in Canada', *Canadian Ethnic Studies*, vol. 29, no. 2, 1997, pp. 4–7.

33 This seems to echo the notion of a 'community of communities' that Bhikhu Parekh once discussed. But the idea, at least in the authors' minds, is a Canadian one articulated well by former Canadian Prime Minister Lester Pearson, who said that Quebec was 'not just a province, it is a nation within a nation'. Kenneth McRoberts, *Misconceiving Canada*, Oxford, Oxford University Press, 1997, p. 20.

34 Ibid. For a discussion about whether the Scottish case will become akin to the Québécois one see I. McLean, 'Scotland: towards Quebec or Slovakia?', *Regional Studies*, vol. 35, no. 7, 2001.

35 Lord Goldsmith, *Citizenship—Our Common Bond*, London, 2008, pp. 93–6.

36 Department of Culture, Media and Sport, *The Governance of Britain, Flag Flying*, Consultation, London, 2008.

England and Britain, Europe and the Anglosphere

DAVID WILLETTS

England

IDENTITY is in. Those who thought we would enter the twenty-first century as characterless ciphers, our cultural distinctiveness gone, have been proved spectacularly wrong. Roots, ties, and belonging matter as much as ever.

In England we have celebrated these ties with nothing as vulgar as a clear theory. Instead we offer lists of associations:

It is to be doubted whether one person in that whole assembly had a clear thought in his head. Rather, words and their associations marched in a grand chain, giving hand to hand: England, Shakespeare, Elizabeth, London; Westminster, the docks, India, the Cutty Sark, England; England, Gloucestershire, John of Gaunt; Magna Carta, Cromwell, England.

Or

All the characteristics and activities of a people: Derby Day, Henley Regatta, Cowes, the twelfth of August, a Cup Final, the dog races, the pin-table, the dart board, Wensleydale cheese, boiled cabbage cut into sections, beetroot in vinegar, nineteenth century gothic churches and the music of Elgar.

Those are two of my favourite examples—Vita Sackville-West on the congregation at the coronation of King George V and T. S. Eliot on what makes a national culture. Both tell us that we are members of a club with few explicit rules, or rather rules so subtle that they can only be caught by knowing references. It is this understated but potent sense of shared understandings which has been historically one of the features of Englishness.

But can we get any deeper with an account of our identities that has some intellectual rigour and political bite?

There was one traditional account of our identities which drove a powerful political agenda for the last century but has disappeared in the past decade. Class identity is out. That is why the Labour campaign attacking toffs at the Crewe by-election seemed so strangely out of date. The story of the making of the English Working Class has lost its way in the shopping malls of Bluewater and Lakeside.

Some historians have responded to the collapse of these identities fixed in industrial structures by abandoning a belief in any underlying identity. Instead national identities are 'invented' 'imagined' or 'forged'. The Marxist historian Eric Hobsbawm is the key figure behind this transition. The book he edited, *The Invention of Tradition*, is a conspicuous example of the genre. It is as

 Published by Blackwell Publishing Ltd, 9600 Garsington Road, Oxford OX4 2DQ, UK and 350 Main Street, Malden, MA 02148, USA

if, having lost the certainties of economic determinism, one group of historians reacted by assuming any other identity must deep down be a fake.

This approach is strongly linked to the Blairite project through the important theoretical work of Professor Anthony Giddens. He proposes what he calls 'reflexivity', meaning that our identities are chosen, not unreflectively accepted. It is the political equivalent of Hobsbawm's historiography. This is not surprising because it is a reaction to the same event—the decline of tribal class identities.

New Labour was an attempt to invent a new narrative to plug this gap—and narrative is the key word behind this postmodern project. Smart Blairite political operators saw their task as inventing narratives which gave coherence and purpose to the Labour government. This is the intellectual background to the dodgy dossier and the catastrophic loss of confidence by voters in anything any politician says. A coherent and credible account of who we are, looking out to the real world and our actual experiences is important for the restoration of faith in politics. So here is the challenge: can we offer an account of Englishness which is empirically rooted and conceptually rigorous.

I believe we can. It is right under our noses. It is quite simply the main school of English historical writing from its emergence as a serious discipline. David Hume and Sir William Blackstone are key founding figures. It includes Bishop Stubbs, Sir Henry Maine and F. W. Maitland. Maitland was the mentor of one of the leading founders of the Political Studies Association, Sir Ernest Barker, sympathetically captured in Julia Stapleton's excellent account of him 'Englishness and the study of politics'. This, the dominant strand of both English political thought and of historiography, has almost disappeared from view: it is due for a revival. It emphasises the strength and importance of civil society, our country's historic freedoms, a legitimate role for government in providing equitable justice accessible to all, together with a faith in evolutionary social progress.

This tradition can be renewed by enriching it with the insights of the Cambridge school of family history. Its key thinkers such as Peter Laslett and Alan Macfarlane, offer the most serious and empirically grounded account of what it is to be English. They focus on our social structure, notably our nuclear families. I believe it is our family structure which is the key. It is odd that this has had little impact on the political debate but that is about to change now that so much politics is about social issues and with the emphasis David Cameron is rightly putting on the family.

One reason why this school is out of fashion is that it shows what is distinctive about England. It is the opposite of Linda Colley's fashionable argument that we just happened to take a different turn at the Reformation and after a few centuries as a Protestant island off a Catholic continent can now resume our place as another European country. But we are different. It is not that we are right and Continentals are wrong. But we are different from them, apart perhaps for the Low Countries and Denmark which do appear to share many features of our social structure and our political tradition.

Here is a classic description of how we live: 'The majority of ordinary people in England . . . are rampant individuals, highly mobile both geographically and socially, economically "rational", market-oriented and acquisitive, ego-centred in kinship and social life'. In one survey of 140 English families, fifty-one failed to maintain residence for longer than a generation. There was lots of buying and selling of property. On forty-three occasions the house was passed on within the family of which twenty-four were direct blood inheritance. But there were twenty-one cases of the property being conveyed to someone outside the family and ninety-eight cases of an open market sale. This is a fairly familiar story about life in England. However, this was a survey of thirteenth-century England by the historian Alan Macfarlane in his great book, *The Origins of English Individualism*.

Macfarlane shows that England never had serfs and feudalism in the form they existed on the Continent. It looks as if we have had unusually small nuclear families since at least the early Middle Ages. You left the family home earlier than in most other cultures to be an apprentice or a servant. You then had to save up or get a job well paid enough to get a place to live with your partner, chosen by you not your family. Your parents had no obligation to support you and you had no automatic right to inherit any of their property— unlike inheritance laws in France for example where the children still have an automatic right to inherit the family property. This meant that the support you got from your own family was surprisingly modest. In other words you are individualistic, free from parental authority and need instead other forms of support when things are bad.

Our unusual nuclear families and our distinctive form of civil society are closely linked. With small families you look out to others for support as you cannot rely on a clan. Other countries may have a strong civil society but it is usually based on the extended family or on Church-sponsored social organisations. But ours was more voluntary and open. In the words of a London guild more than a thousand years ago: 'if our lord or any of our reeves can suggest to us any addition to our peace-guild (rather) let us accept it joyfully, as becomes us all and is necessary for us'.

The idea of the corporation was carefully investigated by the Victorian historians such as Maitland and Maine. Macaulay celebrates our civil society with a hint of friendly amusement: 'This is the age of societies. There is scarcely one Englishman in ten who has not belonged to some association for distributing books, or for prosecuting them; for sending invalids to the hospital or beggars to the treadmill; for giving plate to the rich or blankets to the poor.'

Small families need a strong civil society. You turn to a rich network of clubs and friendly societies. And they need markets too. If we need something we can also turn to Yellow Pages, rather than a family member. Instead of using the mutual exchanges of the extended family, you must buy services. This requires commercial transactions, contracts and the marketplace. This makes an economy open and market-facing. We did not have the Industrial Revolution and then become a market society. It was the other way round. We were already the world's first market society and therefore the birth place of the modern industrial economy.

Blackstone has a phrase which brings all this together very neatly—we are 'a polite and commercial people'.

Emmanuel Todd is the key thinker in this fascinating research programme assessing the impact of family structures on political and social arrangements. He has identified other parts of Europe with our distinctive family structure, such as the Netherlands and Denmark, and then casually notes that these happen to be the areas of Europe once held by King Canute. This gives an idea of the timescale over which we have held this family structure. King Alfred's law codes place very weak obligations on families. They are not the laws of a clan society. A recent study of European families by Duranton, Rodriguez-Pose and Sandall showed that these patterns continue to matter today. People in societies with inegalitarian nuclear families like England, Denmark and the Netherlands, are the likeliest to join clubs and associations.

The origins of this family structure are more speculative. But the explanation that seems to me most plausible goes back to the Anglo-Saxons. Benjamin Franklin put it as simply as anyone—'Britain was once the America of the Germans'. We have kept Anglo-Saxon social structures even whilst Roman law made a come back across most parts of the Continent.

Great Britain

So far I have concentrated on England. Let us now turn to Britishness. This is emphatically not the same thing. Scotland has a distinctive history, with a separate legal system and educational arrangements and a different culture. Great Britain provides the political institutions which link these two nations in above all an outward-looking endeavour of trade and conquest—it is the British army, the British Empire and the British pound. That deal has made both nations different and better than they would be on their own—and in the early excitement after the Act of Union, Scots such as David Hume were willing to describe themselves as living in North Britain.

Britishness is a much weaker cultural identity than Englishness or Scottishness. It is a political identity resting above all on a set of political institutions. This gives it a marvellous openness—there is no ethnic element to it for example. That is why H. G. Wells could say that 'The great advantage of being British is that we do not have a national dress'. But it does present a challenge when British identity is so tied up with a particular set of political institutions—a point we will come back to.

Norman Davies in his powerful book, *The Isles*, helps us to understand that the English model is just one within the British Isles. If I were to date my party's decline in Scotland to any one moment it would be when we stopped running as unionists. That unionist identity reflected the origins of much of the Scottish Party in the Liberal unionist tradition, which merged with the Conservatives after the Liberal split on Ireland. Instead in the 1960s we insisted on giving the Scottish party a more Conservative identity—symbolised in the shift from orange to blue. But there must be a place in the Scottish political debate, just as elsewhere in Europe, for a modern centre right party that is sceptical about the expansion of the state and believes in market economics and the family. This is the space we can occupy in the future.

There are British political institutions and Scottish ones but no English ones. This is the English Question. Kenneth Clarke has recently put forward some excellent ideas that could ensure a distinctive English voice is heard in Parliament without destabilising the entire constitutional structure.

We can pause now to reflect on one of Gordon Brown's favourite thinkers and the great intellectual movement she has popularised—the British Enlightenment. In the past decade Gertrude Himmelfarb has done more than anyone to remind us of the extraordinary flowering of great Scottish thinkers such as David Hume, Adam Smith and Adam Ferguson. How did this small nation produce thinkers who got to the heart of modernity by making sense of markets, contracts and civil society far better than the French? I believe the explanation is the union with England. The British Enlightenment is Scottish thinkers observing English society and economy.

Europe

What about Europe? Where does it fit in? One view is set out in Linda Colley's lively and enjoyable book, *Britons*. As the Marxist faith in class identity falls away so our identity as British is shown to be artificial, but deep down beneath it there is an ur-identity which is European. Her argument that we were forged by the experience of wars against Continental powers must have some truth to it. But it misses the sense that we are different. Indeed this is what the Continental European thinkers such as Montesquieu observed 'I too have been a traveller, and have seen the country in the world which is most worth of our curiosity —I mean England'.

Europe's extraordinary cultural and scientific achievements over the past five hundred years do give Europe a shared identity. But what gave Europe its drive and dynamism was surely its fragmentation and its diversity. This is the argument put most notably in the book *The Wealth and Poverty of Nations* by David Landes. Five hundred years ago China was the world's most advanced and sophisticated society. But the next half millennium saw most of the world's intellectual and scientific advances in Europe. The explanation David Landes offers is that China had a single and powerful political authority. Europe did not. If the prince did not like the scientific experiments you were carrying out or the poetry you were writing you could flee over the border to a different prince who would tolerate them. Trying to build Europe by standardising everything from drinking water to wine bottles is a betrayal of the true source of its greatness.

There are now European political institutions. They present a peculiar challenge to Great Britain for the reason we saw earlier. National identity need not depend on the same features in different countries. One way of observing this is the tourist test. What do foreign tourists want to visit and photograph to capture the distinctive otherness of a different country? When they are in Paris they want to see the Impressionist paintings and enjoy French cuisine but they do not queue up outside the Assemblée Nationale or photograph the Elysée. In Italy it is similarly culture and history which matter. But when tourists are in London they photograph Parliament and stand outside Buckingham Palace and Downing Street—these national symbols are also political institutions. These institutions have a long and continuous history, another reason why we have invested so much in them as sources of pride and belonging. If Europe were being constructed by a harmonised cuisine or a standardised culture it might have proved more controversial in other countries. But Europe as a political project is particularly problematic for Britain because Britishness above all depends on a set of political institutions.

This challenge was answered most radically by John Major in one of the most important and misunderstood speeches on the subject. Here is a famous quote:

The clatter of clogs in the Lancashire mill towns, the to-and–fro of the lorries on the Great North Road, the queues outside the labour exchanges, the rattle of pin tables in Soho pubs, the old maids biking to holy communion through the mists of the autumn morning—all these are not only fragments, but characteristic fragments of the English scene.

This sepia-tinted image of England actually comes of course from George Orwell. He was deliberately quoted by John Major in a speech on Europe to make a rather important and interesting challenge to the conventional wisdom. George Orwell, the radical critic of so many features of our national life, was writing during the Second World War and trying to explain what he felt we were fighting for. As such a stern critic of his country he could not quite give a conventional list of political institutions which made our country great. Instead he gave another one of those cultural lists of associations. He was offering a definition of Englishness that did not depend on Britain's political arrangements.

John Major was quoting this to argue, very boldly, that the process of building Europe was not as much a threat as people feared because the essential cultural features of our national identity would survive. But the trouble is that, as the full quote from George Orwell makes clear, this is a list of English cultural associations. That is why it does not resolve the problem. England at least as a cultural and social entity might survive in a federal Europe. Great Britain could not.

David Willetts

The Anglosphere

Finally in our list of identities, what about the Anglosphere? There is something real here. Even though it has never had political expression, it pops up all over the place from military and intelligence cooperation to surprisingly similar economic structures and growth rates. At its heart is the Special Relationship between Great Britain and the USA but it includes New Zealand, Australia, Canada and, in interesting and complicated ways, Ireland and India.

It is easy to think of the English language as what gives this group its identity—after all it was formerly known as the English-speaking peoples. But this does not tell anything like the whole story. A distinctive and unusually strong civil society is crucial. And we immediately face a strange paradox. Alexis de Tocqueville was one of the first people to see that the youthful USA derived much of its dynamism from its extraordinarily rich and self-reliant civil society. But he is also one of the biggest obstacles to understanding what the USA and England share. The trouble is he suffers from one massive disadvantage—he went to America before he visited England. When he wrote his great book on democracy in America he was completely unaware of the English origins of the American model. In fact he thought that England was trapped in an aristocratic and feudal past and that the vigour of civil society in America was unique. This is a crucial mistake. It has left us all, metaphorically at least, condemned to Denholm Eliot's fate—forever playing butlers in American films.

When he finally visited England, Toqueville was like a proto-Marxist, trying to work out when the revolution which America and France had already experienced would also strike England, leading to the overthrow of the powerful concentrations of aristocratic wealth. He expected some Jeffersonian revolution in favour of agricultural small-holdings. He only came to appreciate that what he had seen in America could also be found in England after two visits—the moment of epiphany coming when he visited my home town of Birmingham in the full vigour of the Industrial Revolution and noted in his diary that they are 'generally very intelligent people but intelligent in the American Way'.

Toqueville thought at first that America was the future for everywhere—and indeed that France having already had its revolution was further on the way than England. But slowly he came to realise that this model was not right. The vigour of civil society in England or the USA is not some universal trend. Why do some countries have a very different civil society from others?

I believe we share a similar civil society because we share that rather unusual family structure which was described earlier. We both have the classic nuclear family. However, quite unusually, this is also combined with an 'inegalitarian' system of inheritance. The Anglosphere family is also unusual in having no special status in property law it is a relationship not a project. But once more there are frustrating misunderstandings between

Britain and America which obscure this crucial point about our shared family structure. Nancy Cott's classic history of the American family, *Public Vows: a History of Marriage and the Nation* talks of the nuclear family as the republican family—seeing it as an example of republican virtue contrasting with the decadence of European families. But the real dividing line is to be drawn differently. American family structure is the same as the English model and very different from much of Continental Europe. The Special Relationship depends on a special relationship.

What Britishness Means to the British

PETER KELLNER

THREE years ago the Commission for Racial Equality commissioned YouGov to conduct two parallel, wide-ranging surveys—one of white Britons, the other of non-white Britons. Against my advice, Trevor Phillips, the CRE's chairman, insisted that we include a simple open-ended question: 'what does the term "Britishness" mean to you?' Respondents were not given alternative answers to tick; they were asked to give their own unprompted answers in their own words.

I warned Trevor that the responses would provide nothing of interest. They would wander all over the place and provide no coherent pattern for us to analyse. Trevor rejected my warning. As he was the client who was paying for the survey, we went ahead.

Trevor turned out to be right. I was wrong. When we coded and added up the responses, they revealed something highly significant. Broadly speaking, most answers fell into one of two categories: either geography/tradition (e.g. place of birth, monarchy, pride in British achievements) or values (e.g. democracy, fairness, free speech). That was, perhaps, predictable. What was striking was that by two-to-one, white respondents opted for geography/tradition, while non-white respondents, also by two-to-one, opted for values.

Here are some typical responses:

Holding certain values, beliefs and behaviour which people who live in Britain tend to display. For me, the best of Britishness would be a belief in the rule of law, fair play, moderation in politics: 'common decency'. However, the worst traits of Britishness are: a) lapses in civic consciousness such as hooliganism and public drunkness and b) philistinism

non-white respondent

Being America's lapdog, falling manufacturing business, football yobs, soft touch for immigrants (legal & illegal) & no national pride

non-white respondent

Someone whose great grandparents were born in Britain. Persons who put Britain before themselves. Persons who, if their families are recent arrivals, are prepared to accept the British way of life and laws above their natural instincts. When in Rome do as the Romans do . . .

white respondent

Stiff upper lip, slightly conservative, fish and chips, tea, history, old Empire

white respondent

 Published by Blackwell Publishing Ltd, 9600 Garsington Road, Oxford OX4 2DQ, UK and 350 Main Street, Malden, MA 02148, USA

Examining the answers I discovered something about myself. Had I been surveyed I would have placed myself firmly on the values side of the divide. As I am white and British-born, is this simply because I have a centre-left outlook on life? Or, could it be that my outlook has been influenced more than I realised by my family origins—the fact that my Jewish, Austrian-born father came to Britain at the end of the Second World War, having volunteered from Palestine to join the British army in order to help democracy defeat Nazism? He ended up British by choice, not British by birth. It may well be that his particular brand of British patriotism rubbed off on me.

This reflection prompts a wider point. Meanings in political debate can be far more slippery than we realise. Words with apparently unambiguous definitions turn out to carry a variety of different sentiments, depending on the roots, circumstances and standpoint of the person using them. 'Britishness' certainly falls into this category. It means different things to different people. As other YouGov research shows, the range of attitudes goes way beyond the differences between white and non-white Britons.

In July 2005, a YouGov survey for the *Daily Telegraph* tested thirty-five words and phrases that are sometimes, or frequently, associated with Britain. In each case we asked people how important it was in defining 'Britishness'. Table 1 shows how many people said 'very important' in each case. The two top phrases were 'British people's right to say what they think' (61 per cent) and 'Britain's defiance of Nazi Germany in 1940' (59 per cent). Four other items scored more than 50 per cent: fairness and fair play; Britain's landscape; scientific and engineering achievements; and British justice.

Those six items straddle the values and tradition/geography divide. But they have two things in common. They are attributes that are relevant to us all, and they are relevant to the modern era. Narrower and older features of Britishness achieve lower scores, as do institutions, a number of which are widely thought to be remote, or not centrally relevant to everyday life today. Note, for example, the monarchy (considered a 'very important' feature of Britishness by 38 per cent), the House of Commons (37 per cent), 'Land of Hope and Glory' (31 per cent); 'God Save the Queen' (29 per cent); The battles of Trafalgar and Waterloo (28 per cent); and Britain's empire (25 per cent). Perhaps the most surprising member of this group is the BBC, which scores a lowly 27 per cent. I suspect that this would have rated more highly between the 1940s and 1970s, when it dominated our viewing and listening more than it does in today's multi-channel times.

Another group that achieves low scores might be termed the John Major category. In 1993 the then Prime Minister said: 'Fifty years on from now, Britain will still be the country of long shadows on cricket grounds, warm beer, invincible green suburbs, dog lovers and pools fillers and, as George Orwell said, "Old maids bicycling to holy communion through the morning mist"; and, if we get our way, "Shakespeare will still be read even in school."' The relevant scores from YouGov's survey are: cricket (16 per cent); warm beer (8 per cent); the Church of England (17 per cent); our weather (23 per

Table 1: How the British define 'Britishness'

Below is a list of phrases which might be used to describe or define Britain and what it is to be British. For each one, please indicate how important you think that word or phrase is in defining 'Britishness'	% saying 'very important'
Most people say 'very important'	
British people's right to say what they think	61
Britain's defiance of Nazi Germany in 1940	59
British people's sense of fairness and fair play	54
The landscape of Britain	53
The achievements of Britain's scientists and engineers	52
British justice	51
Between one third and one half the public say 'very important'	
Our parliamentary democracy	49
People's politeness and consideration towards one another	47
The Royal Navy	42
Having a strong economy	41
Their tolerance of other people and other people's ideas	41
The fact that Britain has not been invaded since 1066	41
British people's stoicism—their ability to 'take it'	40
Britain's role in the world today	38
The Monarchy	38
The House of Commons	37
The Common Law	34
The fact that Britain has not been divided by civil war since the 17th century	33
Between one fifth and one third of the public say 'very important'	
'Land of Hope and Glory'	31
The fact that Britain consists of three countries: England, Scotland and Wales	30
'God Save the Queen'	29
The battles of Trafalgar and Waterloo	28
The BBC	27
Pubs	27
The fact that Britain once had a great Empire	25
William Shakespeare	24
Driving on the left	24
Our weather	23
The fact that we don't have to carry identity cards	23
Double-decker buses	20
Less than one fifth of the public say 'very important'	
Red telephone boxes	19
The Church of England	17
Cricket	16
The motorway network	12
The quality of Britain's restaurants	9
Britain's membership of the European Union	9
Warm British beer	8

Source: YouGov; sample size: 3505; fieldwork: 20th–22nd July 2005

cent); and Shakespeare (24 per cent). Nostalgia, as they say, is not what it used to be. One might add two low-scoring, historically-recent recent traditions: double-decker buses (20 per cent) and red telephone boxes (19 per cent).

Is the explanation for this that there is a sharp generational divide, with today's young adults scorning their parents' cherished view of Britain? No—at least not in the John Major category. In two of the five items in that group, the under 35s are actually more likely than those aged 55 and over to say they are 'very important' aspects of Britishness: warm beer, and our weather. As for the other three 'Major' items, there is little difference between young and old.

There are, though, seven phrases where there is an acute generational divide, with the 'very important' scores among the 55+ age group at least 20 points higher than among the under 35s: our right to say what we think (over 55s: 72 per cent; under 35s: 48 per cent); our defiance of Hitler in 1940 (72 per cent; 48 per cent); our sense of fairness (63 per cent; 43 per cent); British justice (63 per cent; 37 per cent); our parliamentary democracy (60 per cent; 39 per cent); the Royal Navy (55 per cent; 32 per cent) and the fact that we have not been divided by civil war since the seventeenth century (48 per cent; 21 per cent). In various ways, these all relate to the battles fought down the centuries to give us our democratic inheritance.

One pair of items crystallises cause for concern. Whereas three times as many of those aged 55+ apply the label 'very important' to our parliamentary democracy (60 per cent) as to pubs (21 per cent); among the under 35s, the two figures are very similar (39 per cent; 36 per cent). What is not clear from a single snapshot is whether this reflects a long-term shift in attitudes, or a cohort effect (whereby today's younger adults will gradually adopt the stance of their parents as they grow older).

What about today's Britain? More specifically, what do we think about ourselves as a people? YouGov recently posed a pair of questions for *The Political Quarterly*. We listed 12 attributes—six positive and six negative—and asked respondents to say which three or four applied most to British people. The results are shown in Table 2. The virtues scored an average of 34 per cent, with 'democratic' (45 per cent) and 'love animals' (41 per cent) heading the list; 'generous' (21 per cent) was the virtue we least applied to our fellow Britons. The perceived defects were headed by 'drunken' (33 per cent) and 'rude' (22 per cent). But only 4 per cent think of the British as 'mean'. On average, while the virtues scored 34 per cent, the defects scored 18 per cent.

Once again, there are worrying signs of a generation gap. Among those aged 55 and over, the virtues score an average of 41 per cent, headed by 'love animals' (52 per cent) and 'democratic' (51 per cent), while our defects score an average of just 16 per cent (headed by 'drunken', on 27 per cent).

Among the under 35s, however, the highest-scoring attribute is a negative one. 'Drunken' (38 per cent) just pips 'democratic' (37 per cent). Overall, in this age group, our virtues score an average of just 27 per cent, while our defects are not far behind, averaging 21 per cent. Younger adults may be

Table 2: How we see ourselves—and how we think others see us

Thinking about British people, both as they are viewed by the British themselves, and as they are viewed by people from other countries (a) Which three or four of these descriptions do YOU think apply most to British people? (b) And which three or four of these descriptions do you think PEOPLE IN OTHER COUNTRIES think apply most to British people?	(a) How we see ourselves %	(b) How we think others see us %
Democratic	45	16
Love animals	41	21
Patriotic	37	19
Fair-minded	33	11
Drunken	32	66
Tolerant	29	15
Rude	22	41
Generous	21	7
Arrogant	19	41
Narrow-minded	18	23
Racist	14	31
Mean	4	9
None of these	2	1
Don't know	5	10

Source: YouGov; sample 2,422; fieldwork June 20–23, 2008

almost as proud of Britain as their parents' generation, but they are less convinced that the British people behave well.

We then repeated the list and asked which three or four attributes they thought people in other countries applied to the British. It turns out we are fearful of our reputation. The five highest scoring attributes are all defects; together, the six scored an average of 35 per cent, while our virtues averaged just 13 per cent. Fully 66 per cent of us think the rest of the world regards the British as 'drunken', while 41 per cent say we are perceived as 'rude' and the same number say 'arrogant'. Now, what we believe others think us to be like may be different from the way the rest of the world actually regards us; but it does seem that bad news stories of the way we behave abroad, from football grounds to Mediterranean beaches, not to mention accounts of our recent mad-dogs-and-Englishmen imperial past, have left their mark.

For all that, a large majority of us say we are proud to be British. Our 2005 survey found that the proportions saying they are 'very' or 'fairly' proud are 84 per cent among the under 35s, 85 per cent among the 25–54s and 87 per cent among those aged 55 or older. And non-white Britons (83 per cent) say this almost as much as white Britons (87 per cent).

When we divide the figures between those who are 'very' proud and those who are 'fairly' proud, we find that overall, 50 per cent say they are 'very proud' and 36 per cent 'fairly proud'. Those figures are broadly the same among all groups, with two exceptions: among Scots the figures are: 32 per cent 'very proud' and 44 per cent 'fairly proud'. Among non-white Britons they are 42 per cent 'very proud' and 41 per cent 'fairly proud'. In other words, the totals in both groups saying they are proud are not far short of those of everyone else, but theirs is, to some extent, a more qualified sense of pride.

Pride, of course, can have a variety of roots. Is one of them a sense that Britain today is the best country in any practical sense? To find out, YouGov recently asked how the United Kingdom compared with nine other countries on eight different attributes; in each case, which country is best?

As Table 3 shows, the UK is reckoned to come top on three attributes: we are considered to be the most tolerant, to have the best form of democracy and, curiously, to have the best public services, such as health and education. However, a closer look at the figures shows that, although no single other country is thought to outrank Britain, the totals naming other countries always exceed those naming Britain.

Thus, 35 per cent think the UK is the most tolerant of the ten countries, Sweden, on 12 per cent, comes a distant second. But altogether, 46 per cent name one of the other nine countries. When asked which country has the best form of democracy, 27 per cent say the UK, while other countries total 42 per cent, with Australia, on 12 per cent, heading the pack.

With public services, our surprising first place looks less impressive when we note that just 22 per cent say the UK, while 57 per cent say one of the other countries, with Sweden scoring 18 per cent and Germany, Canada, France, Switzerland and Australia scoring 6–8 per cent each.

With the five other attributes, the UK is not even reckoned to come first. On which has the friendliest people, the UK (13 per cent) is outpolled by Australia (21 per cent) and Ireland (also 21 per cent). Asked which has the hardest-working workforce, Japan (48 per cent) easily leads the field, with Germany (15 per cent) coming a distant second, followed by the UK (13 per cent). In the case of the other three attributes, the UK does not even make it into double figures. Just nine per cent say we are the most patriotic. Here the United States, with a 59 per cent score, enjoys the highest rating of any single country on any specific attribute.

The UK's lowest score is the four per cent who think we have the highest average income. On this we are perceived to come sixth, behind Switzerland, the United States, Sweden, Germany and Japan. Although these figures bear some relation to reality, as Britain's income per head has not led the world for many decades, the differences are also noteworthy. According to the latest OECD figures, the United States clearly comes top, with an average income 44 per cent higher than the OECD average (once both currency rates and domestic prices levels are taken into account), followed by Ireland, 31 per cent above the average, Switzerland (22 per cent above average), Canada (21 per cent), Australia (13 per cent) and Sweden (10 per cent). Britain comes seventh in this group of ten (nine per cent above the OECD average), with

Table 3: How Britain compares with other countries

To which of the following countries do you think each of these statements BEST applies?	%
Is the most tolerant	
UNITED KINGDOM	35
Sweden	12
Canada	9
Switzerland	8
Australia	8
Ireland	3
United States	3
Japan	2
Germany	1
France	1
Don't Know	19
Total non-UK countries	46
Has the best form of democracy	
UNITED KINGDOM	27
Australia	12
United States	7
Sweden	6
Switzerland	6
Canada	4
Ireland	2
France	2
Germany	2
Japan	0
Don't Know	31
Total non-UK countries	42
Has the best public services (e.g. health, education)	
UNITED KINGDOM	22
Sweden	18
Germany	8
Canada	6
France	6
Switzerland	6
Australia	6
United States	3
Japan	3
Ireland	1
Don't Know	21
Total non-UK countries	57
Has the friendliest people	
Australia	21
Ireland	21
UNITED KINGDOM	13

Table 3 (*cont.*)

Canada	10
United States	9
Sweden	4
Japan	2
Switzerland	2
Germany	1
France	0
Don't Know	16
Total non-UK countries	71

Has the hardest-working workforce

Japan	48
Germany	15
UNITED KINGDOM	13
United States	3
Australia	2
Canada	2
Sweden	1
Switzerland	1
Ireland	1
France	0
Don't Know	13
Total non-UK countries	74

Is the most patriotic

United States	59
UNITED KINGDOM	9
Australia	6
Japan	4
France	4
Germany	3
Ireland	3
Canada	2
Switzerland	1
Sweden	0
Don't Know	10
Total non-UK countries	81

Overall provides the best quality of life for ordinary people

Australia	28
Sweden	14
Canada	13
Switzerland	9
UNITED KINGDOM	8
Germany	4
United States	3
France	3
Ireland	2

Table 3 (*cont.*)

Japan	1
Don't Know	15
Total non-UK countries	77
Has the highest average income	%
Switzerland	23
United States	14
Sweden	9
Germany	9
Japan	8
UNITED KINGDOM	4
Australia	3
Canada	3
Ireland	1
France	1
Don't Know	24
Total non-UK countries	72

Source: YouGov; sample 1,641; fieldwork June 26–27, 2008

Germany (five per cent), Japan (four per cent) and France (two per cent) bringing up the tail. So one in six Britons reckon that either the Germans or the Japanese have the world's highest average incomes when, in fact (or, at least, the OECD version of the facts) they are not only way off the pace, but actually have lower average incomes than the British.

What about the best quality of life for ordinary people? This is a concept that goes far beyond economics. Perhaps, when we take into account all the facets of living in Britain today, our pride in being British translates into a sense that we have the best quality of life in the world? Those who think that are in a small minority: just eight per cent. Australia comes top, with 28 per cent regarding it as having the best quality of life, followed by Sweden (14 per cent), Canada (13 per cent) and Switzerland (9 per cent).

The Scots are the least likely group to say the quality of life in Britain leads the world: just three per cent of them think this. And it is not the case that there is a generation gap between the contentedly patriotic elderly and their angry children. Indeed, if anything, the trend is the other way, with 10 per cent of 18–34s saying the UK has the best quality of life in the world, and just seven per cent of the 55+ age group agreeing. Where there is a more orthodox generation gap is in attitudes to tolerance. Forty-two per cent of those aged 55 and over say the UK is the most tolerant of the ten countries; just 28 per cent of the 18–34s agree.

Pride in Britain, then, is more to do with our identity than with any widespread feeling these days that, on any specific measure, Britain leads the world. We are proud to be British chiefly because we are British. Is that glue strong enough to hold us together? Could debates in England, Scotland,

Wales and Northern Ireland cause more of us to amend our sense of national identity? Might a majority of us end up transferring our appreciation of our values and traditions from Britain as a whole to our own country within the UK? These are large questions that are beyond the scope of this article. However, I do hope to be around long enough to measure the answers that the Britons themselves give in the years ahead.

The BBC and Metabolising Britishness: Critical Patriotism

JEAN SEATON

A FEW years ago my husband and I went to a garden party at Buckingham Palace (he was doing a bit of research). These vast fetes are not remotely posh—and are surprisingly democratic events swarming with legions of tea ladies, people who do noble things to be *useful*, volunteers, soldiers, policemen, nurses, with a sprinkling of lawyers, civil servants and industrialists who all mill about, drinking tea and lemonade while brass bands play. Uncomfortable in their best shoes, the chosen potter around the Queen's back garden (municipal, with a scruffy tennis court). The mood is jolly, proud, a tiny bit smug, not particularly deferential and tense from the strain of all that best behaviour (a fit of the giggles is never far away, as it is all so deliciously prurient as one peers at her majesty's compost heap), but above all there is a pervading sense of cheery enjoyment. It is emphatically non-suave.

However I made one startling, observational discovery. Apparently, if you ask several thousand women from every part of the UK to a garden party, they come dressed as an herbaceous border in full riot. Women of every size (mostly large and larger), colour, class, region, profession, age and taste dazzled in frocks smothered in roses and lilies, ferns and poppies, violets and daisies. The Queen was in one, I was in one, we were all in one. Very gorgeous the collective frock looked too: it was not chic—but it made me beam. No assembly of French, American, Chinese or Iranian women would have looked like that. When reaching out for a way to celebrate themselves, the ladies of Britain found a common language. It was a way of representing ourselves grasped unconsciously and all the more powerful for that—we belonged together.

Yet everywhere there is an anxious inspection of national tea leaves for what they might portend (except, of course, we don't drink as much tea as we used to—perhaps even our auguries have become unreliable?). What is 'Britishness'? This is not the first tentatively anxious enquiry into the mystery. It tends to come up when people are uncertain about it—for if you are clear what it is and that you feel it, there is no question to be asked. Despite the revolutions in how we live, are there continuing sensibilities and processes that provide a recognisable architecture to what we want to be?

The problem is not that Britain has changed but rather whether we need it any more. The national project has, it is argued, been unsettled by colliding forces, which play out in confusingly opposite directions. Nevertheless, slightly subversively, one might observe that 'Britishness', and certainly the British constitution, have always been a muddle: we just have a new

 Published by Blackwell Publishing Ltd, 9600 Garsington Road, Oxford OX4 2DQ, UK and 350 Main Street, Malden, MA 02148, USA

emerging muddle which has given some power (but by no means all or the most sensible bits) to a new fairer settlement—messiness sometimes works rather well. However, the great contemporary priority is tidiness and written down-ness. The holy grail of 'transparency' has been understood to mean that codifying everything that moves is seen as a solution to abuses of power, when a code is often merely a map of formal relations—when the abuses might still flourish in the informal practice. Although the worry is that the muddle no longer has any coherence, simply tidying up 'Britishness' will not make it real. Indeed, more than ever, being 'British' is voluntary not necessary.

There are a number of things nibbling and gnawing at our sense of our selves. Firstly there are the physical frontiers of the nation. The British now have almost no grasp of the fact that we are still 'an island nation' (let alone 'this sceptred isle') as people come and go by air not sea, by internet not mail, the vivid apprehension of our coastal edges and what they have meant (and still mean) has almost disappeared. However, the most obvious way that Britishness is under strain is the rise and rise of nationalisms. Scotland and to a lesser extent Wales bustle with novel institutions and apparently 'feel' no Britishness. Scotland apparently wants to be shot of 'us'. Anthony King's mordant and shrewd assessment of the state of the British constitution argues that the devolutionary engine we have landed ourselves with has an in-built friction that will inevitably lead to separation. What about England? (Which, as a child, I just assumed *was* Britain; the titles seemed interchangeable—as they did many writers in the late twentieth century.) King's conclusions are marred by a certain glumness, but despite some acute observations (a reformed House of Lords, the author fears, could wind up comprising 'a miscellaneous assemblage of party hacks, political careerists, clapped-out retired or defeated MPs, has-beens, never-weres and never-could-possibly-bes'[1]), it is more profoundly limited by a blindness to the shifting nature of power in every aspect of contemporary lives. There is a real revolution going on from the music industry, to the mutating publishing trade, to news, and from surveillance to consuming. In every aspect of private lives and societies there is a technologically-driven Wild West frontier re-making old relation-ships of authority. Constitutional change must mirror a new compact that other forces are making with British citizens. The shape of power is changing and what a nation is must change with it.

In addition there are many separatist enthusiasts around in the political and intellectual classes. It is nevertheless perhaps worth noting that at least some of the advocates for the 'break up' scenario tend to ignore Northern Ireland which is far more settled in Ireland and in the EU and in the Union than it has been for thirty years of bloody grinding conflict, not least because as Roy Foster shows in a tour de force of evidence and argument in *The Luck of the Irish*, Ireland has changed out of all recognition—although in fits and starts. He sardonically points out with a certain glee that none of this has happened in any of the ways in which the instigators of the conflict hoped or predicted.

Ireland has become secular, feminised, venal, successful, vulgar and the very last thing it wants or is interested in is Northern Ireland.[2] But perhaps Northern Ireland—for so long the most agitated of the nations—has become an inconvenient and complicating reality that many of the protagonists of dissolution prefer to ignore.

However, while the political geography of the nation is fretfully bothersome (as a Seaton whose mother's maiden name was McKenzie, who spent my Battersea childhood in tartan kilts—along with a brother called Andrew with red hair and freckles, the prospect of being dumped by Scotland and spending the rest of my life in a one party state is a trifle irritating), nevertheless, many other aspects of 'geography' and indeed landscape have disappeared. As Robert Colls points out in his troubled interrogation of national spirit, a 'local' and 'regional' map of Britain recognisable since 1840, at which policies were directed and in which people lived, has been replaced since the Thatcher government by a range of uncoordinated, unlocated 'schemes' and agencies driven by a multiplicity of public/private bodies. What they have instead of 'region' or 'local' is 'efficiency' and they have measured their success by achievement in (sometimes invented) 'markets' not by how they elicit and represent different local interests. Colls observes, 'as forces not entirely of the centre, nor in the centre, yet structured by the centre they came to replace the discourse of "geographical region" or "away from the centre"'. With this new way of talking, the periphery ceased to be just geographical. 'At a time when the centre lost the confidence in its power to order things and the metropolis felt less responsible for the rest of the county, the old national shape began to dissolve. This truly odd condition prevails.'[3] Indeed, the whole landscape of Britain has disappeared since the 1970s as factories became (in a way best captured by the dystopian novels of J. G. Ballard) 'gated communities' and 'lofts' while Methodist chapels—which were the engines of moral and political reform of the industrial revolution and after have become paint shops. Cities and towns and the British countryside have all mutated, died away and sparked to life: yet some public spaces in cities have been re-vitalised in the past decade.

Moreover, surely there are aspects of 'Britishness' that are above locality although shaped by it. The poor (what Orwell called 'the common man', and what we have learnt to call 'the socially excluded' what, I wonder, will Cameron-speak call them?), the unhappy, how we talk to our children (or increasingly and horrifying fail to), the elderly, the changed role of women and the extraordinary challenges for young men, these are everywhere and common. How to think of the best nurture for young lives when children and parents have legal rights but there is no way of discussing in court the only thing a child can thrive in—a home with, however it is constituted, a family, is a shared issue. When we talk and think of the nation surely we also mean such broad sociological realities that together give us the flavour of the life within it. We also mean literature, plays, art, architecture, design, films, dance, music, humour: we mean sensibilities and environments.

The next big challenges to 'Britishness' are the Siamese-twinned issues of the multi-faith, multi-ethnic, multi-ness and the conjoined question of limits to the elasticity of 'Britishness'. Is there a lowest common denominator of consensus about what defines belonging that cannot be breached? Have we fretted too much about diminishing hostility to new pieces in the national jigsaw and not worried enough about whether there is a shared reality? On the one hand there is the problem identified so well by Geoff Dench in his work on the East End, that thirty years of well meaning 'triage' in cash-strapped public services, housing, health and education that have, in rationally allocating resources to the neediest incomers from abroad, accidentally actively disadvantaged a section of the British working class.[4] On the other, there is the problem of including and celebrating many differences.

Finally, to be a nation there has to be a sense of exceptionalism, of a unique inheritance and world view. Often such a concept of destiny has been forged through conflict with an outside force. Raphael Samuel argued 'national sentiment as a historical force can hardly be studied without reference to the demonisation of enemies both within and without'.[5] Yet the last national story that we could tell ourselves that had a legitimate and satisfactory 'us and them' in it—the story of World War Two—fades and loses purchase. A sense of British 'exceptionalism' had been for several generations based on a myth but also a powerful reality and that is now increasingly frail. Nevertheless this 'us versus them' view of national identity is a fairly conventional view, and there can be a more generous interpretation of pleasure in a heritage.

The life of nations depends on how the past is lined up with the present. This seems the great failure and a great opportunity of the moment we are struggling through. One of the things we need to revitalise is an un-embarrassed national history again. 'A nation' claimed Edmund Burke in 1782 'is not only an idea of local extent, but it is an idea of continuity, which extends in time as well as numbers and in space'. Terry, a character in *Whatever Happened to the Likely Lads?* on the BBC, commented in 1973, 'Not one of our memories are left intact'. Most people simply don't know what matters about our history any more. Moreover, in a nation which has always used history to explore itself (just as the French have philosophers, and the Americans have political/economists and Hollywood, we have history) there is a loss of historical memory and ways of remembering. Indeed this is more than ever important as in much of the wider academy at least there has been an almost complete abandonment of 'Britishness' as a source of understanding or study. Some universities, turned into businesses, have ducked the challenging task of re-thinking a fit-for-purpose way of scrutinising the Britishness of disciplines. Thus, despite being equipped with cohorts of able historians, many of whom still aspire to write stylish clear English, we have been dreadful at re-inspecting our history collectively. A coy discomfort at aspects of the story has led us to bury it. We have recently failed to tell children any coherent (let alone interesting) national story. Apart from Hitler and the Tudors, older students learn little of the nineteenth-century struggle for the franchise, and while it is true that all ten year olds learn about an empire in school: it is not ours of course, it is the Incas and the Spanish empire they toil over. Who lives where and how on the streets of Britain is shaped by our history. So surely by now we could confront the awfulness *and* the admirableness of our own imperial past?

Meanwhile 'globalisation', despite being a more peculiar process, with more complex impacts than almost any of the 'theorists' who easily proclaim it have recognised, does mean that we share some cultures internationally—and perhaps lose our own. Yet, conversely, one of the most disturbing aspects the 'globalisation' of the media is that it has lead to cross-continental cultural ghettoes and silos of narrow interests, in which people only encounter the like-minded. 'Nation shall speak unto nation'—the BBC's founding mission is both far easier than it used to be but it is far harder to get people to pay attention to anything other than the familiar and comfortable. Moreover there is a wider sense of tectonic plates moving, Brazil, China and India are storming into the world arena. Where do we fit into this new emerging map, and does anyone care?

There is another problem: this is not about what we may or may not have lost, but that the dominant way of thinking about 'Britishness'. It has become common to see a sense of the nation as a plastic and fluid construct. Linda Colley's stimulating and influential book *Britons: Forging the Nation 1707–1837*, in itself an attempt by someone who, as she explained, was not clear that she would go on living and working in Britain, was a pioneering example of this. In an authoritative and original account she demonstrates that a British identity was 'forged' in the eighteenth century out of popular anti-Catholicism, the real threats of French aggression, but also the comfort of watching successes in wars abroad with little direct experience of the reality at home, and out of a re-worked monarchy. The British state pre-dated the 'idea' of Britain. However, she also argues that there was a material basis to a sense of nationhood, 'For all classes and both sexes, patriotism was more often than not a rational response and a creative one as well'.[6] Elsewhere the notion of the constructed nature of nationality gained ground. Benedict Anderson's definition of nations as 'imagined communities' was influential, as were in a way a wonderful set of essays edited by Eric Hobsbawm and Terence Ranger, *The Invention of Tradition*,[7] which considered, with a glorious wit, the ways in which ideas of nationality were invented and accepted (I learnt that those kilts I had worn were the late survival of a highland fantasy). But while Colley was austerely aware that the enterprise of founding a national collective project was precarious and vital, for many of the other writers, as all national sentiment was really little more than a ruling class trick, there was the sense of the ridiculousness of much national invention, and its ephemeral duplicity.

These ideas were picked up eagerly—and bowderalised. In a world where advertising can mould desires with such ease, why not remake—or 'rebrand' as it came to be called—the nation? Anthony Giddens, who famously thinks history is irrelevant as it happened in the past, with his 'Third Way' was in effect one such immensely powerful, 're-brander', while Mark Leonard's branding Britain another version of the same idea. We are in another bout of 'designer' Britishness now. Thus, what started out as an empirical interrogation of collective processes in the past in the hands of accomplished historians turned into something quite different. It turned into a proposal to 're-design' Britishness. New, more sellable ways to describe us were advanced with breathy excitement, for it was suggested if you could describe us differently, perhaps hey presto, we would be different. It was an essentially propagandistic and certainly ideological view of Britishness, self-consciously shaped for selling us to ourselves and abroad.

The idea was especially attractive because it proposed a way of harnessing the power of the media into a re-invention of our purposes. The media do indeed seep into and chemically alter much of our collective lives and the mix of outlets that we have ended up with says all sorts of things about the national psyche. The British popular press, gaudy, sentimental, ruthless and dispiriting, is increasingly brutal with ordinary lives as well as the more powerful (think Sally Clark, the woman who was wrongly convicted of murdering two babies on the basis of misleading expert evidence for which the expert has lost his job, and a local and national press campaign, for which no one lost their job—or ever apologised). The press tells us little about the wide world we find ourselves in and in increasingly cash-strapped times is marked by a narrow provincialism. Nevertheless it is occasionally savagely truth-telling, more often hysterical and ruthless—as only a wounded beast can be. So while the prospect of 'using' the media to rebrand us looks like a way of managing the media to mould us for more useful ends—even so, you cannot 'remake' Britishness as an advertising campaign. It will not work because—dears—that is not what the 'British' are prepared to put up with. In such stubborn prosaic refusals may still lay a national sentiment we can conjure with.

Indeed, 'Britishness' can only be a co-production. The public has to collaborate—but will only do so in something that is useful and meaningful to them. 'Britishness' cannot be done to us—it has also to bubble up. This is especially the case in times of crisis, which has often been forgotten by the happy-clappy evangelists of re-engineering national identity. 'Britishness' has to be grounded in the soil of contemporary life: even if that is unsettling. Unfortunately, modern political and academic language is saturated with the easy encomiums of the seminar room, in which people 'negotiate' meanings and 'discourses' are 'contested'. But these words disguise the reality of sharply felt losses and brutish triumphs. It is the real needs and desires of the public, not mythologised or convenient ones that is the place to start a proper dusting down of Britishness. Being British is more voluntary than it has ever seemed before, but it has to start from realities.

So is there anything 'British' left? Where can we look for our exceptionalism? Actually, there is more of it around than people think—they look for it in the wrong places. But it is not a set of 'things' or 'essences'. Orwell's British 'Heavy breakfasts and gloomy Sundays' have been swept away in a blizzard of shopping. John Major's maiden aunts on bicycles and warm beer never hit the mark, even then. Early New Labour's Cool Britannia has been spat out. Yet there are qualities which on closer scrutiny endure, although some of which we may find deeply unattractive: that surely is part of the British point.

The 'media' play a special role in representing (and at times whipping up) national characteristics. But what is unusual in Britain is that British 'exceptionalism' has been defined and reinforced by a unique media institution which has played a role in metabolising the nation's sense of itself, but which has also represented 'Britishness' abroad: the BBC. The Corporation may, or may not, survive the next decade of rocky problems, with technology, rapacious international businesses perhaps even more threatening than domestic political vandalism, and a certain capacity for auto-destructiveness, posing a set of inter-related looming threats. Nevertheless inspecting how it has done Britishness is illuminating. The Corporation has an obligation to the nation because it is for the nation—so it has endlessly to try and sort out what the nation is. Mainly the BBC metabolises the nation by worrying about it. It adds reflective anxiety and creative imagination to the problems it confronts. This is clearly a quality in news and journalism: but it is as much an issue in drama and documentary and in the very administrative principles of the thing. In particular it is the 'newsiness' of the programming in general—the way in which news provides moral and political climate for other kinds of creativity—and in turn the embedded nature of news in the wider programme making milieu, that can make for a fertile and sensitive Petri-dish culture. Of course the BBC cannot and does not survive alone, but that perhaps is the point. It is enmeshed in ways of doing things and values elsewhere in other British institutions. So examining what it does tells us something about it, but it may also tell us something more general about the puzzle of us and our present uncertainties.

The Corporation metabolises Britain (when it gets it right) by airing its virtues; by bestowing recognition to groups, issues, achievements and failures; by including the mad aunts and errant teenagers in the family group; by show-casing and polishing up the crown jewels of culture; by washing as much of the dirty linen as it can find right out there in the street and by taking the mickey out of the whole attempt.

The Corporation has been able to do this because it is part of the British 'unwritten' and informal constitution and as such it has related to the British public as citizens but in quite a different way from any other official body. It consumes an alternative set of data about the British people on the move socially, technologically and aesthetically from any department of state: for it lives in the minds and hearts and imaginations of people at play. People have always had to choose to spend their time with the BBC, even though the competition for attention has become far more intense, the Corporation has always had to win and woo. So it has never been able to ignore what the people want for long (although it has sometimes been out of step with the national mood and at other times it has been able to express and lead it). Yet at the same time it is enjoined to engage with the public not only as consumers but as members of an evolving society. So the BBC's sense of the nation is at an angle to any governments'.

The BBC metabolises the nation materially by distributing resources according to a political and citizenship map of Britain not an economic or market one. The argument for this remains simple: in democracies, electorates need to be recognised and informed; now there is plenty of information available but navigating it or having attention focused on the things that matter is far more difficult. Distributing resources has meant access to radio, television and now digital technologies and reshaping the production and ideas map of the country. If the BBC *is* national then it has somehow to be part of the wider nation. This is so 'taken for granted' that it is almost invisible in the British mind yet it has been a powerful engine of integration. A shrewd Ofcom player observed that the whole of the independence tussle was being played out in Scotland 'through the prism of broadcasting'. Yet there is a devilish paradox in the drama unfolding north of the Border: market forces alone would not support an independent production market of any size in Scotland, yet the Corporation is being asked to invest in one. Those campaigning for this are not interested in a better service for any audience but in developing an economic capacity at home. Yet the decision to invest such resources can only come (and is coming rather generously) from the 'British' BBC: the logic of economic and political decisions is quite different.

Then there is the 'representing the nation' to itself. This is in part an issue of representing the bits of the nation to themselves, partly an issue of representing the bits of the nation to the whole and partly a matter of correcting the overall picture by the nuancing that regional perspectives and realities bring. It has done each task variably well over time, sometimes falling into clichés, but at others creatively harvesting local differences and local contributions to enrich the national brew. Some of this is to do with news—putting the nations and regions on the collective mind map as keeping them alert to their own condition is one part of the task. It requires political will.

But metabolising the nation has to be continually reinvented. Take Northern Ireland: the BBC in the 1960s and the early 1970s was part of the problem that was about to erupt. It was staffed solely by members of the protestant community, failed to 'see' the minority community and was unreflectively 'unionist'. But slowly it became more responsive, its staff more representative, the voices it gave access to more varied, and then, as the troubles gathered venom, it evolved into an admirably pioneering institution. This was both a matter of getting the balance of staff, news stories, plays, documentaries and children's programmes appropriately right for the local audiences but also of telling that story to the rest of Britain. Yet, at first when the sensitivity to the variety of Northern Irish voices had improved, another error emerged: an understandable attempt to emphasise the positive distorted the story yet again. The BBC had to learn that it did not exist in order to 'build the peace' or 'build the community'. Later still, visiting journalists from London hungry for a scoop and some drama but who did not appreciate the local consequences of stories had to be managed: they were too unresponsive to local meanings. Another corrective lesson: the BBC did not exist to tell exciting stories that were over-dramatised. Yet, and this is also true, the visiting, observing journalist was also an important part of carrying meanings from community to community. 'Outsiders' brought something to the mix in the province and to the understanding in the mainland. Over time the BBC learnt how to do it—and on the way produced a world class news outfit in the region.

Pat Loughrey, the first Catholic to be appointed to a senior position there and now Head of the Regions and Nations for the BBC, argued that the single most important programme that started the move in Northern Ireland was a phone-in called 'Talk Back', a loud, opinionated, shouting shop at first. There was political pressure to close it down as it was thought to incite inter-communal violence, but the BBC held steady. After 'about five years of both communities screeching poisonously at each other, they got it out of their system, realised there was a space in which they could be heard, and then they started to listen to each other'.[8] This is one key way the BBC does Britishness: by listening to and allowing an arena for the variety of voices that reflect real communities. But in Northern Ireland the struggle to get it right was part of the bigger solution: there are no easy, quick fixes to attempting to be truthful.[9]

Indeed, one of the things the regions need to do is to correct the metropolitan bias of almost everything in Britain. But the process is more complicated than it appears at first inspection. The BBC has to be part of and let the regions speak their minds on issues and pleasures to themselves. One way is to make programmes about them—another way is to make pro-grammes in them. But devolving to the regions only does its transformative, enlarging work if then the regional insights are brought back to amend and correct the whole picture. This is the trick we have to learn more generally and it is more complicated than it looks to get this right. In this way, as one ex-BBC mandarin pointed out, putting production capacity out to the regions was not enough: the regional production needs to be able to engage and catch the attention of the centre and the centre needs it to do so. Thus for example the whole issue of Europe looked different from the shires and the provinces. In the close Westminster village there is traditionally a good deal of hostility to the whole EU policy, and the BBC political and cultural elites are largely, unavoidably, part of that central mind set. Yet reporters working where the EU has brought benefits, out in the valleys of Wales and the Yorkshire Dales, corrected the dominant Westminster-centric view.[10] Indeed, what is true of the regions is true of the world. Going and seeing, bringing back views and understanding is the single most critical way in which the whole BBC news gathering and processing machine contributes to our comprehension of our place in all of the worlds we all live as a part of.

These dilemmas are merely reproduced when dealing with the increasingly diverse communities that live within Britain. An old BBC problem, of what constitutes a representative voice, which stands legitimately for a point of view, becomes especially acute when times are dangerous. The Corporation's determination to represent the Northern Irish 'street' of opinion brought it into conflict with successive governments and took time to get passably right. Yet the inclusion of voices—which does legitimise them—also exposes them to scrutiny. Inclusion is insufficient: every voice must be properly challenged yet inclusion in the national arena of nation remains one of the most important ways of defining the Britishness. Regions, classes, faiths, communities all need recognising.

Yet what vision of Britishness does the BBC work with? It is perhaps easier to see the kinds of interpretations that have to be balanced in something less contentious than religion or politics. Take classical music in the BBC as an example of the dilemmas that have to be resolved in practice. The BBC is one of the largest patrons of music in Europe and the world. But working out (and 'balancing') different aspects of Britishness has all sorts of conflicts within it. To render 'British' musical life the best service what must you do? Well obviously you must support orchestras in the centre and in the regions—and keep live music performance and performers vitally alive. But that is not enough. You should also play the repertoire of 'British' music, from the great mediaeval choral tradition, of Tallis and Bird, through Handel and Purcell, to Elgar, Delius and Walton. However, you ought also to be rediscovering new bits of the repertoire, which at some times the BBC has done almost single-handedly, not just the British repertoire of course, but music in general. However, 'British' music should not just be a heritage trinket so, of course, you must commission new work from new composers, John Tavener, Harrison Birtwhistle and the baby avant-garders, even perhaps at times if no one much listens to it, though finding new ways of presenting music is part of the trick. Meanwhile 'British' music must not get out of touch with the world, so you must also get the best foreign performers and conductors to play here and continually relaunch great music at the audiences. However, then there is the obligation to nurture young British performers and musical life in the schools. 'Young Musician of the Year' was invented brilliantly to do just this when a BBC producer noted with dismay that there were few young British performers appearing in international competitions. It worked: and can somebody please un-dumb it down right away? Today's one-size-fits-all populism with ignorant 'celebrity' presenters asking accomplished young people asinine questions and an interference with the judging system so that the most 'news-friendly' performer wins—not the most skilled—gets in the way of the real capacities and interests it is capable of encouraging and displaying. The principle of 'recognition' is one that governments have no purchase on—yet is a powerful, necessary cultural tool.

Occasionally the whole balancing act of allocating money and attention hits the rocks of invention. The BBC has always cared obsessively about the quality of sound it has put out, but in the 1970s a new musical kid on the block was the 'early music' movement with performances on original instruments. Unfortunately, as few had built or played sackbuts for several hundred years, they tended to sound—well—odd. But it was British movement—so, after some resistance the doughty BBC producer (a wonderful breed) grasped it—with lots of expensive rehearsal time. But when all of that is sorted into an acceptable division of resources and energy there is another big problem: how do you balance your obligation to interest as many people as possible and to the music and its development? The answer is all of the above, but in addition replayed in the shifting sands of contemporary musical history and taste. Balancing what is best for 'Britishness' is no easy task. It is a complex business of money and imagination.

Yet there is another paradox of Britishness: it is often best done when it is not attempted at all. Thus the BBC World Service wonderfully represents the British interest best, precisely in so far as it is not pursuing a 'British' agenda or indeed British 'interests'. It does it by doing impartiality, balance, and it arrives at them through hard won, necessarily imperfect, properly objective judgements. In many ways it (and the 'mothership of values' of the larger BBC) relate to the world on our behalf by setting standards. The receiving audiences will use the World Service because it is useful and accurate for their lives, not because it represents a 'British' voice. Indeed, the perception that it is inflected by our interests damages it. This commitment to trying very hard to describe reality as opposed to influencing it has been the basis of the World Service's authority. Perhaps what is true abroad (or indeed increasingly at home because of the way in which such services now include diaspora audiences scattered throughout Britain), is also true of how we need to see 'Britishness', not as a set of things or values. It is not that 'the beer is bitterer, the coins are heavier and the grass is greener, the faces knobblier and mild'[11] but rather a set of processes which engage us in our contemporary reality.

David Hendy's sparkling, thoughtful account of Radio Four, *Life on Air*, makes a similar point. It is 'how' public service broadcasting processes thoughtful playfulness that matters more than the passing scenery of programmes which reflect continuities but also changing tastes and agendas. In representing the nation, the 'immense variation in tone' from the warm homeliness of the shipping forecasts to the cerebral investigations of *In our Time*, have been part of 'Diversification which was embedded as a fundamental goal' in the station's purposes. Radio Four embodied in 'one service a variety of ways with which the nation could view itself. It provides a national kaleidoscope'.[12] The author Lynne Truss put well the odd sense of community it can engender, 'The idea that other listeners, in other kitchens, in other baths, in other traffic jams, are yelling at the same thing is a comforting notion'. Thus the World Service and Radio Four both show the way to some qualities, of fair representativeness, that are not things or even values but habits of mind, processes, that are far more pervasive than any of the end-of-Britain doom-mongers appreciate. Perhaps the thing is not to 'do' Britishness at all.

One of the last great successful inspections of Britishness was as a consequence of the Second World War, when a series of writers defined national characteristics in ways which critics have spent many years dismissing. Yet some aspects of them are more relevant to a very much changed Britain than appears at first sight. Not the modesty, or the class structure, let alone the cups of tea or the boiled cabbage. In 1957, Nickolas Pevsner, the great architectural historian, gave a series of BBC Reith lectures on the 'Englishness of English Art' (by which, being a German, like many of the most anglophile of postwar thinkers, he endearingly claimed he meant, 'just the most commonly acceptable name for that which is the essence of Britishness'). The lectures became a smash hit, selling out by their millions. For Pevsner, whose dry yet utterly comprehensive catalogue of vernacular architecture sought to distil the qualities of national life built in local bricks and mortar, the defining quality of British culture was an emphasis on narrative and preaching. It was, he claimed, epitomised by Hogarth with his great, popular, morality tales—criticising in Gin Lane and The Rake's Progress the corruption of British society. But, Pevsner notes that the most effective British artistic sermon 'is the recounting of what a sharp eye sees around it'. The hallmark of the British spirit, he claimed was 'Keen observing and quick recording together with an intense interest in the details of the everyday world and a preference for personal experience'.[13] But he also claimed to see (in our great Cathedrals along with extreme length and height) qualities of 'detachment as against passionate single mindedness', although he also argued that the nation's 'rationalism and matter of fact-ness' was matched by an enduring penchant for the 'romantic, weird and the irrational'. Meanwhile George Mikes (a Hungarian this time) observed on a Home Service programme that 'the British will not tell you a lie, but would not dream of telling you the truth'. He also added, that in Britain 'If you go for a walk with a friend don't say a word. If you go with a dog never stop talking to him . . .'[14]

Of course this elaboration of empiricism, open mindedness and critical scrutiny was part of an image of Britain widely shared then. Karl Popper's *Open Society*—a stern injunction to keep an open mind and to exercise vigilance against falling into thought ruts and complacency and to bear the discomfort of challenging argument was an immensely influential underpinning to all of this exploration. In many ways the BBC at its best also puts some of these habits of mind into practice: sceptical, evidence-driven, committed to the possibility of understanding others, and in as far as it tries to continually push the boundaries of what we might be.

For perhaps there is no easy answer to 'Britishness'—and the recognition is in itself part of the answer. You *could* invent civic ceremonies but we have quite good ones around the place: the Queen's Jubilee (for example) was not supposed to be going to be popular but the people, as far as could be discerned, rather enjoyed it. You *could* do something with flags but I for one will certainly not be swearing allegiance to any fluttering bit of civic religion. You *could* make the contract between us and the state more explicit. You certainly ought to do something about interpreting our history again: without polite omissions. You must represent the voices and instincts that exist within the national arena. You absolutely must permit, encourage and develop creative, imaginative energy. Museums and children reading great books for fun (not dull, pointless reading schemes), artists, theatres and dancers all have much to add to our sense of what matters. But do not try to tidy the 'Britishness' up. After all, one enduring quality is our national hypocrisy. In as far as the BBC has found ways to be part of a national discussion about our condition, redistributed resources, tried to balance—however inadequately—competing claims, puzzled and questioned whether it is doing the right thing, learnt by trial and error, and above all attempted to avoid ideological capture for all of the 'purposes' people would like to impose on it, then it has indeed, most usefully 'metabolised' Britishness.

George Orwell, that quintessentially most British of writers, is also the least parochial. What he wrote in the middle of the last century still resonates and alerts readers everywhere to their predicament. Perhaps he also provides a way to see the contemporary quandary of our national identity. Writing in the 1930s he claimed that Britain was 'the most class ridden society under the sun. It is a land of snobbery and privilege, ruled largely by the old and silly'. It was like a family, but one 'with the wrong members in control—and cupboards stuffed with skeletons'. He was pitiless about its double standards, snobbery, pomposity, xenophobia, inability at languages and the terrible social divisiveness that separated the comfortable from the needy. As Ben Pimlott argued about Orwell, 'Being "British" we have to be reminded, perhaps does not mean that the list is full of things we approve of. Orwell sniffs orthodoxy at a hundred yards and having sniffed it, seeks to upset its adherents',[15] yet Orwell also 'refused to scorn qualities of common sense, empiricism and toleration'. Elsewhere, Orwell distinguished between patriotism as 'devotion to a particular place and a particular way of life, which one believes is the best in the world but has no wish to force on other people', and nationalism (which he said could be applied to ideologies like communism and fascism as well as nations) 'which is inseparable from the desire for power. The abiding purpose of every nationalist is to secure more power and more prestige, not for himself but for the nation or other unit in which he has chosen to sink his own individuality'. Orwell was, in short, a critical patriot and everything he wrote was an extended polemic on the side of seeing the truth—however ugly—in ourselves. It was an embarrassing, awkward intimacy with ourselves that Orwell proposed, but it was above all a state of mind, a way of looking at the world that was fleshed out in his invitation to be critical, find shamefully distasteful—and yet appreciate that which was individual.

Perhaps the only way forward in our current national quandary—and yet one (and that is the delight) that is part of a long history that is distinctly British—is a stroppy-minded, slightly resigned toleration and defence of where we are as a nation. And it is in this slightly bleak describing, recognising, relishing and laughing at our accurate condition (even if that is a somewhat dissolving condition) that really lies doing 'Britishness' better—because this is the place from which we can hope for better. Orwell wrote of Britain, 'There is something in it that is continuous, it stretches into the future and the past, there is something in it that persists, as in a living creature. It has a flavour of its own.'[16] We may or may not need to go on 'being British'—but we do all need to go on being critical, open minded realists—if we can. And remember, no one had told the girls at the Queen's party to gird themselves in blossom—they did it spontaneously. They were neither fashionable nor part of a plan—they just did being British.

Notes

1 Anthony King, *The British Constitution*, Oxford, Oxford University Press, 2007.
2 Many intellectuals of devolution, from Tom Nairn and Neal Ascherson onwards have been devolutionionists, partly because of gleeful hostility to the British past.
3 Robert Colls, *Identity of England*, Oxford, Oxford University Press, 2002, p. 333.
4 Geoff Dench, Kate Gavron and Michael Young, *The New East End,: Kinship, Race and Conflict*, London, Profile Books, 2006.
5 Raphael Samuel, 'Nationalism and the British', History Workshop, Oxford, 1985, p. 28.
6 Linda Colley, *Britons: Forging the Nation 1707–1837*, London, Yale University Press, 1992, p. 15.
7 Eric Hobsbawm and Terence Ranger, *The Invention of Tradition*, Oxford, Oxford University Press, 1984.
8 Pat Loughrey, The BBC, author's interview.
9 This is based on interviews in Northern Ireland for the history of the BBC.
10 Interviews with Stephen Whittle about the relocation of religious programmes to Manchester, for the history of the BBC.
11 George Orwell, 'The lion and the unicorn' in *Orwell's England*, London, Penguin, 2001, p. 23.
12 David Hendy, *Life on Air: a History of Radio Four*, Oxford, Oxford University Press, 2007, p. 395.
13 Nickolas Pevsner, *The Englishness of English Art*, London, Hutchinson, 1957, p. 47.
14 George Mikes, 'How to be an Alien', BBC Home Service, 1959.
15 Ben Pimlott, introduction, *Orwell's England*, London, Penguin, 2001.
16 George Orwell, *England, Your England*, London, Secker and Warburg, 1953, p. 195.

Don't Mess with the Missionary Man: Brown, Moral Compasses and the Road to Britishness

GERRY HASSAN

> . . . we long for that most elusive quality in our leaders–the quality of authenticity, of being who you say you are, of possessing a truthfulness that goes beyond words.
>
> Barack Obama, *The Audacity of Hope*[1]

Introduction

ONCE upon a time one way people used to judge politicians was by the words they used: in books, pamphlets, articles and speeches. Politicians cared passionately about the words they used, knew they would in part be judged by them, and attempted to create that 'quality of authenticity' to show their words linked to a set of values and view of the world.

Looking at the pantheon of Labour politicians through the party's history, a number of its leaders in its early years—Keir Hardie, Ramsay MacDonald, John Wheatley and James Maxton to name but four—straddled the world of thinking and writing about politics and acting as politicians.[2] This tradition has continued—with later R. H. Tawney, R. H. S. Crossman and Tony Crosland—attempting to define a modern sense of the socialist credo. More recently, Michael Foot can be seen within this tradition, while pre-Diaries Tony Benn showed in his work the paucity of much of his thinking[3]; the same can also be said of Tony Blair's few writings which show a politician with only the most superficial understanding of ideas.[4]

Another strand of political writing centres more on national leadership and the power and integrity of character. This can be seen in the industry of American Presidential hopefuls and their books: the modern brand of which began with J. F. Kennedy's *Profiles in Courage*.[5] Nowadays it is *de rigueur* for American Presidential prospective candidates to have their life story or vision put in book form whether it is Hillary Clinton, Barack Obama or Rudolph Giuliani.[6] These books offer a very different concept of politics to the Labour style of writing: being about the centrality of personality, the importance of charisma and the practice of positioning in party and national contests.

Gordon Brown's writings have their roots in this earlier concept of the Labour politician as someone combining writing and thinking about politics with the act of being a politician. They have in the course of over thirty years shifted terrain, focus and style, bringing more and more to the fore the

 Published by Blackwell Publishing Ltd, 9600 Garsington Road, Oxford OX4 2DQ, UK and 350 Main Street, Malden, MA 02148, USA

importance of character: both Brown's and others as a leitmotiv of change, most recently seen in his invoking of JFK with his own version of 'Courage'.[7]

This essay aims to position Gordon Brown in this context—and explore the main manifestations of Brown's moral compass leading up to his contemporary fascination with Britishness.[8]

Gordon Brown: the missionary man

Gordon Brown has consistently throughout his public life presented himself as a politician with a moral mission and compass and his thoughts, writings and public interventions from the earliest age have reflected this.[9]

First wave Brown: the age of 'Red Brown'

In the 1970s Brown portrayed himself himself as a young radical whose moral mission coalesced around the ideas of socialism and political economy. Examining Brown's writings in these areas it is revealing that these are not in fact that radical. Instead, in their concept of 'socialism' these are writings shaped by the conventional Labour ethos of time memorial. The introduction to *The Red Paper* essays sees Brown cite a plethora of 'new left' heroes: Gramsci, Freire, E. P. Thompson and others, but this appears window-dressing compared to the references to 'Scotland's socialist pioneers' such as Keir Hardie, Wheatley and Maxton.[10]

This is a political view very close to the ethical socialism of the early Labour movement—one that is short of detail and programmatic policy and full of exhortation and rhetoric.[11] There is a general feeling in Brown's writing at this time of what was a very fashionable view in certain circles—that the reformism of recent Labour governments had failed and needed to be transcended. However, the strategy he offers is one which appeals more to emotion and a cumulative radical challenge to capitalist rationale: a sort of left Fabianism without the detail.

It was also very different from what passed for radical left thinking at this time. All of Brown's biographers from the hatchet job of Tom Bower to the hagiography of Paul Routledge emphasise this as the time of 'Red Brown'.[12] However, it becomes obvious reading Brown that such writers have never made a comparative analysis of left writing at the time. The contributions of various left groups of the period—such as the Institute for Workers' Control—are filled with detailed proposals for advancing the power of organising labour and challenging capital.[13] Brown's radicalism of the period looks positively lame by comparison, an act of posturing and going with the grain, without one single specific policy recommendation.

There is also in the Brown of the 1970s little detailed understanding of political economy whether at a British or international level despite Brown's reputation at the time and subsequently. Instead, there is a wide, but shallow understanding of the economic literature of the time and regurgitating of numerous facts and figures. A useful comparison can be made between Brown and the detailed work of Stuart Holland and Michael Barrett Brown which developed a sophisticated model of capitalism and the challenge of corporate power to democracy.[14] All of this is referenced in passing by Brown but the substance of it eluded him.

Second wave Brown: supply side Socialism man

A decade later the Brown of the 1980s positioned himself as the self-appointed champion of Labour's eternal values. At this point, Labour's humiliation in 1983 called for a reappraisal of the party's policies and how it conducted and presented itself. Brown's writings show a distinct shift—from numerous references to 'socialism' in his earlier phase to its replacement by frequent mentions of 'social democracy'.

His main moral crusade at this point coalesces around the idea of 'social justice'—the subject of a collection edited with Robin Cook and his maiden speech in the House of Commons.[15] Central to this was challenging the harsh, uncaring consequences of Tory 'enterprise culture' and giving a voice to the disadvantaged and victims of government policy. Brown stated at the time that he believed 'making the case for social justice is not the same as solving the problem of poverty'.[16]

Within all Brown's contributions on social justice at this time it is interesting to note how little of interest or originality he had to say, but how he made it go a long way. He was neither 'new left' Brown nor old fashioned labourite, but by 1983 this wasn't controversial but instead the mainstream majority of Kinnockite Labour.

Subsequently Brown began to branch out to develop a more detailed account of the failures of Thatcherite economics. This concentrated on the short-termism of British industry, its failure to invest and the need to develop a long-term approach to investing in people, education and skills. At this point from Labour's election defeat in 1987 onwards the party through the process of the Policy Review began its long haul to reposition itself as a pro-business party.[17]

Brown became a rising star in Labour and published a book, *Where There is Greed* which attempted to coherently critique Thatcherite economics. The book contains little of originality, but repeats the mainstream left view of the Conservatives. Brown openly advocated 'a new supply side socialism' centred on 'efficiency and fairness'.[18] What is more interesting are the omissions and silences with no cogent critique of the City and the power of finance capital, and little acknowledgement of the long-term structural weaknesses and imbalances in the UK which culminated in Thatcherism.

Third wave Brown: the man next door

The third wave of Brown's thinking contributed to the ascent of New Labour. His moral mission still coalesced around ideas of the economy and social justice to deliver Labour's historic goals of full employment, ending poverty and widening opportunity for all.

Brown's thinking on the economy and social justice had shifted significantly from his critique of Thatcherism in the 1980s. His approach to the UK economy had now become based on a mix of second generation neoliberalism along with investment in skills and education to make workers more competitive and efficient in the world economy. This was a very functionalist, determinist mindset which seemed devoid of any real heart, soul and emotion.

To soften this very unappealing world Brown remained convinced of a concept of social justice which was now defined more narrowly than before. It was now focused on the priorities of ending child and pensioner poverty, but omitted talk of the super-rich, the responsibility of those who were 'winners' in society, or the gaping inequalities between rich and poor.

In the early days of New Labour's reign Brown began to turn to the idea of Britishness as a third pillar in his moral mission. This was partly due to the recognition of the changing nature of the union, but part was due to a realisation that his economy and social justice messages were neither distinctive nor that appealing.

Brown's discovery of Britishness

Thus Brown's emerging story of Britishness has been a slow burning one and not one which has been a constant in his political life. In the period of 'Red Brown' as he pontificated and fine-tuned the nuance of his rhetoric, he attempted to articulate a 'third way' between an unconditional Scottish nationalism and British unionism. He stressed that Scottish socialists should not support Scottish independence which 'postpones the question of meeting urgent social and economic needs', but nor should they 'give unconditional support to maintaining the integrity of the United Kingdom and all that entails—without any guarantee of radical social change'.[19] In later years, this subtle positioning seems merely to have been grandstanding and point-scoring on the part of the young Brown to differentiate himself from his elders in the party.

In *The Politics of Nationalism and Devolution*, Brown's neglected and forgotten book with academic Henry Drucker, Brown addressed the failure of Scottish devolution in 1979 and looked to identify ways it could succeed at a Scottish and UK level. The most interesting and revealing proposal that Brown elucidated is that he makes the controversial case for 'in/out voting' or 'English votes for English laws' as it has become known post-devolution. He states that this would in all likelihood lead to a 'semi-permanent Tory majority' in the Commons, which he recognises would be 'no small prize', but believes worth paying for a 'Scottish Assembly'.[20]

One of the main consistencies of Brown's writings which the previous section indicated has been his lack of original thinking, saying anything radical at all, and yet, somehow giving the appearance of the exact opposite. Brown has been able through the years to write at great length and provide no hostages to fortune to future Tory researchers!

The exception of this example is traceable to the book being co-written with Henry Drucker, but Brown sanctioned all of its contents. The book also contains the beginnings of an outline for a coherent programme of reforming the British state which was radical and far ahead of its time: something Brown was never to show any real interest in beyond rhetoric. Thus, it outlines the case for proportional representation in the Scottish Assembly, consideration of sweeping reform at a British level and challenging Treasury centralism: issues which could not exactly be seen as close to Brown's heart.[21]

Brown's discovery of and identification with Britishness involves a number of factors. It came about at the politically expedient point in the emergence of New Labour, the development of its constitutional reform programme, and Brown's visible presence as the 'premier-in waiting'. The theme of Britishness allowed him both to address the subject of the UK in flux, and develop a Brown credo which went way beyond his Treasury brief or his usual subjects of the economy and social justice. This latter-day odyssey attempted to do a number of things.

First, Brown has attempted to provide a good story of Britishness—about culture, civilisation and enlightenment. Britishness has for long been a subject of embarrassment or scorn to progressives and Brown sees this as a self-defeating position vacating a huge terrain of territory, symbols and history to the Tories. Instead, progressives need to reclaim these areas so that the Union Jack can become 'a flag for all Britain—symbolising inclusion, tolerance and unity'.[22]

Second, it is a story about domestic progress attempting to connect Britishness and the story of free health care, education for all and widening opportunity. In this, institutions such as the NHS, BBC and British Council are seen as having a vital role in transmitting progressive values synonymous with Britishness.[23]

Third, it articulates an account of progress across the nations and peoples of these isles which emphasises and celebrates the uniqueness of the United Kingdom. This perspective stresses that the multicultural, multinational basis of the UK is unprecedented and claims the UK in typically modest (almost quasi-Thatcherite rhetoric) terms as the most successful union of its kind anywhere and anytime in human history. Brown put this in an interview in 1999:

I see Britain as being the first country in the world that can be a multicultural, multi-ethnic and multinational state. America, at its best, is a multicultural and multi-ethnic society, but America does not have nationalities within identifiable political units in the way that Britain does. We have a chance to forge a unique pluralist democracy where diversity becomes a source of strength.[24]

Fourth, it is about the United Kingdom's role as a force for good in the world. This emphasises Britain's role in a series of alliances and institutions, which due to its history and values allow it to address issues with more influence than its size on international aid, debt relief and world poverty, along with freeing trade to aid Africa and the developing world. Moreover, by Britain's position sitting in a nexus of institutions from the Commonwealth to UN Security Council, IMF, WTO, GATT and others it has the capacity due to its history and understanding to bring a moral dimension to international issues.

Fifth, Brown's aim in this aspires to interweave Labour's story with that of the United Kingdom: to tell a peoples' story rather than a traditional account. In the Labour story the state was used as a lifting hand to bring people out of poverty, to give them wider opportunity and hope, and to banish the blighted prospects and aspirations which had disfigured generations of working class communities. Brown and Douglas Alexander articulated this in their defence of the union at its 300th anniversary: 'The union in 2007 is now clearly founded on social justice'.[25] For much of the postwar period, Labour's story became that of the British political system and elite (and one the Conservatives bought into), and Brown sees his mission on Britishness as to make this 'progressive consensus' more explicit and secure.

Finally, this was a mission informed by the growing crisis of democratic legitimacy and involvement which characterised the British political system. The Britishness agenda fed into an increasing recognition by government of the need to support and encourage volunteering and people contributing to helping others in a way which acknowledged the difference this made to the civic life of Britain. This tied into discussions about the potential of citizenship, from breaking with the old culture of people being subjects to immigrants passing citizenship tests and taking 'Oaths of Allegiance'.

What is the story of the re-emergence of Britishness?

The wide-ranging and daunting list of areas which Brown has attempted to address begs the wider question of why he chose to embark on this journey in the first place. One of the most significant reasons is the damage that the Thatcherite revolution has inflicted on the beliefs and confidence of social democracy. This has resulted in New Labour's core concepts (and later-day Brown's too) of the economy and social justice being barely decipherable from the other mainstream political parties. They have all positioned themselves in the narrow centre ground of the post-Thatcherite/Blairite environment.

Therefore, Brown's account of Britishness is an attempt to combine a synthesis of the Labour story of Britain which reached its apex in the 1945–70 period with an embrace and advocacy of the post-Thatcherite view of the world. This uneasy and conflicting alliance mirrors the strange mix within

New Labour itself: elements of social democratic policy within a wider neoliberal polity.[26]

Second, Labour has historically had a problem with the British state.[27] Its main traditions have involved an uncritical embrace of the state as 'neutral' and a force for progressive ends. Labour's history from its arrival as a minority government in 1924 and more pronouncedly from 1940 when it entered the Churchill wartime coalition saw it as a party become incorporated into the Westminster political system which thus influenced its ethos and outlook. All through Labour's travails with devolution first in the 1960s and 1970s and subsequently post-1997, the party aimed to square the circle of supporting devolution and maintaining the integrity of the central state.

Third, alongside this has been Labour's understanding of the territorial dimensions and nations of the UK. Despite British Labour having its origins in Scotland, Wales and outlier groups of the British political system, it quickly bought into the dominant political system's understanding of the UK. This was an account which emphasised despite there being four nations in the UK the homogenisation of the territory, common interests and values and saw 'Britishness' and its association with socio-economic allegiances of class and background transcend place.

The British political establishment, Labour included, have long understood the UK as a unitary state: a place with one centre of power and authority. However, the UK is not and never has been a unitary state, but is instead what is known as a 'union state'.[28] This involves a complex set of different arrangements allowing for local, regional and sub-national differences and importantly, the preservation of pre-union rights in the case of Scotland. However, the political classes have more and more clung to the idea of the UK as a unitary state with grave consequences for the way the centre acts and sees politics and power.

From Labour's concept of the state and nations comes its attempt to stand up to the challenge of Scottish and to a lesser extent Welsh nationalism. The electoral forces of the SNP and Plaid Cymru threatened Labour in its once safe heartlands and thus its prospects for a British-wide coalition forming a government. Labour's answer to this was first shaped by an ad hoc response and expediency, but post-1997 the party's commitment to Scottish and Welsh devolution became more thought through and convincing. The establishment of the Scottish Parliament and Welsh Assembly with nationalist parties as the main challenge to Labour required a new way of presenting the case for the union.[29]

The Scottish and Welsh challenge had a direct bearing on the party's anxiety on 'the English Question'. Scotland and Wales had grievances and a 'democratic deficit' pre-devolution; some argued that England had this post-devolution. The asymmetrical union that characterises the UK has to some shifted its inconsistencies and anomalies from Scotland and Wales to England; some regard this as a perennially British situation which most

English people seem to be willing to put up with for the moment; others see this as an intolerable situation.

This is focused around 'the West Lothian Question'—Scots MPs voting on such issues as education and health for England which does not affect their constituencies.[30] This has a political salience when Scottish Labour MPs provide the crucial votes for foundation hospitals and top-up student fees in England which are not being introduced by the Scottish government.[31] This has led to calls for identifying what legislation in front of Parliament is 'English' and 'English votes for English laws'—something Brown once saw the point of.

The contemporary Brown now sees this as something which needs to be headed off—not by English regionalism or an English Parliament or anything which fundamentally changes the order. Brown's exploration of Britishness is despite not directly dealing with England, an attempt to identify a set of values and stories which unite the English into the UK.

Brown's credo hopes to address growing concerns in society about immigration and multiculturalism. A new narrative evolved under New Labour which saw multiculturalism as placing too much emphasis on diversity and separate development and too little on integration and common values.[32] The search for a set of British values was seen as a means of articulating an inclusive British citizenship.

This was also related to anxieties over the 'war on terror'. Increasingly, the Blair and Brown governments talked and acted tough on dealing with 'suspected terrorists' and challenged civil rights and liberties. A more subtle track of addressing these concerns saw British authorities stress the importance of winning the battle for 'the hearts and minds' of British Muslim communities by emphasising common British values.[33]

Then, of course there is the personal dimension behind all this. Gordon Brown is a Scotsman representing a Scottish constituency post-devolution. He is the living embodiment of 'the West Lothian Question'. In the period before Brown became Prime Minister a host of polls and surveys showed a growing English and British set of anxieties about the state of the union. One indicated that 76 per cent of British respondents thought the current situation with Scots MPs able to vote on English matters was unfair.[34] All of this mattered to Brown as he waited to become Prime Minister of the UK.

The omissions of the Britishness agenda

There are profound problems and omissions about Brown's Britishness agenda. For one, it is systematically silent on the structural weaknesses and lack of democracy in the British constitution. The political re-ordering of the last thirty years which has seen the rise of the centralist Thatcherite/Blairite state is not fundamentally questioned by Brown, but instead actively embraced. All of Brown's rhetoric as chancellor and PM on the perils of centralism, command and control and the need for localism is just that, and the examples of localism and devolution he chooses as examples are ones where the centre still has power and decides the rules (such as Sure Start and English RDAs).

This illustrates Labour's historic and contemporary failure to understand the importance of 'constitutional reform' even with a government which was supposedly committed to such a programme. The Blair government began with much pomp and hype in its 'New Britain' days to enact a programme of reform with the aim of renewing and modernising British democracy.[35] Brown talked of the British tradition of adaptability and willingness 'to embrace, not fear constitutional reform'[36]; Britain would move 'from an over-centralised and uniform state—the old Britain of subjects—to a pluralist and decentralised democracy—the new Britain of citizens'.[37]

It was clear from early on that Blair had no interest in this at all and Brown had little beyond rhetoric, with no coherent set of reforms. This became even more self-evident after the 9/11 attacks when the government began to vandalise parts of its own constitutional reform programme, seeking derogation from the Human Rights Act for example to detain 'suspected terrorists'.

Another weakness lay in the relationship between England and the UK. Brown consistently laid claim to an English tradition and lineage of human rights and standing up to arbitrary power citing Magna Carta, the Peasants' revolt, English Civil War and Bill of Rights as British traditions.[38] This is a terrain requiring subtle reading and analysis, and there is a powerful narrative within British progressive thinking which claims English radical traditions as British: one only needs to think of Tony Benn's constant incantation of the Levellers and Diggers or Michael Foot.[39] There has to be recognition that English struggles do play a huge part in what it means to be British, witness David Davies' resignation from the Conservative Shadow Front Bench citing the importance of Magna Carta in his battle with the government over extending detention to forty-two days.[40]

Brown's confusion of England and Britain does seem to be a deep, seismic one which illustrates that he has problems with both concepts. His vision of 'a Britain of regions and nations' is one where Scotland, Wales and Northern Ireland are nations and England is a collection of regions.[41] England in Brown's Britain seems forever silenced and forbidden to speak in its own collective national voice, yet is co-opted and claimed for the greater British story.

London to take one example in Brown's thinking just did not seem to exist. This was true of the London that was the imperial capital of the Empire and centre of power and administration in the British state. It was also true of the city of the twenty-first century which saw itself as a reinvented 'city-state' and global player.

'The English problem' can be witnessed in the numerous writers and authorities Brown trundles out to show the historic importance of liberty in our political culture. These include Edmund Burke, William Wordsworth, William Hazlitt and George Orwell who speak about English liberty, character, culture and politics. At some points, Brown is on very thin ground misquoting or inaccurately citing some of the above, most obviously when he changes Orwell's 'English genius' into 'the British genius'.[42] However, at other times when he has cited the people above or for example Winston Churchill on Britishness, it is more that the person Brown is citing is using 'English' as interchangeable with 'British'.[43] This is complex territory, but it is clear that Brown errs in a manner which is at times simplifying and misrepresenting some of the most influential figures in British history and appropriating them to his cause of redefining Britishness.

Brown's Britishness agenda scandalously either neglects or tries to offer an apology for the British past associated with empire, colonialism and imperialism. Thus, the darker side of British history upon which so much of the country's trade, commerce and wealth was based: slavery, rape, torture and genocide, barely get a look-in; the British state just before the 200th anniversary of its abolition in the British Empire called it a 'crime against humanity' and expressed 'deep sorrow' that it ever happened which stopped just short of a full apology or offering any redress.[44]

Brown has been on even more controversial ground trying to reclaim the British Empire as a force for good. Such views were once seen as enlightened and uncontroversial with the Empire presented as a means by which 'backward peoples' and nations would attain civilised standards.[45] Brown does not go that far of course, but he has stated that we should stop apologising and instead feel pride about the Empire: 'the days of Britain having to apologise for our history are over . . . we should celebrate much of our past rather than apologise for it'.[46] In a contemporary setting, such claims should really form no part of any centre-left politician's thinking, and it shows how far Brown has travelled that he has articulated such opinions.

The articulation of a good news story about Britishness by Brown led to the omission of some of its more negative aspects and history; Ireland for example has been completely ignored. The British state's treatment of Ireland from conquest and colonisation to brutal repression and two bitter wars in the last century involving British armed forces, is passed over in silence by Brown. The UK government eventually realised it could not achieve a military victory over the IRA resulting in the Anglo-Irish Agreement, Downing Street Declaration and under Labour, Good Friday Agreement.[47] This entire terrain clearly has implications for the British state and Britishness and yet Brown's credo is one in which the island of Ireland just does not register.

The construction of Britishness offered by Brown is a strangely insular creation which tries to ignore that national identity is never just about internal characteristics and relationships, but external relationships as well. Britishness is influenced by the set of concentric circles it finds itself located in the idea of 'England as a world island' situated in the worlds of union, Commonwealth, Europe and Anglo-America.[48] These mirror Churchill's historic grasp of postwar Britain within three worlds—Empire, Europe and

Anglo-America with the UK playing a role in all three which allowed it to avoid having to make a decision about its role.[49]

The Brown vision encounters problems with regard to UK relations with the European Union and Atlanticism. Both of these have reshaped what the UK is in the postwar era, the nature of state and polity, and how the UK practices self-determination and sovereignty without the British political classes being upfront about the consequences. Europe now frames a large part of UK legislation passed by the UK Parliament, whereas Atlanticism now permeates the British political, military and security elites and is one of the defining pillars of British postwar identity. Brown chooses to remain silent on the consequences of these two relationships for Britishness.

Brown's fatal embrace and the crisis of Social Democracy

Brown's articulation of a British credo has to be seen as part of his eternal quest to see the world in terms of moral missions and crusades. His discourses on Britishness came relatively late in his political life, only really appearing in a sustained way with the emergence and ascendancy of New Labour and its decade in office. However, any hope that this would be linked to the beginning of a programme of fundamental constitutional reform and altering in a far-reaching way the manner in which political power is held and practised in the UK was soon dissipated by Brown's actions as Prime Minister.

The actions of Brown as Chancellor and Prime Minister seem to point to his interest in Britishness being mere window-addressing and political camouflage. Brown was not interested at all in changing the Westminster power system which sees the executive dominate the legislature, hold unprecedented centralist control and reach over aspects of British domestic life, and the manner in which politics and power is conducted. There was no inclination that the Thatcherite/Blairite state was suffering from 'overload' or that the old checks and balances which once made the British constitution the envy of many had been eroded and broken.

Instead, Brown's promulgation of Britishness is about shoring up the discredited status quo and maintaining Westminster's hold and power. It is an attempt to develop a counter-story to the calls for systematic reform, and prevent any serious redistribution of power in the UK political system which fundamentally rebalances the centre-local relationship and gives local government a new voice and respect, which develops a new centre which stops trying to extend its reach into every part of the UK, and which comes to a new accommodation with Europe and checks the obsession of our political classes with Atlanticism.

One pivotal political area Brown wishes to avoid in these deliberations is any discussion about the location of Britishness: about what it is, who speaks for it, and where it places itself in the world in a geo-political sense. And it is these kinds of conversations which are needed to give meaning to any debate.

Fundamentally, the emergence of Britishness has to be located in the crisis of social democracy as the political and governing philosophy of New Labour. The social democratic outlook has been battered, bruised and diminished by the experience of New Labour and the Blair and Brown governments, and yet at the same time both administrations have retained the means by which Labour in office undertook its politics and polity: namely centralism and command and control. Once upon a time this was a means to the end of the promise of a socialist commonwealth (à la Attlee), but now it has become about the sheer brutalities of power and maintenance of neoliberalism.

This journey also marks a personal one for Gordon Brown in his writing, thoughts and how he sees himself as a politician. It represents a profound shift from the politics of values and ideas in the 1970s to that of the politics of character and the individual in the twenty-first century. Brown's transition from referencing socialist, usually British thinkers in the 1970s, to his embrace of centre-right and liberal thinkers today mirrors this change. He has shifted from eulogising James Maxton and John Wheatley to British writers such as Adam Smith and John Stuart Mill and American ones including Gertrude Himmerlfarb and James Q. Wilson.[50]

This is a shift from seeing the world from a socialist perspective to one informed by a liberal and centre-right perspective. It can also be seen in Brown's book *Courage* which contains the portraits of eight people 'driven and sustained by higher ideals' not one of whom is connected to the Labour Party or wider socialist tradition.[51]

Yet, for most of the last thirty years Brown has managed to present himself as an ideas man, deeply committed to thinking, intellectual concepts and looking to address the serious issues of the day. Sadly, there is little in his writings, thoughts or actions in office which give serious sustenance to this. His journey is an example of 'the paradox of authenticity in our political culture' where politicians present a manufactured version of themselves which gives the pretence of being 'authentic'.[52]

Gordon Brown's politics represent a fatal embrace of the governing orthodoxies of the last few decades: of social democracy's compromise and collusion with neoliberalism, and the failure of the Labour Party to attempt to make the political weather after Thatcherism. It is in this wider tragedy and story that Brown's interest and exploration of Britishness has to be seen.

Notes

1 Barack Obama, *The Audacity of Hope: Thoughts on Reclaiming the American Dream*, Edinburgh, Canongate, 2007, p. 66.
2 Kenneth O. Morgan, *Labour People: Labour Leaders and Lieutenants, Hardie to Kinnock*, Oxford, Oxford University Press, 1987.
3 Tony Benn, *Arguments for Socialism*, London, Jonathan Cape, 1979; *Arguments for Democracy*, London, Jonathan Cape, 1981.

4 Tony Blair, *Socialism,* London, Fabian Society, 1994; *New Britain: My Vision of a Young Country,* London, Fourth Estate, 1996; *The Third Way: New Politics for the New Century,* London, Fabian Society, 1998.

5 John F. Kennedy, *Profiles in Courage: Decisive Moments in the Lives of Celebrated Americans,* New York, Harper and Bros, 1956.

6 David Greenberg, 'Reading the candidates', *Dissent,* Fall, 2007, http://www.dissentmagazine.org/article/?article=939

7 Gordon Brown, *Courage: Eight Portraits,* London, Bloomsbury, 2007.

8 For another perspective on Brown's thinking on Britishness and the future prospects of the UK see: Gerry Hassan, 'Brown and the importance of being British', *Renewal: A Journal of Social Democracy,* vol. 16, no. 1, 2008, pp. 13–24.

9 Gerry Hassan, 'Labour's journey from Socialism to Social Democracy: a case study of Gordon Brown's political thought', in Gerry Hassan, ed., *The Scottish Labour Party: History, Institutions and Ideas,* Edinburgh, Edinburgh University Press, 2004, pp. 195–218.

10 Gordon Brown, 'Introduction: the Socialist challenge', in Gordon Brown, ed., *The Red Paper on Scotland,* Edinburgh, Edinburgh University Student Publications Board, 1975, p. 19.

11 Norman Dennis and A. H. Halsey, *English Ethical Socialism: Thomas More to R. H. Tawney,* Oxford, Clarendon Press, 1988.

12 Tom Bower, *Gordon Brown,* London, Harper Collins, 2004; Paul Routledge, *Gordon Brown: The Biography,* London, Simon and Schuster, 1998.

13 For example: Ken Coates and Tony Topham, eds., *Workers' Control: A Book of Readings and Witnesses for Workers' Control,* London, Panther Books, 1970; Ken Coates, ed., *Essays on Industrial Democracy,* Nottingham, Spokesman Books, 1971.

14 Stuart Holland, *The Socialist Challenge,* London, Quartet Books, 1975; Michael Barrett Brown, *From Labourism to Socialism: The Political Economy of Labour in the 1970s,* Nottingham, Spokesman Books, 1972.

15 Gordon Brown and Robin Cook, eds., *Scotland: The Real Divide: Poverty and Deprivation in Scotland,* Edinburgh, Mainstream, 1983; House of Commons, 27 July 1983, cols. 1226–44.

16 Gordon Brown, 'Introduction', in Brown and Cook, p. 20.

17 Eric Shaw, *The Labour Party since 1979: Crisis and Transformation,* London, Routledge, 1994, Chapter. 4.

18 Gordon Brown, *Where There is Greed . . .: Margaret Thatcher and the Betrayal of Britain's Future,* Edinburgh, Mainstream, 1989, p. 10.

19 Gordon Brown, 'Introduction: The Socialist Challenge', in *The Red Paper,* pp. 8–9.

20 H. M. Drucker and Gordon Brown, *The Politics of Nationalism and Devolution,* London, Longman, 1980, p. 127.

21 Drucker and Brown, pp. 127–9.

22 Gordon Brown, British Council 70th Anniversary Annual Lecture, London, 7 July 2004.

23 Brown, 70th Anniversary Annual Lecture.

24 Quoted in Steve Richards, 'Interview with Gordon Brown', *New Statesman,* 19 April 1999.

25 Gordon Brown and Douglas Alexander, *Stronger Together: The 21st century case for Scotland and Britain,* London, Fabian Society, 2007, p. 25.

26 Alan Finlayson, *Making Sense of New Labour,* London, Lawrence and Wishart, 2003.

27 Gerry Hassan, 'Labour, concepts of Britishness, "nation" and "state"', in Gerry

Hassan, ed., *After Blair: Politics after the New Labour Decade*, London, Lawrence and Wishart, 2007, pp. 75–93.

28 Stein Rokkan and Derek Urwin, 'Introduction: Centres and Peripheries in Western Europe', in Stein Rokkan and Derek Urwin, eds., *The Politics of Territorial Identity: Studies In European Regionalism*, London, Sage, 1982.

29 Gordon Brown and Douglas Alexander, *New Scotland, New Britain*, London, Smith Institute, 1999; Brown and Alexander, 2006.

30 Tam Dalyell, *Devolution: The End of Britain*, London, Jonathan Cape, 1977.

31 The Labour government won the vote on foundation hospitals in England by 302 to 285—a government majority of 17 on 19 November 2003. It won the vote on student top-up fees by 316 to 311—a majority of five on 26 January 2004 with 46 Scottish Labour MPs voting with the government, five against and three abstentions.

32 See as an example of this: David Goodhart, *Progressive Nationalism: Citizenship and the Left*, London, Demos, 2006.

33 Gordon Brown, 'Securing Our Future', Speech to Royal United Services Institute, London, 13 February 2006.

34 *YouGov Survey Report April 2007*, London, YouGov, 2007, pp. 4–5.

35 Robert Hazell, ed., *Constitutional Futures: A History of the Next Ten Years*, Oxford, Oxford University Press, 1999; Anthony Barnett, *This Time: Our Constitutional Revolution*, London, Vintage, 1997.

36 Gordon Brown, 'Annual Spectator/Allied Dunbar Lecture', Queen Elizabeth II Conference Centre, London, 4 November 1997.

37 Gordon Brown, Speech to the Smith Institute conference on Britishness, 15 April 1999.

38 Gordon Brown, 'The Future of Britishness', Speech to the Fabian Society 'The Future of Britishness' conference, London, 14 January 2006.

39 Tony Benn, *Arguments for Socialism*, 1979, p. 146.

40 David Davies, *The Times*, 19 June 2008.

41 Gordon Brown, Speech to University of Manchester Institute of Science and Technology, 26 January 2001.

42 Gordon Brown, Speech to the Smith Institute, 1999. Brown was misquoting George Orwell's famous 'The Lion and the Unicorn: Socialism and the English Genius' published in 1941.

43 For a perspective which takes a less forgiving line of Brown's use and confusion between 'English' and 'British' see: Simon Lee, 'Gordon Brown and the 'British way', *The Political Quarterly*, vol. 77 no. 3, 2006, pp. 369–78.

44 David Smith, 'Blair: Britain's "sorrow" for shame of slave trade', *The Observer*, 26 November 2006.

45 Bernard Porter, *The Lion's Share: A Short History of British Imperialism 1850–2004*, London, Longman, 2004 4th edn.

46 Quoted in Martha Kearney, 'Brown seeks out "British values"', *BBC News*, 14 March 2005.

47 Brown has mentioned the Good Friday Agreement once in his contributions on Britishness: 'So devolution does not create new identities; it gives existing identities an institutional form, whether it be Scotland, Wales or Northern Ireland. This is made explicit in the Good Friday Agreement, which for example states "the birthright of all the peoples of Northern Ireland to identify themselves and be accepted as Irish or British or both."' Brown, Speech to the Smith Institute, 1999.

48 Andrew Gamble, *Between Europe and America: The Future of British Politics*, London, Palgrave Macmillan, 2003, p. 30.
49 Gamble, *Between Europe and America*.
50 George Orwell is the exception Gordon Brown continues to quote from the centre-left in his contributions on Britishness.
51 Brown, *Courage*, p. 1.
52 Greenberg, 'Reading the candidates'. The quotation cited is about American political culture, but the point is easily transferable to ours.

Britishness and the Future of the Union

ROBERT HAZELL

Introduction

THIS chapter looks at Britishness through the prism of a number of current political concerns: the SNP's plans for Scottish independence, Gordon Brown's interest in a British statement of values, the English Question and the government's proposals for a British Bill of Rights. The questions running through the chapter are: Is the Union in danger? From whom? And how best to defend it?

The defence of the Union is itself defensible because at least for now, it is supported by a majority within all parts of the Union. One of the underlying principles of the Union, to be discussed shortly, is the principle of consent and the right of self-determination. That is not something recognised by many nation states to apply within their own territory; but it does apply within the UK. (And in Canada: see the judgement of the Supreme Court in *Reference re Secession of Quebec*, [1998] 2 S.C.R. 217.)

So to the first question: Is the Union in danger? Until recently this could be dismissed as reckless talk, indulged in only by wild academics like Tom Nairn or journalists such as Iain McWhirter, talking it up to sell their publications; or by politicians like Alex Salmond, stirring things up to promote the nationalist cause. Now, although Scottish independence must still be judged highly unlikely, there is less confidence about this than there was. For the first time the Union is perceived to be in danger: but the danger to the Union lies more from within, from clumsy defence by unionists, than from the challenges from the nationalists without.

The five stepping stones to Scottish independence

Six years ago the Constitution Unit produced a book on Scottish independence, called *Scottish Independence: A Practical Guide.*[1] It was the product of a year long research project in which we charted the legal and constitutional path to independence. Our starting point was, what if an SNP government is elected in Scotland with a mandate to seek independence? What should happen next? What are the stepping stones the SNP government should follow along the road to independence? And what would be the consequences for Scotland if it achieved independence: what difference would it make in today's globalised, interdependent world?

We made one fatal mistake in that project in relation to its timing. Our book came out in 2002, five years too early. But it is time to resuscitate our

Published by Blackwell Publishing Ltd, 9600 Garsington Road, Oxford OX4 2DQ, UK and 350 Main Street, Malden, MA 02148, USA

conclusions, and to put them back into public debate. There is a general assumption, particularly in the media, that if the Scots vote Yes in an independence referendum, Scotland will automatically become independent. But in fact it is only the beginning of the process. The book identified five stepping stones on the road to independence, each of which could potentially become a road block. Alex Salmond needs to negotiate each one successfully before Scotland can achieve independence.

The first stepping stone is that a referendum cannot be held without legislative authorisation. The SNP would need to get a majority in the Scottish Parliament for their referendum bill. At present there are 50 members of the Scottish Parliament in favour of independence (47 SNP MSPs, plus two pro-independence Scottish Greens, plus Margo Macdonald). Against there are 79 members of the three unionist parties: Labour, Conservative and Liberal Democrats. If the unionist parties vote against the bill, the referendum cannot be held. But following Wendy Alexander's call to 'bring it on',[2] can Labour now vote against? Her extraordinary outburst suggests that Labour might now be willing to knock down this first hurdle for the SNP, and open the first gate for them.

The second hurdle is the referendum itself. Opinion polls have consistently shown support for independence remaining at around 25 to 35 per cent over the last ten years. Even if those figures improve as the referendum approaches, what people say in opinion polls and what they do when confronted by a ballot paper are two different things. The 2004 referendum on regional government in the North East provided dramatic evidence of that.

Third, the referendum proposed by the SNP would simply authorise the Scottish government to start negotiations with the British government about the terms of independence. Some of the terms will be deeply unwelcome. The Scots would no longer receive transfers from the British taxpayer which enable them to enjoy levels of per capita public expenditure some 20 per cent higher than in England. And Scotland would have to re-apply for membership of the EU. It is a difficult question of international and EU law, but the better view is that in international law the rest of the UK would be the successor state which would remain in membership, and Scotland would have to re-apply.[3]

The SNP dispute this. Their August 2007 white paper *Choosing Scotland's Future* maintains that an independent Scotland would continue to be a member of the European Union, but they acknowledge that there would be 'negotiations on the detailed terms of membership' (para. 3.21). Recognising the need for negotiations must include recognising the possibility that those negotiations might fail, so even on their terms, renewed membership is not guaranteed. Other EU member states like Spain might block the negotiations, for fear of encouraging the independence claims of their own national minorities, in the same way (and for the same reasons) that they signalled their unhappiness at the prospect of independence for Kosovo. There are half a dozen EU states in this position.[4]

Whether Scotland was offered fast track re-entry would depend crucially on how strongly the UK supported Scotland's application. That in turn might depend on the outcome of the negotiations on other big issues: North Sea oil, division of the national debt, the future of the defence bases on the Clyde. These are just some of the bigger issues. The Czech-Slovak velvet divorce in 1992 required 31 Treaties and over 2000 separate agreements. Their equivalents for Scotland and the UK would take a long time to negotiate. Once concluded they would constitute the terms of independence, on which the people of Scotland deserve a separate vote.

The need for a second referendum

A second referendum on the terms of independence should be the fourth hurdle to clear before Scotland becomes independent. The SNP contest the need for a second referendum. The reason why a second referendum is needed is the principle of consent; but it must be *informed* consent. Basing democratic authorisation solely on the first referendum, on the initial question of principle which enables the Scottish government to enter into negotiations, is not sufficient because the information at that stage is not available: it is like agreeing to buy a house without knowing the price or having a survey. The people of Scotland deserve better than that; and the UK government is entitled to insist on a second referendum to test whether the people of Scotland want independence on the terms that have been negotiated before agreeing to pass the necessary legislation at Westminster.

Westminster legislation is the fifth and last hurdle to be cleared. Independence can be granted only by Westminster: it is not within the competence of the Scottish Parliament unilaterally to declare independence. Perhaps surprisingly, it is the lowest hurdle of all. Successive British prime ministers, including staunch opponents of devolution like Margaret Thatcher and John Major, have nevertheless recognised the Scottish people's right to self-determination. So did supporters of devolution like Donald Dewar.[5] Unlike the situation in Northern Ireland, there is no formal statement by the British government recognising the Scottish nation's right to become independent from the UK; but having accorded that right to the people of Northern Ireland (and reaffirmed it in section 1 of the Northern Ireland Act 1998), it would be difficult to deny the same right to the people of Scotland. And having recognised Scotland's right to self-determination, it would be difficult to deny the same right to the people of Wales. The Union rests ultimately on consent, and the component nations have the right to self-determination; but the UK government has the right to insist that any test of consent is based on the principle of informed consent.

Brown on Britishness

If Wendy Alexander was short sighted in calling on Alex Salmond to 'bring on' the independence referendum, her party leader is short sighted as well, but in a different way. His interest in Britishness goes back a long way, with numerous speeches on the subject, extending as far back as fifteen years.[6] But it is always essentially the same speech, going through lists of core British values. For Brown the core values are liberty, responsibility, fairness, creativity, enterprise, public service, the welfare state, diversity and equal opportunity. Some have observed that these are universal values in any modern democracy, with nothing distinctively British about them. To that criticism can be added another: that trying to build a society or a nation simply upon the basis of shared values is like trying to construct a one-legged stool.

Where Brown misses something is in omitting the *interests* and the *institutions* which bind the British together, as well as their values. Nation states exist to defend interests; and values and interests find expression through institutions of the state and of civil society. By considering all three sets of factors Brown would be able to provide a more comprehensive, balanced and rounded account of unionism and Britishness. A brief sketch can illustrate what I mean.

Institutions of Britishness

Institutions which symbolise Britain and Britishness include the key political institutions, the major public services and institutions of civil society: the Westminster parliament, the Monarchy, the new Supreme Court, the judiciary, common law, the BBC, British Council, civil service, armed forces and the National Health Service. And in civil society, institutions which represent Britishness and express British values include the Church of England, the Church of Scotland, the Church in Wales and other churches and faith groups; and a whole range of voluntary organisations, from national welfare bodies such as Age Concern and the NSPCC, to specialist bodies like Amnesty or Oxfam.

Some of these state institutions have lost the automatic legitimacy and authority they once enjoyed, and with it perhaps some of their power to bind the nation together. That in part lies behind the Blair government's modernisation agenda, including the creation of the new Supreme Court and Brown's interest in strengthening Parliament. There is also a need to re-examine the extent to which these 'British' institutions are differentiated between the four territories of the UK. The BBC constantly re-examines the balance between its UK-wide programming and its differentiated programmes in Scotland, Wales and Northern Ireland: controversy continues over the six o'clock news in Scotland and the question of whether the devolved governments should have more say over broadcasting policy.

Interests which bind Britain together

Interests can be divided into 'hard' and 'soft' interests. Hard interests include prosperity and security, especially in terms of the basic human interests of safety, food, shelter, survival. These interests are still primarily protected at nation state level. It is the UK state which provides the institutions for defence, national security, foreign policy, macro-economic management, pensions and social security, and all the funding for the welfare state. The Calman Commission on Scottish Devolution will be reconsidering the balance between reserved and devolved functions, but it is unlikely to recommend any fundamental change in responsibility for defence and national security, tax and welfare spending, financial transfers between the different parts of the Union and financial redistribution between different classes in society. Those are, and are likely to remain, the responsibility of central government at the UK state level.

But there is another set of interests which might be called 'soft' interests. By this is meant the shared experience of Britishness on a personal and popular level: how Britishness is represented and how it is felt in our everyday lives. This would include the shared experience of Britishness in ties of history, sense of place, shared culture, high and low, and shared interests in sport. Introducing this set of 'soft interests' goes way beyond Gordon Brown's frame of reference. But if the focus is left too narrowly defined it may miss a whole range of important factors which help to explain what binds modern Britain together.

So to sum up: Britain and Britishness rest not just on shared values, but on shared interests and shared experience and a common set of institutions to give expression to those shared interests. The government's interest in developing a British statement of values risks being a peculiarly abstract exercise (and in that respect, strangely un-British); but more important, it risks missing some of the most important and most basic of the things which bind us together.

Rebalancing the institutions of the British state

Many of the institutions of the British state need to adapt post-devolution. In particular, central government needs to adapt to cope more effectively with the challenges of devolution. Now that there are nationalist parties in power or sharing power in Scotland, Wales and Northern Ireland, it is more important to make the machinery of central government fit for purpose.

The first difficulty is that there is no capacity to think about devolution in the round, because there is no single minister in Whitehall responsible for devolution strategy. Instead there are half a dozen centres responsible for their different bits. There are three separate centres in the Scotland Office, Wales Office and Northern Ireland Office, responsible for their respective bilateral relations. In England the new Department for Communities and Local Government continues to be responsible for regional policy; and the new Department for Business, Enterprise and Regulatory Reform continues to be responsible for Regional Development Agencies. The new Ministry of Justice retains nominal responsibility for overall devolution strategy. And the Cabinet Office has responsibility for coordinating devolution policy, and the Nations and Regions team in the Treasury.

This fragmentation worked—just—when there were Labour-led governments in London, Edinburgh and Cardiff, but is now a serious handicap. Gordon Brown recognised the need for a more coherent devolution strategy, and in late 2007 he appointed Jim Gallagher to be Director General for Devolution in the Ministry of Justice and Cabinet Office. But he needs to go much further and merge the separate territorial Secretaries of State. They are part of the old pre-devolution structures in Whitehall which have no place in the post-devolution world. They perpetuate the piecemeal approach which sees devolution as a set of bilateral relationships. Until we have a single Secretary of State for the Union, or the Nations and Regions, the government will never be able to think about devolution in the round.

Making that change will have a beneficial knock-on effect in Parliament. Reflecting the fragmented structures in Whitehall, the House of Commons has three separate Select Committees for Scottish, Welsh and Northern Irish Affairs. In the Lords the Constitution Committee has tried to take a more synoptic view, and in the Commons the Justice Committee is doing likewise in its 2007-08 inquiry into Devolution: Ten Years On. But we need a permanent committee responsible for devolution as a whole rather than the three separate territorial committees. That would happen if we had a single Secretary of State.

Rebalancing in Whitehall: intergovernmental relations and devolution finance

There are three more things the UK government needs to do to manage devolution effectively and in the round. The first is to revive the Joint Ministerial Committee (JMC) for managing intergovernmental relations with the devolved governments. Following repeated requests from Alex Salmond, the UK government began grudgingly to take this in hand in 2008. Paul Murphy, the Secretary of State for Wales, did the rounds of the devolved governments to discuss the working arrangements. The first plenary JMC (of First Ministers) for five years was held in June 2008, chaired by Jack Straw, but the plan seems to be for the main business to be done in what is dubbed a JMC (Domestic). The 'domestic' format was suggested by the Scottish government in 2007, and might take various forms (or have changing ministerial attendance) depending on the issues under consideration.

Second, the government needs to prepare for a review of the Barnett formula which determines the funding of the devolved governments. At UK government level the main forum for discussing these issues is the Calman Commission, which has appointed an independent expert group chaired by Anton Muscatelli to 'assess the strengths and weaknesses of the present system of financing devolved expenditure . . . and any alternative fiscal options which might provide improved financial accountability'.[7] The Treasury are preparing a memorandum for the Commission on the operation of the Barnett formula, which may offer some indication of the government's willingness to move on the issue. If unwilling, they may come under pressure from the Tories, who have indicated their support for an updated needs assessment.

The English Question

Third, the government needs to have a better answer to the English Question. The English Question is partly about representation and voice (the Campaign for an English Parliament, and the call for English votes on English laws), and it is partly about grievances (the differentials between public spending in England and the devolved nations, in particular Scotland). The differential public spending could be addressed by a review of the Barnett formula. Representation and voice is harder. The government wishes to introduce English Regional Committees at Westminster, to scrutinise the new Regional Ministers. The Commons Modernisation Committee is conducting an inquiry into what form these committees should take. Should they be Select Committees, with permanent staff and scrutiny powers; or Grand Committees, which are just occasional talking shops? Should they reflect the political balance in their region, in which case some would have a Conservative majority; or should they reflect the political balance of the House as a whole? The committees are likely to be as weak as the Regional Ministers they scrutinise, which points to them being Grand rather than Select Committees.

Answers to the English Question are more likely to come from the Conservatives than from Labour. The Conservatives flirted with the idea of an English Parliament under the leadership of William Hague, but they soon switched their policy to English votes on English laws, which was in their manifesto in 2001 and 2005. How to implement English votes on English laws is being considered by the Conservative Democracy Task Force headed by Kenneth Clarke MP. In October 2007 Sir Malcolm Rifkind claimed to have found an answer, by proposing that English laws would be scrutinised by an English Grand Committee at Westminster.[8] Is this the magic answer which has eluded all previous searchers? And can it be made to work? It seems unlikely. The difficulties remain formidable, at both a technical and a political level.

The technical difficulty is identifying those English laws which would be referred to Grand Committee. Strictly speaking there is no such thing as an

English law, in the sense of a Westminster statute which applies only to England. Many statutes vary in their territorial application in different parts of the Act. Is the Speaker to identify in advance those parts or clauses which apply only to England, and rule that those parts be referred to Grand Committee? His rulings will be hotly contested. If the Conservatives are hoping that Parliamentary Counsel could draft statutes differently, separating out all the English provisions into England only bills, then they really need to take a year's worth of the statute book to demonstrate how this might be done.

If the technical difficulties are daunting, the political difficulties are even greater. Proponents of special procedures for English laws tend to under-estimate just what a huge change would be involved. An English Grand Committee would effectively create two classes of MP, ending the traditional reciprocity whereby all members can vote on all matters. It could in time lead to the creation of an English Parliament within the Westminster parliament. And after close fought elections, the UK government might not be able to command a majority for its English business, leading to great political instability. These political difficulties cast doubt on the likelihood of English votes on English laws ever becoming political reality. It may be significant that David Cameron, in his speech on the Union given in Edinburgh last December, made no mention of English votes on English laws.[9]

What might be giving him pause? By ending the equal voting rights of all MPs, the Conservatives could no longer claim to be unionist, but would have become an English party. An English party does not sound like a party of government. The Conservatives might find it more expedient to reduce the numbers of Scottish and Welsh MPs, than to attempt the more complicated task of trying to restrict their voting rights. Research done by the Constitution Unit shows that Scottish and Welsh MPs have seen their workloads reduced since devolution, significantly so in terms of their postbags, which suggests that it would be justifiable to reduce their numbers.[10] Following the precedent set during the first Northern Ireland Parliament from 1922 to 1972, their numbers might be reduced by one third. This was also Conservative policy in their 2005 manifesto, but little noticed at the time. It would not eliminate the possibility of Scottish and Welsh MPs voting on English laws, but it would further reduce the likelihood of their votes being able to tip the balance.

British Bill of Rights, and British statement of values

Another big issue in the next general election is going to be the debate about a British Bill of Rights. It is important to understand where each side is coming from. David Cameron started the debate in a speech given in June 2006 in which he proposed repealing the Human Rights Act and replacing it with a British Bill of Rights. At the time Blair and Cameron were outbidding each other in their denunciations of the Human Rights Act, following a High Court decision which had ruled that a group of Afghan hijackers could not be deported back to Afghanistan.[11] Cameron got the headline he wanted 'Tories to repeal Human Rights Act', and suggested in his speech that a British Bill of Rights might make it easier for the UK to disapply some of the stricter requirements of the European Convention on Human Rights, the ECHR. In the short hand of the human rights world, he is seeking a British Bill of Rights which could be ECHR minus. The lawyers in his team advise that is not possible without leaving the Council of Europe, and it will be interesting to see how the Conservative working party on this subject squares that particular circle.

The Labour party has a long standing commitment to a British Bill of Rights. In the 1997 manifesto, incorporation of the ECHR into UK domestic law was going to be stage one, with stage two being the development of a British Bill of Rights. But with Blair's manifest lack of enthusiasm for any aspect of the constitutional reform agenda stage two was quietly dropped, and the government rested on its laurels after the passage of the Human Rights Act in 1998. What has led to the change of heart? For Brown, it is part of the Britishness agenda; but he is also more committed to human rights than Blair, as part of his wider commitment to constitutional reform generally. There has been no more sniping about the Human Rights Act since Brown became Prime Minister. He genuinely wants to introduce a British Bill of Rights, which he sees as a possible precursor to a written constitution.

The lead minister giving effect to Brown's policy is Jack Straw. He was also the lead minister who introduced the Human Rights Act ten years ago, which was shaped and drafted in the Home Office. Ten years on he is concerned that the Human Rights Act has not more strongly taken root, and anxious to secure his legacy. He knows that any British Bill of Rights has to be ECHR plus, and his speeches on the subject are quite explicit about that.[12] So in the government's consultation document on a British Bill of Rights, the section to read with greatest interest is the 'plus'. It is likely to be quite thin, and hedged about with caveats; but the enterprise should not be dismissed on that account. It is a worthwhile project in its own right to try to re-incorporate the ECHR, if in the process the British people can be persuaded to take it to their hearts, so that the tabloids can no longer denounce it as a nasty foreign plot.

But Jack Straw faces some quite big difficulties. The first is the government's determination to launch at the same time a consultation exercise on a British statement of values. This is to be discussed by citizens' juries up and down the country, culminating in a Citizens' Summit of 500 to 1000 people, and the result presented to Parliament. There risks being no result; or the result attracting media and public derision. It seems an artificial exercise. It would be far better for the deliberative forums to be given a real political task, of drafting a British Bill of Rights. To persuade the British public to take the new Bill of Rights to their hearts, there does need to be something big which captures the public imagination and engages the public directly in shaping and crafting the Bill of Rights. The recent Citizens' Assemblies in British Columbia and Ontario show that given a real political task (in their case, devising a new electoral system) ordinary people can rise to the challenge and grapple with technical complexity and political trade-offs, and come up with carefully worked through conclusions and recommendations.

But it is not going to happen that way here. The main reason is Jack Straw's other difficulty, which is that the government is running out of time. There are only two legislative sessions left in this Parliament. If the government are to get a British Bill of Rights onto the statute book before the next election, they are forced into an old style, top down consultation of the classic kind, with a green paper in summer 2008, three months or so for responses, white paper and bill. One other difficulty which could spoil this timetable is the devolved governments. The Scottish government has already signalled its opposition to a British Bill of Rights. In Northern Ireland the Human Rights Commission has been consulting on its own Bill of Rights for the last seven years. Scotland and Wales could start their own rival debates about the content of a Bill of Rights—and indeed the statement of values—and what was intended to be a unifying exercise could end up being divisive. When the devolution complications are added to the array of institutional actors who will need to be consulted—the judiciary, the new Commission for Equality and Human Rights, the parliamentary Joint Committee on Human Rights—the target of achieving a British Bill of Rights this side of the next election seems very ambitious indeed.

Conclusion: the five Cs to defend the Union

In conclusion, what advice can be offered to the British government on how best to defend the Union? The conclusions from this chapter can be summarised under five Cs: consent, custodianship, constitutionality, consistency and confidence.

The most important principle underlying the Union is consent. It is a voluntary union, and the UK government should recognise (as it has in the case of Northern Ireland) that the nations comprising the UK are free to leave the Union if they wish.

That imposes on the UK government important obligations as the main custodian of the Union. It needs to uphold the principles of constitutionality in the path to independence for Scotland. And to uphold the principle of consistency, the UK government should engage fairly and equally with all the devolved governments, and ensure fair and consistent representation in the UK parliament and fair distribution of territorial finance according to need.

Finally, confidence. The UK government can and should be far more confident about the future of the Union than it appears to be. The Union rests on much broader and firmer foundations than the government seems to realise. The panic which gripped UK ministers in the summer of 2007 after the formation of the SNP government was extraordinary. They confused the threat to their party with a threat to the nation. They need to calm down, be a lot more confident, and—to add one more C—get a comparative perspective on all this. In federal and devolved systems like Canada and Spain constitutional debates about independence and autonomy go on all the time. The nationalist threat cannot be thwarted by bringing on an early referendum as if that could decide the question once and for all. The Scottish Question will always be with us. We lived with the Irish Question for a century, and the Northern Ireland Question for nearly half a century. It is one of the main responsibilities of the UK government to be the custodian of the national question, and to manage these issues in a calm, confident, consistent and constitutional way.

Notes

1 Jo Murkens, Peter Jones and Michael Keating. *Scottish Independence: A Practical Guide*, Edinburgh: Edinburgh University Press, 2002.
2 BBC Scotland, *Politics on Sunday* 4 May 2008.
3 Murkens, Jones and Keating, *Scottish Independence*, chapters 6 to 8.
4 Simon James, 'Kosovo could end Scotland's European dream', *Financial Times*, 26 February 2008.
5 Murkens, Jones and Keating, *Scottish Independence*, pp. 12–13.
6 For analysis and extracts from Brown's speeches see Robert Hazell et al, *Towards a New Constitutional Settlement: An Agenda for Gordon Brown's First 100 Days and Beyond*, London, The Constitution Unit, June 2007, chapter 2.
7 Commission on Scottish Devolution, press notice on independent expert group, 11 June 2008.
8 'Tories will hand crucial powers to English MPs', *Observer*, 28 October 2007.
9 David Cameron, 'Stronger Together', speech on the Union in Edinburgh 10 December 2007.
10 Akash Paun, 'Lost souls in the lobbies? What backbenchers from Scotland and Wales do in post-devolution Westminster' in Alan Trench ed., *State of the Nations*, Exeter, Imprint Academic, 2008.
11 10 May 2006, Mr Justice Sullivan.
12 Jack Straw, Mackenzie-Stuart lecture, Cambridge, 25 October 2007.

Devolution, Britishness and the Future of the Union

CHARLIE JEFFERY

Devolution and union: are values enough?

GORDON Brown is the only senior UK politician to have devoted sustained attention to the implications of devolution for 'Britishness'. In his series of speeches on Britishness, extending back to the late 1990s, he has generally noted that while devolution might seem to offer a challenge to the cohesion of state and society in the UK, that challenge is contained by shared values of Britishness. His British Council Annual Lecture in 2004 put the point forcefully:

Take devolution and nationalism. While the United Kingdom has always been a country of different nations and thus of plural identities . . . the issue is whether we retreat into more exclusive identities rooted in 19th century conceptions of blood, race and territory, or whether we are still able to celebrate a British identity which is bigger than the sum of its parts and a Union that is strong because of the values we share and because of the way these values are expressed through our history and our institutions.[1]

Brown's claim serves as a riposte to the pro-independence nationalism of the Scottish National Party and though it is put intemperately (the SNP does not articulate its nationalism as one of blood and race), it is an intriguing one. The values he talks about in the speech—standing firm for freedom and liberty against tyranny, a sense of duty and fair play, openness to new ideas and new influences—are indeed shared across the component parts of the UK. The British Social Attitudes survey and its counterparts in Scotland, Wales and Northern Ireland provide the most authoritative data on UK public attitudes. They consistently show that citizens across the UK think in much the same ways about their sense of obligation to one another, and about the roles that the state should be performing collectively on behalf of all. Table 1 gives one example through a question designed to tap values on social solidarity, in Brown's terms the British sense of fair play. It shows that differences between the UK nations are small and any year-on-year variations follow no obvious territorial pattern.

Whether these commonalities add up to something that helps bind the UK together, as Brown suggests, is less clear. It is a fair bet that if the same question were asked of citizens in different parts of France, or Spain, or Germany, some similar pattern of answers would be found. Henderson and McEwen made a similar point when they compared the fissiparous pressures

 Published by Blackwell Publishing Ltd, 9600 Garsington Road, Oxford OX4 2DQ, UK and 350 Main Street, Malden, MA 02148, USA

Table 1: 'Ordinary people do not get their fair share of the nation's wealth' (% agree / agree strongly)

	1999	2000	2001	2002	2003	2005
Scotland	58	71	61	64	54	57
England	60	61	58	61	60	55
Wales	61	–	61	60	59	–
Northern Ireland	62	60	55	62	59	52

Sources: British Social Attitudes, Scottish Social Attitudes, Welsh Life and Times Survey, Northern Ireland Life and Times Survey, Devolved Election Studies.

of sub-state nationalism in the UK with the Quebec–Canada relationship: they found that the 'values' claimed by the Parti Québécois as the foundations of Quebec nationhood 'are virtually indistinguishable'[2] from the values promoted by those committed to Canadian unity. A recent Eurobarometer survey across the European Union underlines the point, finding that 'most Europeans say that they can differentiate a set of collective European values' and that these 'largely overlap with a broader set of global western values'.[3] In other words, the existence of common values within a state does not necessarily underpin a shared commitment to the same state as Brown suggests; those values may simply express a broader set of commonalities shared across western democracies. That Scottish and English (and Welsh and Northern Irish) citizens have broadly the same values clearly does not stop them from having and pursuing different constitutional preferences. To press the point further: if Scotland became independent, it would not stop having in common with the rest of the UK the values that Brown singles out as 'British'.

Brown does, though, point to a different way in which values may underpin union: when they are embodied in institutional structures that express and contain union. In particular he focuses on the BBC and the NHS as archetypal institutions of Britishness. Both were singled out in a speech Brown made to the Smith Institute in 1999[4] (and in similar phrasing in later speeches) as examples of how resources can be pooled to general benefit. The BBC 'was created by a Scot, but healthy devolution should not obscure the fact that it is a service that operates for the whole of Britain, is paid for by a sharing of costs by all the people of Britain and is seen as a defining feature of Britain'. Similarly,

when people talk of the National Health Service whether in Scotland, Wales or England people think of the British National Health Service: here national is unquestionably 'British'. And its most powerful driving idea is that every citizen of Britain has an equal right to treatment regardless of wealth, position or race and, indeed, can secure treatment in any part of Britain.

There is much to Brown's claims here. The BBC and the NHS are iconically British, and do express values shared across the UK's internal boundaries; recent survey research on attitudes to the NHS has for example shown that 'what matters to the public is much the same in Scotland as it is in England'.[5] But while the BBC and NHS may still embody shared *values* the practice of nearly a decade of devolution has weakened their *institutional* cohesion across the UK. Even if citizens identify the 'national' in the NHS as British, in reality there are now four increasingly distinctive national health services in the UK. From headline issues like prescription charging, the licensing of treatments for use in the NHS, and free personal care for the elderly through to underlying questions of organisation and philosophy, the four services do things in different ways and deliver different priorities and outcomes (as indeed they did, to lesser extents, before devolution). And while the BBC remains institutionally (British) national it now is under increasing pressure to diversify to reflect more systematically the territorially distinctive arenas for public debate, culture and entertainment that have become consolidated in the decade since devolution.

This institutional centrifugalism would seem to jar with the shared values that people across the UK claim. It is increasingly fostering policy outcomes that vary across the four UK nations, within healthcare and broadcasting, but also in many other policy fields. There are plenty of indicators that citizens do not much like these variations: from regular controversies about postcode lotteries in the delivery of public services, through mischievous opinion polling suggesting that the people of Berwick-upon-Tweed would prefer to reunite with Scotland to enjoy what they perceive as more generous public services there than in England, to the more reliable scholarly analysis of the British Social Attitudes survey about public preferences for territorially uniform public policy. Yet shared values are now confronted increasingly by (and have no obvious capacity to prevent) unshared outcomes across the four nations of the UK. This dissonance reflects a failing the Britishness debate has barely touched on, yet is arguably fundamental to prospects for the future of the UK union: the design and operation of the post-devolution political system.

The dynamics of disconnected union

To be blunt: the post-devolution political system was not designed as an integrated system of government. This lack of integrated design is a long-standing tradition in UK government. The UK state grew (and in Ireland later contracted) through a set of relationships between England and the other nations in which England has always been the sole common denominator. The UK state has always been asymmetrically organised, with a generally and over time increasingly uniform approach to public administration in England, and different sets of distinctive arrangements for public administration, with varying degrees of policy discretion and institutional underpinning, in the other nations. The relationship of the English core and the other nations has always been a piecemeal one; changes to administrative arrangements in, say, Scotland did not lead to equivalent changes in Wales or (Northern) Ireland.

Relationships have always been bilateral and partial, not multilateral and statewide. The UK union has always been curiously disconnected as between its non-English parts.

That tradition of disconnection was continued in 1997–99. Different UK government departments introduced reforms for Scotland, Wales and Northern Ireland (with a half-hearted and then aborted attempt to add English regional reforms following in the period 2002–4). Those reforms were introduced for different reasons in different places, and were discussed in government and Parliament for the most part as discrete issues. This characteristically piecemeal approach has a number of consequences which underline and exacerbate the centrifugal tendency noted above.

First, approaching each reform as a discrete renegotiation of the relationship of one part of the UK to the UK as a whole carried with it the danger of spillovers, that is unanticipated consequences of reforms designed to meet a need in one part of the UK for another. James Mitchell has highlighted the most obvious example: while devolution in Scotland met a Scottish need (to relegitimise the UK system of government after a protracted period of being governed in Westminster by a Conservative party that was increasingly weak in Scotland), one consequence has been to open up perceptions in England that Scottish devolution is unfair to the English[6]:

- in terms of political representation (the West Lothian Question);
- in the distribution of resources (Scotland, for historic reasons unconnected to the devolution reforms, has a block grant from the UK Treasury which awards more public spending per capita than England); and
- in terms of policy provision (where post-devolution policy innovations in Scotland like reduced prescription charges and fee-free higher education are not available in England).

In consequence, there has been further debate about how to address these perceptions of inequity, including proposals to restrict Scottish MPs' rights at Westminster and/or to devolve fuller tax-raising powers to Scotland so that public spending in Scotland is financed more fully by Scottish taxpayers and less by the general UK taxpayer. The risk is, of course, that addressing these spillovers of Scottish devolution into England in the same piecemeal way as the earlier Scottish reforms were introduced will add further spillovers, for example concerning perceptions of unfairness in Scotland about 'second class' status at Westminster, or emulative demands in Wales for tax-raising powers, and so on. The prospect is one of continual flux.

A second consequence of the piecemeal approach to reform in 1997–99 concerns the relationships between England and the rest. England is one of the most centralised political units among liberal democracies. It is also, in relative terms, very big: around ten times the size of Scotland, seventeen times the size of Wales and thirty times the size of Northern Ireland. The combination of one unit of large size and centralised government alongside smaller units with extensive devolution is, in comparative terms, unique. It brings with it its own spillovers. Irrespective of the formal distribution of powers, decisions taken by Westminster for England inevitably spill over into areas of devolved responsibility given England's predominance on the UK's single market, single welfare state and single internal security area. They do so all the more given the ways that the government of England is fused (and often confused) with the government of the UK in the institutions of Westminster and Whitehall. Moreover, where UK institutions act for the UK as a whole the mindset of decision-making is, logically enough, dominated by the largest part, England, and equally logically neglectful of interests outside England or effects in devolved settings. Finally, because it is in this way 'captured' by English interests UK government is ill-placed to arbitrate concerns or conflicts over spillovers between jurisdictions.

That this mix of devolution outside England and centralisation of England was not understood as an integrated system of government is confirmed, third, by the practices the UK uses for coordinating the work of its different governments. These have projected forward an approach to the accommodation of different territorial interests inherited from pre-devolution UK government. That approach sees coordination as an ad hoc process, lubricated by assumptions of Civil Service collegiality, referred to ministers only in case of dispute, and carried out entirely beyond public view. It was, no doubt, appropriate to the pre-devolution situation. It functioned more or less adequately from 1999 to 2007 when Labour led governments at the UK level and in Scotland and Wales (and when Northern Irish devolution was in the main suspended), and disputes could be managed within the Labour party 'family'. But it appears unfit for purpose now the SNP provides the Scottish government, Labour is in coalition with Plaid Cymru in Wales, and Northern Ireland devolution, with its distinctive party system, is in operation again. Ad hocery and non-transparency do not appear well-suited to managing the growing number of intergovernmental disputes, especially between Scotland and the UK, allowing accusations of duplicity and grandstanding to be made on both sides. More importantly, there is minimal provision in this practice of intergovernmental coordination for identifying and pursuing *common* interests shared between governments across jurisdictions.

To put this last point another way, there is no apparent sense of the need, or desirability, of the UK's different governments to join together to make policy across their different jurisdictions *for the union as a whole*. This is a striking absence. It expresses the fourth consequence of piecemeal devolution: the purpose of union, in its post-devolution form, is unclear and under-articulated. The UK operates after devolution as a collection of governments working side by side in a sense by default, rather than because they are joined in some kind of common endeavour in service of the citizens of the UK. Gordon Brown's discussion of British values is an attempt to suffuse this disconnected political system with some kind of commonality, but for the reasons discussed above is flawed and insufficient. What needs to be added to the mix is a more explicit articulation of the shared *interests* that all UK citizens might draw from the union in its new, post-devolution form. A glance at other devolved and federal systems gives some pointers. Germany and Australia operate systems of fiscal equalisation based on commitments that all citizens should enjoy similar levels of provision of public services, despite the existence of a tier of decentralised government. Canada and Belgium have significantly more decentralised and diverse sub-state governments, but in each case diversity is bounded by continued commitments to statewide 'social union' in Canada and a statewide social security system in Belgium; diversity is highly prized, yet still tempered by explicit commitments to statewide solidarity.

The UK has failed to problematise the balance between the commitment to diversity that devolution embodies, and the commitment to solidarity and equity that continued union implies. There has been no general articulation of the balance of interests that might best be secured for citizens at a statewide scale, and those that might best be secured for citizens in each of the four nations of the UK. There has been no explicit distinction between policy outcomes that can or should vary across jurisdictions, and those that should not and should be delivered for all citizens no matter where they live. There has been no systematic discussion of the allocation of resources between levels of government as a means of achieving balance between territorial diversity and statewide fairness. As a result, the post-devolution state lacks generally understood, generally accepted rules of the game which might mark out limits of policy variation, offer a general rather than a piecemeal framework for addressing the concerns and relationships of the UK's component nations, consider more systematically the government of England and connect it to government outside of England, and inform a framework of intergovernmental coordination capable of pursuing statewide objectives and balancing them against devolved autonomy. In sum, the UK has failed to identify how 'Britishness'—in this sense some conception of the interests shared by all citizens, across all UK-level, English and devolved jurisdictions—can be understood, debated and delivered by the post-devolution political system.

Options for a new Britishness

Can this be fixed? There are two directions to a 'new Britishness' in the post-devolution political system, the first involving more union, the second less. The first would involve mechanisms and techniques for expressing and guaranteeing shared statewide interests more explicitly. This might involve:

- Guarantees of minimum or common standards of policy provision in some policy fields for all citizens. The UK currently has common standards in the field of social security. Equivalent guarantees might be established— though inevitably with wider margins of variation around the common core or from the minimum level—in health, education and other policy fields.

- Mechanisms to express union more explicitly in the UK's territorial financial arrangements. These might include a system of fiscal equalisation to replace the Barnett system, in which differential territorial need was compensated as an expression of solidarity between the different parts of the UK. The purpose of such systems is to ensure sub-state governments have roughly the same fiscal capacity to provide public goods and services, not to provide uniform goods and services. Additional mechanisms could be used to ensure uniformity if deemed desirable in particular policy fields by the UK's governments: some element of fiscal transfers could be made conditional on achieving agreed UK-wide priorities; or UK and devolved governments could agree to combine resources to joint-fund shared priorities.
- Policy-making for the union by intergovernmental agreement. The UK's approach to intergovernmental coordination could be modified to add a policy development role to meet objectives across jurisdictions. This would need to provide much fuller guarantees of devolved government input, not least in agreeing any minimum or common standards, the terms of fiscal equalisation, or areas for conditional or joint funding. It would also need a more systematic distinction of the UK-wide and England-specific roles of the UK government, with more systematic consideration of the government of England (as distinguished from the government of the UK) nudging the UK in the direction of a federal system.

Any movement in this direction of more union, more 'Britishness', in the operation of the devolved political system would require a subtlety of thought often lacking in UK constitutional debate: though such measures would increase the capacity for union-wide government in areas formally devolved outside of England, they would not automatically imply a loss of function of devolved governments. Rather—assuming effective guarantees on inter-governmental policy-making—devolved government would add functions by having a greater grip over the central UK state. Moreover, establishing elements of union-wide decision making into which devolved and UK governments are bound is not incompatible with further devolution of policy-making powers or fiscal autonomy. Indeed, introducing mechanisms for more union might most easily be achieved as part of a package deal including further devolution.

The second direction of possible change is one involving less union. This direction of change would follow the logic of centrifugalism in the current arrangements and institutionalise it more explicitly. This logic could involve the further devolution of powers to the non-English nations and the establishment of fuller degrees of fiscal autonomy without the balancing measures of the 'more union' route. The logic would imply continued and growing diversification of policy portfolios in the different nations of the UK, weak (or weakening) intergovernmental coordination, and perhaps reduced representation of the devolved nations at the UK centre. A result would be a further and fuller diminution of commonalities and solidarities—that is, an acceptance of significantly greater asymmetries—between the different nations of the UK. The institutional direction would not be that of federalism, but one of two other routes:

- The establishment of Scotland, and perhaps Wales and Northern Ireland, as 'special status' nations of the UK or, in academic jargon, 'federacies', 'political arrangements where a large unit is linked to a smaller unit or units, but the smaller unit retains considerable autonomy and has a limited role in the government of the larger one'.[7]
- Scottish (and perhaps Welsh and Northern Irish) independence.

There might ultimately be little practical distinction between special status devolution within the UK and independence. A special status Scotland might have very extensive or even full fiscal autonomy, full control over domestic policy (though no doubt hedged by reciprocal arrangements on cross-border portability with the rest of the UK), and growing international engagement (for example in trade promotion and development aid). An independent Scotland might well retain the pound sterling and by implication remain subject to UK monetary policy; it would certainly in this field and more generally still have to reckon on spillover effects on its policy autonomy arising from the size and economic weight of neighbouring England. An independent Scotland might recast the UK as the union of Scottish and English crowns which existed for the century or so prior to the union of the Scottish and English states in 1707. There would no doubt be some level of cross-border portability and reciprocity of citizenship rights with the rest of the UK, over and above that which exists, for example, between the UK and the Republic of Ireland. And common EU membership would provide an additional context for continued borderlessness between Scotland and the residual UK. Scottish independence in a contemporary British Isles/European Union setting would not, in other words, be anything like the '19th century conceptions' Gordon Brown pointed to in his 2004 Britishness speech; it could still embody a continued 'Britishness' of economic interdependence, shared currency, joint crown and common citizenship.

Outlook

Which kind of 'Britishness' the UK might be headed towards—a recast system of government with a more systematic approach to union or something looser somewhere in the grey area between special status and independent statehood—is a moot point. The UK currently has three constitutional forums under way or in planning. The SNP's 'National Conversation' in Scotland rules out the status quo, highlights the SNP's preference for independence, but is open to further-reaching devolution (as a kind of interim measure en route to independence). The unionist response in Scotland, the Calman Commission on Scottish Devolution, rules out independence and has a remit focused on more devolution alongside measures to reaffirm union. The All-Wales Convention was launched in mid-2008 and has the task of facilitating a wide debate in Wales on the possible move of the National Assembly to adopt 'full law-making powers', that is something like the current Scottish model of devolution.

None of these forums appears likely to endorse the status quo. Only the Calman Commission has a remit which has elements of 'more union', albeit from a Scottish-UK perspective rather than a union-wide one. All of them have a limited focus on one or other part of the UK. None of them is concerned with the establishment of an overarching balance of purposes between union-wide and devolved government. In other words, each is offering yet more piecemeal change. The picture is no more systematic at UK level. Mystifyingly, none of the initiatives that have spun out of the 2007 Governance of Britain Green Paper have identified arrangements for governing the post-devolution union as a challenge for and priority of Britishness. Nor do the Conservatives appear to be thinking systematically about the relationship of devolution and union. They appear either (as in Labour's Governance of Britain initiative) to be bracketing out territorial questions from their debate on renewing democracy (in Ken Clarke's Democracy Task Force), or to flirt with partial and piecemeal fixes to English concerns about the perceived advantages the Scots have after devolution.

The continued absence of a systematic approach to the territorial government of the UK, and the existence of various forums for discussion of one or other nation's concerns, point to a continuation of the centrifugal dynamic of the UK's strangely disconnected union. The prospects for institutionalising a sense of union-wide Britishness—the identification of shared interests across the jurisdictions of the UK's governments—in the operation of the post-devolution political system appear at best distant; there appears to be no credible counterbalance to the UK's post-devolution centrifugalism. And continued centrifugalism suggests, more or less by default, that a much looser kind of Britishness is set to evolve, perhaps as a set of relationships between autonomous nations contained within a single state, perhaps as a set of unusually close and interdependent relationships between two or more different states.

Notes

1 G. Brown, British Council Annual Lecture, 7 July 2004, at http://www.hm-treasury.gov.uk/newsroom_and_speeches/press/2004/press_63_04.cfm.
2 A. Henderson and N. McEwen, 'Do shared values underpin national identity? Examining the role of values in national identity in Canada and the UK', *National Identities*, 2005, pp. 173–91.

3 European Commission, *Eurobarometer 69. Public Opinion in the European Union*, at http://ec.europa.eu/public_opinion/archives/eb/eb69/eb_69_first_en.pdf.
4 G. Brown, Speech at the Smith Institute, 15 April 1999, at http://www.hm-treasury.gov.uk/newsroom_and_speeches/speeches/chancellorexchequer/speech_chex_19990415.cfm.
5 R. Ormston and J. Curtice, 'Attitudes towards a "British institution": comparing public views of the NHS in England and Scotland', *Scottish Affairs*, 2007, pp. 50–73.
6 J. Mitchell, 'Devolution's unfinished business', *The Political Quarterly*, 2006, pp. 465–74.
7 R. Watts, 'The United Kingdom as a federalised or a regionalised union', in A. Trench, ed., *Devolution and Power in the United Kingdom*, Manchester, Manchester University Press, p. 243.

Englishness in Contemporary British Politics

RICHARD HAYTON, RICHARD ENGLISH and
MICHAEL KENNY

THE NOTION of Englishness is an increasingly salient one in contemporary political and cultural life, and one that extends far beyond the now customary display of the St George's Cross at major sporting occasions involving an England team. That we are currently witnessing a growing commitment to English nationalism and deeper and wider identification with Englishness, as opposed to Britishness, is becoming part of the political wisdom of the age, and feeds into an increasingly vexed debate among politicians and commentators about the constitutional, political and cultural status of the United Kingdom and the identity and future of 'Britishness' itself. This theme is most obviously linked in political terms to the landmark reforms associated with the granting of devolution to Scotland and Wales in 1999, though a new mood of English nationalism was discernible as far back as the early 1990s, and was gathering momentum well before New Labour came to power in 1997.[1]

Quite how widespread is this stronger identification with Englishness, and how new is the idea of belonging to an English rather than a British nation, represent important questions that have been rather buried beneath the sounds of the trumpeting or denouncing of this purportedly new phenomenon. While a full examination of the historical dimensions and depth of identification with Englishness is beyond our remit here, this article seeks to put the case for the adoption of a greater sense of historical proportion about these changes, and challenges the widely held presumption that the rise of Englishness necessarily signals the death-knell of the values and identities associated with Britishness and the legitimacy of the UK's polity. We engage these questions by separating out and providing some critical reflections upon three of the main characterisations of English nationalism that dominate thinking in elite political and cultural circles. None of these, we maintain, is adequate to the task of providing an intellectually robust, historically proportionate or politically wise framework for policy-makers and politicians. In conclusion, we point towards the merits of a rather different reading of, and approach to, Englishness for the political elite in Westminster, a paradigm characterised by a commitment to adaptive reform, constructive engagement with English identity and an awareness of the values and benefits still attached to British and United Kingdom institutions and traditions. A commitment to a strongly held sense of Englishness and the desire to articulate and explore English national identity is by no means a

Published by Blackwell Publishing Ltd, 9600 Garsington Road, Oxford OX4 2DQ, UK and 350 Main Street, Malden, MA 02148, USA

novel feature of British cultural life, nor is it necessarily an indication of the demise of Britishness. The politics of national identification and cultural attachment in Britain does not have to be seen as a zero-sum game.

The politics of English nationalism

The Labour government elected in 1997 has overseen the most far-reaching reform of Britain's constitution over the last century. Whether this programme represents a continuation of the supple and adaptive traditions which some commentators have long celebrated as the hallmark of governance from Westminster, or amounts to a shorter-term politically-driven effort to breathe new life into the ailing Union, or entails a defensive response to the declining legitimacy of Britain, remains the subject of considerable debate. The political reasons given for the devolution of some executive responsibility to, and the creation of legislative bodies in, Scotland and Wales, related to the desire to head off some of the long-held grievances that had fired nationalist movements in both countries. New Labour's election manifesto promised to 'meet the demand for decentralisation of power to Scotland and Wales, once established in referendums' and argued that doing so would strengthen the Union and remove the threat of separatism.[2]

Very little was said about England and the English when these changes were introduced. However, in the years since devolution, three different grievances with these new arrangements have been aired on their behalf. These concern: the apparent absurdity of Scottish MPs at Westminster being able to vote on matters that only affect England—the continuing conundrum known as the West Lothian Question; increasing disaffection about the markedly different proportions of public expenditure incurred per capita in England compared with Scotland; and the emergence of marked differences of attitude and policy toward the public funding of education, healthcare and other services in Scotland.

Some of these putative injustices and affronts to English sensibilities have been sharply noted in recent years. As Conservative politician and commentator Boris Johnson has put it, the Scots might be regarded as building their New Jerusalem with English money.[3] Another leading right-wing commentator, Simon Heffer of the *Daily Telegraph*, expressed his disaffection regarding post-1997 devolution in typically crisp terms: 'I felt not just that I was being denied an identity. I felt that I was being denied proper participation in what was now a reconstituted democracy of these islands . . . I realised I didn't mind not having a say in what was happening in Scotland, but there had to be a *quid pro quo* for that, and that meant that the Scots didn't have a say in what went on here.'[4]

Yet, whether the incensed character of the writings of right-wing populists such as Johnson and Heffer accurately reflects the sentiments of the English populace is harder to assess. Specifically, there is little evidence that the greater self-identification with England which some opinion polls have tracked across this period means that the new Englishness is as defined by grievance and political resentment as these figures tend to assume. Fiscal inequities between England and Scotland have not assumed any consistent political priority, though for obvious tactical reasons, the Conservatives in Parliament are beginning to press this issue more forcefully now that the government is headed by a Scottish MP. More important perhaps, is the potential for grievance about these issues to become conjoined with other contentious issues where a sense of English tradition is involved—the issues mobilised by the Countryside Alliance, or hostility towards the EU.

Few mainstream figures have associated themselves unambiguously with the politics of English resentment, whilst the Conservative party as a whole has been wary since 1997 of making capital out of the West Lothian Question. However electorally attractive the idea of stoking-up English complaints about the burdens of devolution may be, its own historic commitment to the Union has tended to dampen down Conservative radicalism. As the party's last national election manifesto declared, 'Conservatives believe that the Union of England, Scotland, Wales and Northern Ireland brings benefits to all parts of our United Kingdom'.[5] As such, with the exception of a few fringe campaign groups, the tiny UK Independence party, and on the far-right, English post-devolution grievances have not yet found a home within British party politics.

Now confronted with a Scottish Prime Minister, and a potentially tighter public spending settlement, the Union may face a greater legitimacy crisis in the form of heightened English resentment than has hitherto been the case. Yet for all its imperfections, the post-devolution constitutional position has some merits, and may prove more long-lasting than some assume, as the least-worst option currently available in constitutional and fiscal terms. The other main reform scenarios—either re-organising the business of the House of Commons so that only English MPs vote on English matters, or the more radical idea of an English Parliament which would match the Scottish Parliament and Welsh Assembly—come with a tangle of political and constitutional complexities and risks. Nor is the do-nothing option necessarily out of harmony with British opinion: as John Curtice has shown, this has been the most consistent frontrunner in the opinion polls since 1999.[6]

Some observers, from left and right, see the rise of political Englishness as an unavoidable consequence of the inexorable waning of the values and traditions of the British.[7] The English, Richard Weight argues, 'invested their Englishness almost wholly in the idea of Britain'.[8] As the traditions and values of Britishness cease to have the cultural pull they once did—with Gordon Brown's generation perhaps the last to feel an uncomplicated and proud sense of being British—it is suggested that Englishness emerges, confused and disorientated into the light of day. For social theorist Krishan Kumar, 'having for so long resolutely refused to consider themselves as a nation or to define their sense of nationhood [the English] find themselves having to begin from scratch'.[9] Britishness and the defunct British state should be abandoned, asserts Weight, not least because 'the United Kingdom was primarily established to further the quest for Empire, and with the loss of Empire went its raison d'être'. Separation would help to free England from its imperial past, and afford the left the opportunity to develop a radical alternative vision, wresting patriotism from the right.[10]

A small but perhaps growing body of political opinion is beginning to call for a careful re-engagement with Englishness in the context of devolution, primarily to offset the perils of populist nationalism. Former minister David Blunkett, for example, sees the chance to develop a new progressive form of Englishness that is not seen as a threat to Scotland but is 'compatible with a civic value-led sense of Britishness' and 'is strengthened from its position in a multinational Union'.[11] Blunkett's confidence that a rejuvenated idea of Englishness can be accommodated within a Unionist framework is significant in this regard. This kind of sentiment clearly played a role in animating the development of plans, in the first Blair administration, to grant some executive powers to regional authorities in some parts of England, notably the North West and North East. With the demise of this project, there remains a policy vacuum at the heart of Labour's thinking about the governance of England.

Beyond interventions on some symbolically important, but as yet rather isolated, issues—calls for St George's Day to become a public holiday being one example—none of the parties displays any kind of confidence or willingness to bring Englishness into the heart of its strategic and policy thinking. Fearfulness and the hope that English nationalism will quietly subside have been the abiding watchwords of the political elite. With the ascendancy of Gordon Brown to Prime Ministerial office, and his apparent willingness to deliver a further phase of constitutional reform, the Tories may edge closer to mobilising English nationalism. At the same time, David Cameron has been keen to emphasise his Unionist credentials, and to distance himself from 'sour Little Englanders'.[12] He does not, however, look likely to drop the Conservative pledge of 'English votes for English laws' adopted by the party under William Hague, even though some suggest that such a move 'raises the prospect of a UK government being unable to govern England, its largest constituent part'.[13] As one eminent historian suggests, the pull of English nationalism may prove too strong for the Conservative party to resist:

It's clear, I think, that for David Cameron—if ever he wins power—what he should do is float off completely Wales and Scotland . . . and just say, 'We're the English party', because their chances of winning England are so much greater than their chances of winning Britain. And that, I suspect, is why Gordon Brown is now so worried about that prospect, and why it's the left which is talking up Britishness, because paradoxically the party that provided devolution has finally woken up to the fact that it actually needs these votes in the countries it's in the process of devolving, whereas the Tories have woken up to the fact that they should stop defending interconnectedness between England and two countries which have never done them much good. So I think Englishness has a particular *political* salience. It would be a very good Tory future, and therefore Britishness has to be, in a sense, the Labour future. And so I think in that sense what we have really got here are a set of stalking horses for a rather brutal and potentially, I think, hugely interesting political battle.[14]

At present, then, Englishness has become salient within British politics without becoming a vehicle for mainstream political mobilisation. Its motifs, anxieties, and grievances continually recur in British political life, and find their ways into a host of different, apparently unrelated policy issues. But taken as a whole, the political parties, and their most proximate media commentators, appear either unduly optimistic or unduly worried about the likelihood that English nationalism will mutate into a small-nation resentment at its position within a larger multination entity. The essence of political nationalism lies in an organised communal struggle for power,[15] and 'new Englishness' has—as yet—failed to realise such proportions. Despite this, however, there has been a powerful set of arguments deployed in relation to an explicitly *cultural* Englishness, and to these we now turn.

Englishness as a cultural identity

Alongside the popular celebration of symbols of Englishness in the theatres of international sporting competition, a more considered re-examination of England's culture and history has been underway since the early mid-1990s. This is a process that has been most visibly developed by leading political and media commentators, including figures like Jeremy Paxman, Andrew Marr and Billy Bragg;[16] and has found expression in a number of landmark popular television series and books published by a band of public historians. Figures like Simon Schama, David Starkey, and Niall Ferguson have reached an immense audience through their polished and popular TV histories of the English/British past.[17] This theme has surfaced too in popular fiction and cinema in this period,[18] and stretches as well into the academy. Englishness and the idea of English national identity have been the focus of major historical studies in recent years, and are now established as themes of great interest to historians, literary scholars and social scientists.[19]

This cultural outpouring is marked at times by a combination of sharpened anxiety and lingering cultural self-confidence—hallmarks perhaps of the current state of English national identity. In combination with the apparent weakening of the hold of national myths, narratives and values associated with the once-mighty British nation, these developments have prompted an extended moment of cultural introspection on behalf of the English. At times this has involved a display of pride and confidence, based on a recognition that Englishness is the dominant strain within Britain: in Simon Heffer's words, 'Englishness is probably, should be, 85% of Britishness'.[20] And scholarly opinion outlines the historical basis for such a view. The English, observes Krishan Kumar, 'always remained the dominant group in the making and the maintenance of the empire (as of the United Kingdom).

Hence they could think of it, rightly or wrongly, as "their" empire—or, at least, they could take pride in what they could consider a predominantly English creation, in the sense that it was mainly English culture that was spread worldwide through the empire'.[21]

While there is clearly an overlap between this extensive enquiry into the English past and the character of its people, and the political nationalism described above, the two are also quite distinct in kind. Political nationalism involves organised struggle towards the achievement of some formal goal, usually constitutional, institutional or state-centred. Cultural nationalism may be less goal-orientated and more reflective of a sense of communal identity and self-image. While these two phenomena are, historically, often entwined, they thus possess different emphases.[22] Here, it is the cultural-nationalist notion of England as a community united by shared culture and a distinctive historical story that has been central. The attempt to capture what is supposedly essential or distinctive in the national character of the English, clearly arises against a backdrop of a host of socio-economic and geo-political changes, as well as some ongoing pressures, notably the impact of American values and culture. But the genre to which these cultural commentators and national historians are contributing is perhaps best understood as a very long-standing, if over-looked one.

Peter Mandler's recent history of English national identities reminds us of the patchwork of different versions of England's history and character that have been invoked across this period.[23] Some of these have long fallen out of use. Others, however, remain very much alive in the contemporary cultural consciousness. Patrick Wright observes the durability of a sense of English-ness which is deeply connected with an idealisation of the south-eastern landscape and which is characterised by aversion to modernity. Not all of the fragments of Englishness that get recycled in later times travel well. As Wright again observes, Baldwin's plough teams, or 'Orwell's more static list of smoky towns, clattering clogs, red pillar-boxes, autumnal mists and bicycling old maids', seem 'threadbare and sadly exhausted' when revived in a different era.[24] This particular vision of England has also informed the heritage industry Englishness that Wright has railed against elsewhere, maintained by the National Trust ('an ethereal kind of holding company for the dead [but not gone] spirit of the nation'),[25] and which he regards as both a source and reflection of the nostalgic misuse of history for political ends. But Wright's Englishness is itself reliant on the idea of characteristics, particularly the persistence of the propensity to nostalgia, which he seems to regard as the defining trait of current English identity.

The quest for meaningful answers to increasingly pressing questions about who the English are and what they have in common, almost invariably takes a historically inclined form. 'England' is continually re-imagined through two genres of historical recollection. One of these involves a mythical melange of memories of leaders, battles, and periods from the past that embody a tangle of differing narratives and values relating to the supposed 'character' of the

English. The second relates to more generalised attributions of characteristics to the people of England, typically identified in relation to the pre-modern past. Alongside these discourses there has emerged a growing disquiet, expressed in literature, film and song, about England's current inhabitants' increasingly troubled relationship with these versions of the past. Thus Julian Barnes's satirical novel *England, England* takes as its central theme the paradox that the English are torn between the hankering to reconnect with our mythical understanding of our national past and the tawdry kitsch that characterises today's market-led efforts to re-create what went before.[26]

Whether these perspectives offer a historical narrative and cultural account that is adequate to the current needs of England and the English, are questions that deserve more sceptical enquiry within the academic and political worlds. Despite the multiplicity of accounts of the English/British past that have been propounded from within the media and academy, English historical understanding remains tied to a remarkably selective set of (largely mythical) stories and icons. The recurrent mythology of the English destined to be an island race defined by hostility to rival European powers—with Nazi Germany playing the role filled since the late eighteenth century by Catholic France—remains remarkably prevalent; and totally ill-equipped as an intellectual template for a people seeking to come to terms with its status as one nation in a multinational political structure.

The two different relationships with the English past which this wave of cultural self-assertion offers us, have some worrying limitations. Narratives that seek to draw morals and point to lessons from the heroic deeds or narrow escapes of England/Britain, often provide shrill and under-developed accounts of who the English should and could be in the present. Equally, the lingering suspicions of intellectuals (of both right and left) towards the idea that England's current inhabitants might engage in fruitful dialogue with their national past, typically rests upon the conviction that Englishness is inescapably parochial, exclusionary and chauvinist.

But the diversity and lingering resonance of the historical and cultural manifestations of Englishness observed by commentators like Wright, Marr and Mandler, signal the potential for more pluralistic and adaptive political accounts of Englishness in the twenty-first century. The radical presumptions that Englishness was essentially expressed through Britishness until recent times, and in its current forms bears the imprint of the cultural and ethnic characteristics of the Empire, have been extensively assailed in the historical scholarship of the last twenty years.[27] Just as other imagined national communities and cultures subsisted within and alongside Britishness for several centuries, so too, it can be demonstrated, did a relatively autonomous and organically developing sense of Englishness. This provided sustenance for some powerful political identities and visions over the same period. Disallowing a healthy dialogue with the rich treasure of writings, thought and political deeds that were done in the name of Englishness over the last two centuries, is just as unlikely to cement a robust and flexible identity for today's inhabitants as is the nostalgic idealisation of a select number of episodes from this past.

Britannia in peril?

Located at points across the political spectrum is another view of Englishness which regards it as a threat not only to the Union but to the core values of the British. Traditionally this standpoint is most closely associated with the Conservative and Unionist party, but in more recent years, particularly since devolution to Scotland and Wales, it has been voiced most clearly by Labour. Whilst in 1997 it was the outgoing Conservative Prime Minister warning that the British people had just '72 hours to save the Union', in 2007 it is the incoming Labour Prime Minister, goaded by Conservative jibes about his Scottishness, who is forced to articulate his Britishness.[28] From this perspective, the 'new Englishness' is associated with the 'Little Englander' populism of Mrs Thatcher in her most Europhobic form, and is regarded as a contingent, opportunistic, and potentially dangerous political force. British-ness, by contrast, is preferred either for the civic and/or institutional values ascribed to it, or for the sense of morality it is seen to embody.

This notion that Britain, and a variably defined 'Britishness', are under threat is a misguided and rather unsatisfying response to the (re)emergence of a more vocal English identity, and is best seen as a further symptom of the declinist mentality which the British political elite has tended to adopt since the late 1960s.[29] Peter Hitchens's gloomy assessment links the passing of the imperial age with a declining sense of Britishness, and—his greatest concern—the moral degeneration of the nation. Hitchens is uneasy about the recent movement towards identification with 'the narrower loyalties of the UK's smaller nations' and the concurrent turn from Britishness.[30] His concern with this trend is partly cultural—English identity has been tarred for Hitchens by the 'mobs of fat, beery men' who wave St George's flags at England football matches[31]—but it is also political. Calls for greater sub-national autonomy are not, contra Heffer, a chance to revive a deeper, ancient England, but part of a continental/left-wing plot to 'abolish' Britain and create a European superstate. The United Kingdom as a whole is 'far too big and powerful to be swallowed whole into the bland blend of the new multicultural Euroland' so must first be broken up. The issue of European integration is the ultimate bogeyman, as it 'unites all the threads of the cultural revolution into one. The things which made Britain different were the things which made it different *from the continent*'.[32]

For more centrist commentators such as Marr, such shifts are not neces-sarily causes of lament, but may offer the opportunity to forge a more civic form of Britishness better suited to twenty-first century life. Britishness—despite its current travails—remains for many liberal writers a more attractive national identity than Englishness. In part, this is because members of various ethnic and immigrant minority groups have found space within the broad set of values, laws and attachments which the British identity encompasses. More generally, this approach reflects the shift in perception to the idea of Britishness as a set of values—such as tolerance, pluralism and fair play— as opposed to substantive moral and cultural traditions, within liberal circles.

Others are less convinced that Britishness is quite this accommodating or indeed vacuous. For a number of public historians, re-telling the history of the British, and indeed calling for the 'national story' to be told more forcefully, coherently and unapologetically in British schools, is a vital prerequisite of a renewal of national identity. Though sometimes articulated in very recognisably nostalgic or conservative tones, this kind of perspective is interestingly one on which historians of varying political hues agree. Tristram Hunt, for example, argues that: 'We need schools to teach a history syllabus which inculcates a sense of identity beyond race and religion; something of a common culture; and a sense of ownership in the institutions and functions of the British state and civil society together with the ideals and history they embody'.[33] From a rather different angle, David Starkey concurs on the importance of a collective cultural memory, without which 'any notion of community, value or stability vanishes and we become merely individualised flotsam and jetsam'. The problem, he suggests, stems from the fact that 'we have overdone the critical element of history . . . With our perpetual questioning of history, partly from a Tory point of view, partly from a Marxist point of view, partly from a postmodern point of view, we have really lost a sense of the larger generalisations about our past'.[34] All of these commentators make a powerful connection between the ahistorical mindset that prevails in British culture, and the importance of history as a source of national identity and belonging. What pervades these calls for a more sonorous grand narrative is an anxiety that British identity is in decline, and a fear that its absence will be filled with an unsettling mix of atomised, consumerist individualists, with no loyalty to their nation; and the kind of grievance-fuelled nationalism described above.

In January 2000, Home Secretary, Jack Straw, warned of the 'potentially very aggressive, very violent' nature of English nationalism, which he feared would be increasingly articulated following devolution. In the same debate, the leader of the Conservative party, William Hague, described it as 'the most dangerous of all forms of nationalism that can arise within the United Kingdom, because England is five-sixths of the population of the UK'.[35] Such fears have informed the unwillingness of politicians to engage with Englishness, even as the integrative glue of Britishness has weakened. But this conception of Englishness, and the idea that where it apparently divides, Britishness can unify, deserves to be sceptically received. In its place, there is a strong case for a concerted re-evaluation of the relationship between British and English identity, and a consideration of how a positive vision of Englishness can complement, rather than threaten, a rejuvenated civic Britishness.

Conclusion: engaging Englishness

Two years ago, Gordon Brown noted that 'almost every question that we have to deal with about the future of Britain revolves around what we mean by Britishness'.[36] The identity debate, he suggested, has implications far beyond merely the question of constitutional reform, but affects public policy issues as diverse as immigration, the European Union, globalisation and terrorism. In the current post-devolution context, however, we suggest that such issues can only be fully addressed through a politics that is not only framed in terms of Britishness, but is willing to engage positively with an increasingly self-conscious Englishness. Merely to hope for a recovery of the idea of Britishness fails to acknowledge the transformative affect of the new Englishness on British politics, and is likely, if pursued in isolation, to fortify the kind of grievance-fuelled nationalism described above.

What principles and values should inform such a political engagement? Below we sketch three different ideas that together could give shape to an important political-cultural, and not just constitutional, agenda on these issues. Firstly, and most pressingly, engagement with Englishness suggests a readiness to contemplate the next stages of constitutional reform in a manner that engages with Englishness from within a Unionist perspective. Labour's programme of constitutional reform has, as noted above, had very little to say about the position of England. The only seriously debated proposal, for elected regional assemblies with very modest powers, has been taboo in political circles since the northeast region resoundingly defeated the idea in a referendum in November 2004. Yet it would be quite extraordinary if the radical transformation of the United Kingdom constitution, from its historic, uncodified, organic past to a future form 'created by deliberate human agency',[37] were to take place without serious consideration of the status of the largest constituent part within it. Justified in terms of a call for democratic renewal, any such programme would need to address not only Westminster constitutional questions, but the emasculated status of local government, and the powers exercised by the quangocracy bequeathed by the Conservatives in 1997 and expanded by Labour since.

In his early days as Prime Minister, Gordon Brown has demonstrated a refreshing willingness to pick up the torch of constitutional reform. Yet for all of its scope, the *Governance of Britain* Green Paper[38] betrays a degree of uncertainty about the English Question. In his accompanying statement to the House, Brown clearly excluded as unworkable the current Conservative party policy of English votes for English laws, but made little progress beyond this condemnation.[39] Only the tentative step of creating ministers for the English regions, possibly scrutinised by regional select committees, is proposed. In an intriguing paragraph, the Green Paper notes that, 'A large part of what we describe as Britishness traces straight back to our own civil war, its ultimate resolution in the Declaration of Rights of 1689 and the Acts of Union. Our relative stability as a nation is reflected in a relative lack of precision about what we mean to be British'.[40] The confidence and perspective provided by this invocation of British history could well be extended into a parallel discussion of the prospects for a review of the system of English governance (providing an overview of the complex body of public authorities, elected bodies and institutions that currently wield authority over the English). There are potential hazards here for sure, but adopting a purely defensive stance also entails significant risk. Undertaking a process of review that complements the historic reforms which the Green Paper could yield, may provide a valuable way forward for Brown's administration.

Secondly, it is worth bearing in mind the durability and adaptability that have been characteristics of Britishness since its 'invention' in the late eighteenth century.[41] Against the presumption that the end of Empire, the rise of the European Union and the major changes in personal morality that have swept across British society since the 1960s, necessarily mean the demise of a meaningful British identity, it is perhaps worth recalling that for many inhabitants of these isles some sort of dual pattern of identification to nation and state has for a long time been the norm. And while some of the props of British culture and nationhood have undoubtedly waned in the late twentieth century, this does not necessarily signal the demise of an appreciation of, as opposed to a deep attachment to, the merits of the institutions, traditions and governance provided by the multinational state that is the United Kingdom. As David Cannadine recently observed,[42] a rather hard-headed sense of the benefits that come from the British state—in terms of security, economic stability, shared cultural interests—has proved remarkably durable, even if some of the sentiments and sense of being that cultural nationalism provides are no longer available from Britishness. The possibility worth retaining here is that a dual sense of identification—proudly English and happy to be a member of the UK—may well bed down as a more normal pattern of personal identification than the jeremiads and cheerleaders for English nationalism tend to imagine. As Robin Cohen has noted, having 'an elaborated, multi-layered identity is not the same thing as not having one at all'.[43]

Although the UK attracts little of the emotional and fashionable enthusiasm commonly associated with Scottish, Welsh, Northern Irish/Irish or English sentiment, it continues to possess an appeal to many people within each of these national constituencies, often for very practical and economic reasons. And while many of the elements of traditional British identity have been eroded or greatly altered—Protestant religion, monarchy, empire—this could be said to have produced a refashioning rather than disintegration of what it means to be British. Here, the example of Northern Ireland may be instructive. In the six counties, the decline of each of these elements of British identity has caused, not the ending of Ulster unionist Britishness, but rather its reformulation in different but equally committed form.

Thirdly, as the brief survey above demonstrates, a cornucopia of historical and cultural accounts of Englishness have been proffered over the last decade and more. By themselves these writings do not amount to the basis for a new English identity, but they do provide some valuable starting points from which the development of a more positive and pluralistic political English-ness may begin. Such an outlook would reach, for example, beyond the rather bucolic and nostalgic imagery of England that has pervaded much of the literature in previous decades.[44] Engaging with the multiplicity of historical narratives of England, and being open to less familiar and newer ones, offers the best hope for the emergence of a progressive Englishness that can provide a meaningful sense of belonging for those who identify this as their primary source of national allegiance. As Andrew Marr has warned, 'unless England is recognised and given a new sense of its own security, then all the hopes for a liberal, open, democratic and tolerant future are in danger'.[45]

Since Marr wrote those words, the pressures on those who wish to promote a sense of Britishness have only increased. As Philip Norton demonstrates, the effect of devolution on attitudes to independence has been the opposite of that hoped for by its architects.[46] But proponents of Britishness, fearing the ugly face of English nationalism, have, by and large, failed to engage with the rise of more self-conscious identities in the constituent nations of the United Kingdom. Whilst an increasingly political Englishness comes with attendant risks, the best hope for the survival of the Union, and the political-legal concept of Britishness, is to be found in the promotion of the two as complementary, rather than conflictual, identities. Such layered identities within more flexible states might even be seen as a practical means of reconciling the tensions of political organisation and cultural identity within a liberal framework. A modern, vibrant, English identity need not be a British loss. Indeed, the future strength of the democratic, civic Britishness that Gordon Brown wishes to advance is substantially dependent, we suggest, on the nature of the Englishness accommodated within.

Notes

1 This phenomenon is the subject of research projects that the authors are currently undertaking, funded by the British Academy (grant no. SG44212) and the Nuffield Foundation (grant no. SGS33586). We would like to acknowledge our gratitude to both of these bodies. We would also like the thank Guy Lodge and the editors of *PQ* for their insightful comments. For a more extended consideration of some this article's themes, see also: Richard English, Richard Hayton and Michael Kenny, *Beyond the Constitution? Engaging Englishness in Post-devolution Britain*, London, Institute of Public Policy Research.

2 Labour Party, *Because Britain Deserves Better* (Election Manifesto), London, Labour Party, 1997.

3 Boris Johnson, 'Scots can build Jerusalem, but not with English money', *Daily Telegraph*, 1 February 2001.

4 Simon Heffer, interviewed by Richard English and Michael Kenny, London, 5 March 2007. See also Simon Heffer, 'A Tory answer to the West Lothian Question', *Daily Telegraph*, 30 November 2005.

5 Conservative Party, *It's Time For Action* (Election Manifesto), London, Conservative Party, 2005, p. 21.
6 John Curtice, 'What the people say—if anything', in Robert Hazell ed., *The English Question*, Manchester, Manchester University Press, 2006. p. 121.
7 Andrew Marr, *The Day Britain Died*, London, Profile Books, 2000.
8 Richard Weight, *Patriots: National Identity in Britain 1940–2000*, London, Macmillan, 2002, p. 10.
9 Krishan Kumar, *The Making of English National Identity*, Cambridge, CUP, p. 269.
10 Weight, *Patriots*, p. 727.
11 David Blunkett, 'A New England: An English Identity within Britain', Speech to the Institute for Public Policy Research (IPPR), 14 March 2005.
12 David Cameron, 'I will never take Scotland for granted', Speech in Glasgow, 15 September 2006.
13 Sue Stirling, 'Now let us turn to the English question', *The Independent*, 1 May 2007; See also Guy Lodge and Katie Schumuecker, 'Union Blues', *Parliamentary Monitor*, 22 July 2007.
14 David Cannadine, interviewed by Richard English, London, 20 June 2007.
15 Richard English, *Irish Freedom: The History of Nationalism in Ireland* London, Macmillan, 2006.
16 Jeremy Paxman, *The English: A Portrait of a People*, London, Michael Joseph, 1998; Marr, *The Day Britain Died*; Billy Bragg, *The Progressive Patriot: a Search for Belonging*, London, Bantam Press, 2006.
17 Simon Schama, *A History of Britain*, London, BBC Books, 2003; David Starkey, *Monarchy: From the Middle Ages to Modernity*, London, HarperCollins, 2006; Niall Ferguson, *Empire: How Britain Made the Modern World*, London, Allen Lane, 2003.
18 See for instance Julian Barnes' *England, England*, London, Jonathan Cape, 1998; and the independent film, *This is England*, 2006, directed by Shane Meadows.
19 Kumar, *The Making of English National Identity*; Julia Stapleton, *Political Identities and Public Intellectuals in Britain since 1850*, Manchester, Manchester University Press, 2001.
20 Simon Heffer, interviewed by Richard English and Michael Kenny, London, 5 March 2007.
21 Krishan Kumar to Richard Hayton and Michael Kenny, 5 June 2007.
22 English, *Irish Freedom*, pp. 11–21, 431–506.
23 Peter Mandler, *The English National Character: the History of an Idea from Edmund Burke to Tony* Blair, New Haven and London, Yale University Press, 2006.
24 Patrick Wright, 'Last Orders', *The Guardian*, 9 April 2005.
25 Patrick Wright, *On Living in an Old Country*, London, Verso, 1985, p. 56.
26 Julian Barnes, *England, England*, London, Jonathan Cape, 1998.
27 Mandler, *The English National Character*; Stapleton, *Political Identities and Public Intellectuals in Britain since 1850*.
28 George Jones, '72 hours to save Union, says Major', *Daily Telegraph*, 29 April 1997; BBC News, 'Brown lifts ban on national flag', 6 July 2007, http://news.bbc.co.uk/1/hi/uk_politics/6276280.stm
29 Richard English and Michael Kenny eds., *Rethinking British Decline*, Basingstoke, Macmillan, 2000.
30 Peter Hitchens, *The Abolition of Britain*, London, Quartet Books, 2000, p. xxiii.
31 Peter Hitchens, 'Why I can't wait for it to be all over for England', *Mail on Sunday*, 2 June 2002.

32 Hitchens, *The Abolition of Britain*, pp. 347, 364 (original emphasis).
33 Tristram Hunt, 'Stop endless lessons about Nazis. Tell us our national story instead', *The Observer*, 10 June 2007.
34 David Starkey, 'What history should we be teaching in Britain in the 21st century?', History in British Education (first conference), Institute of Historical Research, London, 14–15 February 2005.
35 BBC News, 'English nationalism "threat to UK"', 9 January 2000, http://news.bbc.co.uk/1/uk/596703.stm
36 'Roundtable: Britain rediscovered', *Prospect*, 109, April 2005, p. 20.
37 Vernon Bogdanor, 'Constitutional reform in Britain: The quiet revolution', *Annual Review of Political Science*, 2005, p. 73.
38 Cm 7170, *The Governance of Britain*, London, Stationary Office, 2007.
39 Gordon Brown, 'Change is essential for Britain's future', Statement to the House of Commons, 3 July 2007. Downloaded from: http://www.labour.org.uk/gordon_brown___s_statement_on_constitutional_reform
40 Cm7170, para. 184.
41 Linda Colley, *Britons: Forging the Nation 1707–1837*, New Haven, Yale University Press, 1992.
42 Interview with Richard English, June 2007.
43 Robin Cohen, 'The incredible vagueness of being British/English', *International Affairs*, vol. 76, no. 3, 2000, pp. 575–83.
44 See for instance, Roger Scruton, *England: An Elegy*, London, Chatto & Windus, 2000.
45 Marr, *The Day Britain Died*, p. 230.
46 Philip Norton, 'Tony Blair and the Constitution', *British Politics*, 2007, vol. 2, no. 2, 2007, pp. 269–81.

The Wager of Devolution and the Challenge to Britishness

ARTHUR AUGHEY

THE LABOUR government's concern with Britishness is multi-dimensional but with a common theme of cohesion—social cohesion, especially within England, where the questions of immigration, asylum-seekers and ethnic diversity are most acute, and multinational cohesion within the United Kingdom. The government's objective, as it is the objective of everyone who takes the integrity of the United Kingdom seriously, is to make of Britishness 'a good house to accommodate various identities of minorities as well as majorities'[1] where the aim is not assimilation to a 'mono-culture' but development of 'a stronger sense of why we live in a common place and have a shared future'.[2] This chapter concentrates on only one of these aspects, the multinationalism of the British Question.

The Canadian political theorist James Tully, reflecting on a decade of constitutional transformation in Europe, observed that 'multinational democracy appears to run against the prevailing norms of legitimacy for a single-nation democracy and is condemned as unreasonable or abnormal by both the defenders of the status quo and the proponents of secession'. That thought would provide little succour to a British government determined to make the case for the multinational Union. However, Tully also entered the more hopeful qualification that legitimate multinational democracy runs only against 'the norms of single nationhood, not the norms of constitutional democracy' and these constitutional norms, he thought 'fortunately for the future', are not necessarily but merely 'contingently related to the old ideal of a single-nation polity'.[3] That remark does provide some hope for the government's policy and for the future of the United Kingdom. In that short passage Tully identified the defining question in the Britishness debate. Is the future of democratic politics in the United Kingdom to be nationalist or multinationalist? This is a tricky question, tricky because the answer is uncertain and politicians do not like uncertainties of that sort. The complex elements of the question may be approached initially and elliptically by way of a familiar joke.

The joke is the (likely) apocryphal story of an American academic visitor to Oxford who is shown around the colleges from Balliol to Magdalen. When asked his opinion, he replies that the colleges were impressive, the traditions magnificent, their history marvellous but it would have been nice to see the university. The moral of this story is that he had failed to see that the colleges are the university but that the university, whatever the strength of collegial loyalty, has an identity through the colleges but one that is larger than them

 Published by Blackwell Publishing Ltd, 9600 Garsington Road, Oxford OX4 2DQ, UK and 350 Main Street, Malden, MA 02148, USA

and recognisably 'Oxford'. This moral is applicable in political form to the United Kingdom and that it is not *simply* a joke was confirmed by an American participant at a recent European Consortium for Political Research workshop on Constitutionalism and National Identity who asked consistently: how can one speak of a British constitution when there are only specific pieces of parliamentary legislation relating to different countries? Here seems to be an appropriate starting point for reflections on Britishness because the story illustrates a relationship between the particular and the universal which may be rephrased as the relationship or negotiation, as Tully outlined it, between the national and the multinational. This is not a new condition, of course, but it has a renewed significance today.

When attempting to clarify the character of modern Britishness it is important to deal with one misreading. The 'old order' is often thought to be a United Kingdom rather like 'Oxford without the colleges', a refusal to recognise properly the distinctiveness of the 'multi' in the multinational Union. It is a misreading to be found, for example, in Mark Leonard's *Britain TM: Renewing our Identity* which argued that this renewal could not tolerate the 'exclusive' British nationalism of the past.[4] In *Understanding the United Kingdom*, Richard Rose[5] wrote that only a too-clever-by-half exclusive Britishness 'would create a state with two separate legal systems (one Scots and the other for England, Wales and more or less for Northern Ireland), have two different state churches, or govern one of its parts by "temporary" direct rule' (Northern Ireland). He wrote also of the 'asymmetry' of these 'multiform institutions' and also of England's rather anomalous place within the United Kingdom. Asymmetry itself is clearly not new in British constitutionalism nor is it the recent enormity that some have claimed.[6] Rose's point was to indicate the distinctive success of the United Kingdom in sustaining political cohesion despite these differences and asymmetry. However, it is true that there was a view of British politics which not so much denied but discounted the multinationality of the Union and its assumptions conditioned much of the academic thinking about Britishness and the constitution in what may be called the social democratic years of the post-war United Kingdom. Indeed, the work of Rose and others in the 70s and early 80s was intended to re-assert a territorial dimension to British politics which this view occluded. It assumed three principles of political association which were unity, simplicity and commonality.

Jean Blondel proclaimed the first in his widely read standard text *Voters, Parties and Leaders*[7] where he argued that the United Kingdom was a unitary state. Peter Pulzer[8] most famously and succinctly stated the second when he announced that class was the basis of British politics and all else was embellishment and detail. And Hugh Seton-Watson[9] complained about the third when he observed that the political class in Whitehall and Westminster 'think in bureaucratic categories, use bureaucratic language and are on a different wavelength' from the national sentiment of those they governed. The consequence was that the British political elite appeared incapable of thinking seriously about constitutional reform, something that was also noted by Nevil Johnson in his subtle study *In Search of the Constitution*.[10] For much of recent history, then, this was the alter ego of nationalism, a sort of non-nationalist nationalism, or what Richard Rose also called 'unthinking union-ism'. It fostered a political outlook which meant that 'unionist as much as nationalist ideology in the UK' insisted 'that anyone claiming the right of self-determination must secede, there being no intermediate position'.[11] Or, as McLean and McMillan[12] recently argued, it reflected a primordial unionism, one fixated on the absolute sovereignty of Westminster. Devolution of course has transformed these principles of association and those assumptions of uniformity now seem like echoes from another world. Nevertheless, they do sometimes haunt the imagination of those in politics at the centre and certainly haunt the minds of those who would sometimes dream of redeeming the 'mistakes' of devolution and reversing the changes since 1998. One can be reasonably certain that the narrative of uniformity as a meaningful statement of Britishness is now irrecoverable, if only because it was anyway such a transient form of political self-understanding. When one considers from a longer historical perspective the constitution of the United Kingdom (that is, its character rather than its rules of association) then it can be said to comprise three key elements: contingency, complementarity and solidarity.

Contingency meant both the cultural and national composition and the geographical extent of the state. The British nation, for Ernest Barker,[13] was 'an amalgam of the different species and stocks which have wandered into our island' and there is 'always a mixture from whatever angle you look', a view that calls to mind Oakeshott's comment that politics is attending to the arrangements of 'a set of people whom chance or choice have brought together'.[14] Here, first, was an acknowledgement of what today would be called the ethnic diversity of the United Kingdom, not a 'community of communities' as the Parekh Report[15] called it, but a community of fate. Secondly, the United Kingdom was 'multinational' but there was no certainty that it would hold together as a state. Writing at one of the lowest points in British fortunes during the Second World War, Barker admitted that it remained 'a question of the future whether the contained nationalities will aspire to any system of autonomy or Home Rule'.[16] In short, the extent of the state was contingent and that view should be compared with the fashionable assumption today that the Second World War represented some high point of British unity from which there has been only inexorable decline (for an example of that thought see Weight[17]). As Richard Rose insightfully described it, the British state is a 'Crown of indefinite domain' and that domain (as the secession of Irish Free State had demonstrated) was of contingent extent.

The qualification of the historical and compositional contingency of the state was an assumption that for all their differences, the nations of the multinational Union complemented each other. For example, Dicey and Rait argued that the Anglo-Scottish Union of 1707 had 'destroyed everything which kept the Scottish and the English apart; it destroyed nothing which did not threaten the essential unity of the whole people; and hence, and lastly, the supreme glory of the Act, that while creating the political unity of it kept alive the nationalism of both England and Scotland'.[18] It was through representation at Westminster that political unity was secured and it was through the accommodation of diverse and distinctive institutions, practices and cultures that distinct national identity was kept alive. This is what Barker called the British 'mixture of unity and diversity' which he thought was bound to baffle and puzzle the inquirer, as it did baffle Norman Davies in *The Isles*[19] for whom such bafflement could only mean the United Kingdom's dissolution. However, diversity and variety could be understood (or 'celebrated' as contemporary liberals would write) as complementary in the sense of contributing to collective strength and in the sense of the individual nations getting more 'by being included in the wider scope of the United Kingdom'.[20]

Thus, what diminished the contingency of British politics and helped to secure the complementarity of national difference was the operation of solidarity. Solidarity could be expressed in a number of ways—a sense of kinship, a sharing of economic burdens and financial resources; a mutual political culture; in short, a shared conversation that bound together the nations of the United Kingdom. This shared conversation meant accepting, as Oakeshott put it, that there exists 'a flow of sympathy', a sense of belonging, between the nations and that this flow is worth preserving.[21] That older narrative seems more in tune with contemporary circumstances, of course, but it is not entirely adequate to present circumstances. For example, Barker thought that nationalism in Scotland and Wales to be arrested as yet at the 'stage of a vague and academic ideal' and that it did not represent the 'general feeling' in either country. That cannot be said today, especially in Scotland, nor is it certain that participation in the British conversation is accepted so widely. And devolution was the policy thought appropriate to address those changes in sentiment

The constitutional wager of devolution

Devolution was a constitutional wager but not an irrational one. It was a wager based on a study of political form and probability, what Oakeshott would have called 'an earthy step-child of practice', a response to a particular problem or set of problems, rather than the application of a theoretical constitutional template. Though it might be stretching things a little to make this claim, there was indeed a philosophically idealist sensibility to the policy. One is reminded of Hegel's *Philosophy of History* the appeal of which, according to one scholar, is its profoundly reconciling power. It suggests that 'the good is already fulfilled just in virtue of the fact that it is in the process of being fulfilled'. Moreover, this is so because 'all will be well' and insofar as the all 'is presupposed, or implied, by the achievement of freedom, all is already well here and now'. In short, things 'are as they ought to be because they are on the way to being what they ought to be' and *becoming* can be read as *being*.[22] In the Labour government's original presentation, devolution was certainly a constitutionally conservative understanding wrapped up in radical-sounding form. Though Gordon Brown argued in 1992 that devolution would signal 'a decisive shift in the balance of power in Britain, a long overdue transfer of sovereignty from those who are governed, from an ancient and indefensible Crown sovereignty to a modern popular sovereignty', this radical concession to popular sovereignty was qualified by a vision of Britishness as 'a community of citizens with common needs, mutual interests, shared objectives, related goals and most of all linked destinies'.[23] Here, certainly, was a modification of constitutional circumstances but it remained British in a very traditional and pragmatic way. In this perspective, then, devolution really is as it ought to be—and will remain that way—because it has become already what it ought to be—the United Kingdom as a securely multinational state. Truly, it was designed as a grand policy of reconciling the sovereignty of the 'national-popular' and the constitutional sovereignty of Westminster.[24]

This constitutionally conservative understanding permits a double reading. First, the political purpose of devolution is the accommodation by containment of popular sovereign claims and the bounding of separatist tendencies. This is the reading we find in Lord Falconer's argument that constitutional change was designed to guarantee—by democratic recognition—the rights of the nations within the Union and thereby help to maintain that Union. 'And it has done exactly that. Separatists have been stymied by devolution. And support for separation has flat-lined'. The government, he made clear, was not concerned about the question of 'constitutional symmetry' (by that he meant dealing with the problem of English devolution) but was committed to the practical accommodation of 'difference and rough edges'.[25] That was the argument according to constitutional principle and political justice and that it happened to coincide with party interests, even getting the Conservatives off the anti-devolution hook, was a bonus. Second, even if nationalists were to have success at the polls—and the electoral arrangements were designed to prevent simple majorities—it was hoped that the experience of office would blunt the drive to separation. In the meantime the 'ought' (independence) takes on the shape of the 'is' (a devolutionary settlement) and nationalism becomes complicit in making things work rather than being dedicated to the final, separatist, objective. Here is a narrative which concerns itself with procedures and not with ultimate objectives and elaborates a traditional 'poacher turned gamekeeper' trajectory where the experience and enjoyment of power encourages the suppression of dissent and challenge. Ironically, this may actually be an appealing understanding for nationalists themselves since they are not without hope or evidence that the 'is' (working devolution) will deliver the 'ought' (separation): national independence, yes, but not quite yet. And the greatest irony of them all is that this expectation appears to be most well-founded in Northern Ireland rather than anywhere else in the United Kingdom. So this was the double wager on devolution made by Labour ministers and it seemed to be a sound one.

Unfortunately for the government, there is a second understanding which neatly reverses the politics of 'becoming as being' and promotes a radical politics of secession, 'being as becoming'. In this second, radically transformative understanding, devolution really is as it ought to be because it is on the way to becoming what it ought to be—the break-up of the United Kingdom into its component national parts. Far from contributing to stability and mutual accommodation the elision of 'ought' and 'is' might become another source of instability and national assertion and, far from reconciling nationalists to the 'is' of the United Kingdom, could encourage them to believe that not only *should* Scotland, for example, be other than what it is but also that in a crucial sense it already *is* other than British. In this case the 'ought' (Scottish independence) encounters the 'is' (support for the United Kingdom) as a mere obstacle and that encounter helps to explain the exasperation with expressions of Britishness, those insults to the logic of separation, that one so often finds in nationalist discourse. Equally, on the unionist side, the danger might be that far from reconciling the majority— particularly the English—to the 'is' of the devolutionary settlement, it could encourage the belief that devolution should become *other* than what it is for it has not delivered on what it ought to be. In Scotland, this might mean the unionist parties dancing to a nationalist tune and, in England, a growing sense of grievance married to a further sense of the inevitability of Scottish secession. The consequence of the devolutionary wager, then, would be the rapid attenuation of Britishness and the undoing of the United Kingdom.

What can one make of the wager a decade on? At first glance, it would appear that the appropriate Hegelian reading suggests the hovering of the Owl of Minerva over the devolutionary settlement, at least in Scotland. If one were to read the state of Britishness through the newspaper headlines then one would conclude that the governing wisdom of the last decade—that devolution would strengthen rather than weaken the United Kingdom— appears a complete misreading of the times. And one would think that devolution is no longer the settled will of the Scottish people, that the English are more in favour of separatism than the Scots[26] and that the trajectory of the United Kingdom towards *separatism* is faster than many could have imagined.[27] Moreover, the government's response to these separatist trends often seems disjointed and lacking in credibility. In short, there is now a strong wager that Britishness will become dispensable as people are persuaded that it is more authentic if popular identity finds unique expression in separate, national institutions. The Catch 22 noted by one study is that Brown's concern to make Britishness a political issue may actually be to provoke, in Scotland certainly, the very nationalisation of opinion the Prime Minister seeks to prevent.[28] In short, there has developed an influential separatist narrative which proclaims that the (national) colleges no longer need any (British) 'Oxford' and it is a narrative organised according to three notions: fate, anticipation and imagination. They combine to conceive of Britishness as an identity whose day has already gone and this understanding actually intensifies what can be called the nationalist *anxiety of frustration*. The other side of frustration is irritation with the obstruction of the nationalist project. It reveals itself in an expectation of irresistible advance and this can be called the nationalist *anxiety of impatience*. Let's consider these notions in turn.

Narrative of disintegration

The politics of fate holds that efforts to prop up the United Kingdom will fail and the fatalistic end is already implicit in Labour's Britishness project. The *becoming* of separation is bound up in the *is* of devolution. Why should that be? On the one hand, a multinational union like the United Kingdom is on dangerous ground if identity, as the opinion polls would show, is increasingly associated with its component national parts. On the other hand, its multi-nationality is contradicted by the promotion of a transcendent, institutional British identity. A contrast is made between the emptiness of British political culture—a bloodless Oxford and false cosmopolitanism—and the substance of national peoples—colleges of self-determination and culturally open to the world.[29] Here is a paradox, it is claimed, to which the British state can no longer find a workable solution. As Britishness dies republican self-government will come to life at last and the 'popular nations' will find in the larger political Union of Europe (another inevitability) a more sympathetic and sustaining framework. Tom Nairn, perhaps the most eloquent and longstanding advocate of this view, now gives the United Kingdom a life expectancy of five years.[30, 31] As Rodney Barker[32] once noted, there is indeed a widespread assumption that one is witnessing a movement of the (national) peoples against the (British) state. He was suitably sceptical of this assumption but did acknowledge the attraction of the contrast between the 'populist phenomenon' of national community and the multinational state which allegedly holds together only 'in artificial uniformity'. It is also a thesis which finds some recent support in McLean and McMillan's *State of the Union*[33] which argues that unionism 'always suffered from deep intellectual incoherence', an incoherence only 'masked by its usefulness to politicians and its popular appeal' and now that they both had expired 'can the union state survive without unionism'? Their answer was that it could survive for some time but not forever and they envisaged it lumbering on 'anomalies and all, for at least a few decades more'. That things are not quite as certain or fated as this interpretation claims can be found in a corresponding anxiety of frustration. This anxiety is a measure of nationalist expectation and this very 'lumbering on' of the British Union, despite all the funeral notices, provokes it.

The second related element is the politics of anticipation. It has become common to speak of contemporary politics already being 'after Britain'. Here the becoming of separation already is (at least in the minds of nationalists) and the usage may be traced once again to that inventive melodist of the United Kingdom's break-up, Nairn, whose *After Britain*[34] appeals to a similar constituency as his original *The Break-up of Britain*.[35] It is a constituency not confined to nationalists in Scotland[36] but is one which embraces elements on the left south of the border wishing to explore the possibilities for 'an England after Britain'.[37] In both cases, 'after Britain' is an invitation to anticipate emancipation from old identity constraints and with some urgency because the old order, of course, is rapidly disintegrating. To argue that we are already 'after Britain', as these writers claim, suggests that the fate of Britishness has already been decided, if not yet at the polls, then at the bar of history. Here is a complement to the politics of fate. Of course, it is a view that is not exclusive to the left but finds also articulate expression on the right. According to Simon Heffer, for example, Britain has now become 'simply a geographical entity' and to 'many English people "Britishness" means nothing other than a series of (quite glorious) historical facts' though increasingly a codeword for Labour's (Scottish) exploitation of England.[38] That things are not moving rapidly enough towards the inevitable conclusion promotes a corresponding anxiety of impatience, an anxiety relieved momentarily by unionist politicians using language like 'bring it on'.

What is after Britain, thirdly, is an imaginative arrangement of states linked not by Britishness but by European and global interconnectedness. Globalisation, argues Nairn, means that 'smaller is, if not better, then at least just as good' and it is no surprise that 'the United Kingdom should be the one prime site' for this sort of break-up or downsizing to occur.[39] In *The Break-up of Britain*, Nairn had identified British political culture as a form of arrested development and one which failed the test of modernity. Now Britishness fails the test of post-modernity. For if the old question used to be survival and development in an industrial world the question now is: 'Are you *small and smart enough* to survive, and claim a positive place in the common global culture'. The future is nationalist, not British multinationalist, for it 'demands that differentiation be favoured, be positively fostered, by globalization'. This will not be old-style nationalism but a chance for the individual British nations to participate as equal voices, as 'nations of a new and deeply different age', where they can finally emancipate themselves from British 'self-colonisation', a claim that should appeal as much to the English as to everyone else if only because the English have been denied the possibility of self-government under Labour's constitutional reforms.

This reading posits a static condition, conceding the fact of the Union *pro tem*, and a new dynamic nationalism, signalled by the success of the Scottish National Party (SNP). Partly the intention, best expressed in the statements of the SNP leader Alex Salmond, is to destabilise the Britishness of the English majority by fostering two anxieties. The first is an *anxiety of process* which suggests that the English are being exploited by an arrangement designed to appease national sentiment everywhere but in England. Put simply, the government is buying political quiescence on the 'Celtic fringe' and paying for it with English money. The second and related anxiety, *the anxiety of influence*, concerns the practice of devolution which appears to trap the English electorate in structures inimical to its interest. This is perhaps captured best by the short-hand of the West Lothian Question. Thus, it provokes a mood that would remedy the constitutional inequality which accepts devolution as a (popular) sovereign right of Scotland, Wales and Northern Ireland but denies the same right for England, one which feels that devolution has delivered the worst of all worlds treating 'Scotland and Wales as appendages of England, and England itself as the last vassal nation' of the United Kingdom.[40] It is an English mood that is not yet a movement but it may well become so.

Putting the British case

Contesting that narrative of disintegration has become a personal crusade for Gordon Brown who has proclaimed in numerous speeches and articles that the case for the United Kingdom and its integration needs to be put. The practical question is: how is it to be done? As this article has suggested, it is best done by working according to principles already intimated in the traditions of British political life. Every society, Oakeshott once argued, by the underlinings it makes in the book of its history, 'constructs a legend of its own fortunes which it keeps up to date and in which is hidden its own understanding of its politics'.[41] The legend which needs to be updated and adapted to present circumstances is the legend of the 'Union without Uniformity' as Rose so aptly put it. As he concluded:[42] 'Multiform institutions are consistent with the maintenance of Union as long as all partners to the Union continue to accept the authority of the Crown in parliament'. This reflection is a useful guide to putting the British case and the following seven points represent a brief complement to its generality.

First, despite the chipper certainties of the narrative of disintegration, the United Kingdom is not fated to break up. It is certainly fated to change but that is an entirely different matter. Indeed, it is the anxieties of impatience and frustration one finds in separatist rhetoric which should be noted and this means that political leaders would be best advised to avoid the 'bring it on' approach which suggests not positional strength but positional weakness. Of course, the future of the Union has always been contingent but the culture of complementarity and solidarity is still alive.

Second, it is important to note the distinction between identity and allegiance, something which is not always made clear in ministerial speeches. For example, in a recent keynote lecture, the Justice Minister Michael Wills confused cultural identity with political allegiance, actually reversing their traditional British relationship. British 'identity', he argued, was distinguished from 'other allegiances' to the constituent parts of the United Kingdom. A more accurate rendering would be that a British allegiance accommodates the identities of its different national parts and that this is its great value.

Third, there exists in government rhetoric an emphasis upon 'common purpose' as if this was equivalent to a common allegiance. However, these two notions are also distinct and it would be strange to celebrate a culture defined by diversity and to confuse it with the politics of common *purpose*. One does not require a common purpose to be British, only a common allegiance to the Crown in parliament, as Rose maintained.

Fourth, there is a further ambiguity since the government proclaims at one and the same time 'a values system' citizens *already* know while it also proposes to 'search for a British statement of values' *yet* to be discovered.[43] Probably it would be wise to stop speaking so much of common values and to speak more of those common interests which secure allegiance, a point made effectively by Robert Hazell.[44]

Fifth, sympathetic academics also make—it seems to me—an error by thinking historically of the United Kingdom as a 'project' linked to some external objective designed to serve a particular purpose or purposes. In an otherwise subtle discussion of the United Kingdom, Andrew Gamble[45] has written that 'Britain was always a political project', that the end of Empire 'meant the disappearance of the project' which for so long defined Britishness, that its substitute, the grand project of the American Special Relationship, now threatens to undermine support for the United Kingdom and that even the welfare state, the operation of which has been parcelled out to the devolved institutions, no longer promotes Britishness in the manner it once did. Much of this may be true, but to understand the United Kingdom exclusively as (what Oakeshott would have called) an enterprise association, that is a polity united by a common purpose, is not only to ignore its civic character but also to subscribe to the lure of separatist logic. The civic character of the United Kingdom is found in those procedures and relation-ships which specify the conditions of belonging. Nationalists may ultimately win that argument by convincing citizens that they no longer belong together and that the United Kingdom, like the old Austro–Hungarian Empire, is simply a machine for ill-considered external military adventures. However, that argument has not been lost and much more thought needs to be given to reminding people of the civil association of Britishness, not in terms of 'values', but in terms of relationships.[46]

Sixth, Rose had argued that one of the key integrative elements in the United Kingdom was the party system. The major parties (Northern Ireland excepted) helped to translate territorial concerns into the common (func-tional) language of British politics because to 'give major importance to questions of national identity would distract attention from functional issues' like health, education and economic policy.[47] As questions of national identity *are* paid greater attention, there is the danger that party competition might have the opposite effect, raising and not subduing issues of national allegiance. Despite the operation of devolved institutions, despite the prominence of nationalists in those devolved institutions and despite the different configurations of party support, there continues to exist a British political culture with which citizens across the United Kingdom identify. There have been modifications in the basis of party identification since the early 1980s but this has not displaced the centrality of British party politics. Since no major party leader wishes to promote the disintegrative narrative[48, 49] then it would be logical to introduce a form of PR for Westminster Elections. It would help to address, for example, the cry that 'the Conservatives have no mandate in Scotland', help to make the composition of Westminster reflect better the opinion of the United Kingdom and address (partly) the question of England.

Seventh, the difficulty may lie not in accommodating Scotland, Wales and Northern Ireland but in dealing with this question of England.[50] This could very well turn out to be the crucial element for the future of the United Kingdom. Though there is widespread sympathy for an English parliament, support is neither strong nor deeply rooted[51] and this suggests that English nationalism is a mood, not a movement. Therefore, policy in favour of the Union should be tailored to preventing that mood becoming a movement. PR at Westminster might go some way to addressing the difficulties of an English Grand Committee as suggested by Malcolm Rifkind.[52]

The wager of devolution was probably a necessary one and it has transformed the United Kingdom into a more open conversation about the character of its multinationalism. This conversation now takes place within the democratic arena of assemblies and parliaments, adjusted on the basis of popular politics and it involves an open process of public and institutional negotiation. It is a challenge but a refurbished common citizenship can be sustained within the United Kingdom, one where the acknowledging degrees of national identity need not conflict with sustaining a multinational allegiance. Not only politicians but also the people must want it to continue. They may not in the future but for the moment the vast majority do.

Notes

1 N.-K. Kim, 'The End of Britain?: challenges from devolution, European integration, and multiculturalism', *Journal of International and Area Studies*, vol. 12, no. 1, 2005, p. 75.
2 R. Kelly and L. Byrne, *A Common Place*, London, The Fabian Society, 2007, p. 11.
3 J. Tully, 'Introduction', in A.-G. Gagnon and J. Tully eds., *Multinational Democracies*, Cambridge, Cambridge University Press, 2001, p. 3.
4 M. Leonard, *Britain TM. Renewing our Identity*, London, Demos, 1997.
5 R. Rose, *Understanding the United Kingdom*, London, Longman, 1982, p. 62.
6 M. Keating, 'What's wrong with asymmetrical government?', *Regional and Federal Studies*, vol. 8, no. 1, 1998, pp. 195–218.
7 J. Blondel, *Voters, Parties and Leaders: The Social Fabric of British Politics*, Harmondsworth, Penguin, 1963.

8 P. Pulzer, *Political Representation and Elections in Britain*, London, Allen and Unwin, 1967.

9 H. Seton-Watson, 'History' in C. Maclean, ed., *The Crown and the Thistle*, Edinburgh, Scottish Academic Press, 1979.

10 N. Johnson, *In Search of the Constitution. Reflections on State and Society in Britain*, Oxford, Pergamon, 1977.

11 M. Keating, 'So many nations, so few states: territory and nationalism in the global era', in Gagnon and Tully, *Multinational Democracies*, p. 61.

12 I. McLean and A. McMillan, *State of the Union*, Oxford, Oxford University Press, 2006, p. 246.

13 E. Barker, *Britain and the British People*, Oxford, Oxford University Press, 1942, p. 10.

14 M. Oakeshott, *Rationalism in politics and other essays*, Indianapolis, The Liberty Press, 1991.

15 B. Parekh, *The Future of Multi-Ethnic Britain: The Parekh Report*, London, Profile, 2006.

16 Barker, *Britain and the British People*, p. 14.

17 R. Weight, *Patriots: National Identity in Britain 1940–2000*, Basingstoke, Macmillan, 2002.

18 A. V. Dicey and R. S. Rait, *Thoughts on the Union between Scotland and England*, London, Macmillan, 1920, p. 362.

19 N. Davies, *The Isles: A History*, London, Macmillan, 1999.

20 Barker, *Britain and the British People*, p. 14.

21 Oakeshott, *Rationalism in politics*.

22 J. McCarney, *Hegel on History*, London, Routledge, 2000, pp. 215–16.

23 G. Brown, 'Constitutional Change and the Future of Britain', Charter 88 Sovereignty lecture 9 March 1992.

24 A. Aughey, *Nationalism, Devolution and the Challenge to the United Kingdom State*, London, Pluto, 2001.

25 Lord Falconer, 'Speech to ESRC Devolution and Constitutional Change Programme', Queen Elizabeth II Conference Centre, London, 10 March 2006, available at http://www.dca.gov.uk/speeches/2006/sp060310.htm

26 P. Hennessy and M. Kite, 'Britain wants UK break up, poll shows' *Sunday Telegraph*, 26 November 2006.

27 I. McWhirter, 'End of the UK could be closer than Brown thinks', *The Herald*, 14 May 2007.

28 F. Bechhofer and D. McCrone, 'Being British: A crisis of identity?', *The Political Quarterly*, vol. 78: no. 2, 2007, p. 260.

29 D. Marquand, 'Give us a moral vision for England', 2008, available at http://ourkingdom.opendemocracy.net/2008/01/07/give-us-a-moral-vision-for-england/

30 T. Nairn, 'Union on the rocks?', *New Left Review*, vol. 43, January-February 2007, pp. 131–2.

31 See also the pessimism of Dalyell in 'Tam Dalyell fuels referendum debate', *The Scotsman*, 26 May 2008.

32 R. Barker, 'Whose legitimacy? Elites, nationalism and ethnicity in the United Kingdom' *New Community*, vol. 21, no. 2, 1995, p 209.

33 McLean and McMillan, *State of the Union*, p. 256.

34 T. Nairn, *After Britain*, London, Granta, 2000.

35 T. Nairn, *The Break-Up of Britain: Crisis and Neo-Nationalism*, London, NLB, 1977.

36 M. Gardiner, *The Cultural Roots of British Devolution*, Edinburgh, Edinburgh University Press, 2004.

37 For a concise statement, see M. Perryman, ed., *Imagined Nation: England after Britain* London, Lawrence and Wishart, 2008.

38 S. Heffer, 'The Union of England and Scotland is over', *Daily Telegraph*, 14 November 2007.

39 T. Nairn, 'Globalisation and nationalism: the New Deal?', The Edinburgh Lectures, 2008, available at http://www.scotland.gov.uk/Resource/Doc/923/0057271.pdf

40 G. Young, 'Why do we need an English parliament?', 2007, available at http://thecep.org.uk:80/news/?page_id=202

41 Oakeshott, *Rationalism in politics*.

42 Rose, *Understanding the United Kingdom*, p. 62.

43 M. Wills,'The politics of identity', paper presented to the IPPR, 2008, available at http://www.justice.gov.uk/news/sp260308b.htm

44 R. Hazell, 'The Purpose of the Union', 2008, available at http://www.ucl.ac.uk/constitution-unit/files/events/2008/Keynote_Address.pdf

45 A. Gamble,'A union of historic compromise' in M. Perryman, ed., *Imagined Nation: England after Britain*, London, Lawrence and Wishart, 2008, pp. 38–42.

46 A start has been made by P. Goldsmith, *Citizenship: Our Common Bond*, London, Ministry of Justice, 2008.

47 Rose, *Understanding the United Kingdom*, p. 67.

48 G. Brown, 'The future of Britishness', speech to the Fabian 'Future of Britishness' conference 14 January 2006 available at http://www.fabian-society.org.uk/press_office/display.asp?id=520&type=news&cat=43

49 D. Cameron, 'I support the Union for what it can achieve in the future', speech at Gretna Green 19 April 2007, available at http://www.conservatives.com/popups/print.cfm?obj_id=136389&type=print

50 A. Aughey, *The Politics of Englishness*, Manchester, Manchester University Press, 2007.

51 J. Curtice, 'What the people say—if anything', in R Hazell, ed., *The English Question*, Manchester, Manchester University Press, 2006, p. 138.

52 M. Rifkind, 'Be fair, give devolution to England', *The Times*, 4 November 2007.

Do We Really Need Britannia?

BERNARD CRICK

> ... this sudden sense of knowing her all at once much better was not simultaneously accompanied by any clear portrayal in my mind of the kind of person she might really be. Perhaps intimacy of any sort, love or friendship, impedes all exactness of definition.
>
> (Anthony Powell, *Dance to the Music of Time*)

So SAY I about intimacy with Britannia. To try to define Britishness can be both philosophical and political folly. The philosophical folly arises from the fact, as Arthur Aughey has argued in his profound and searching book *The Politics of Englishness*, that 'a straightforward definition of Englishness' was not required for his study, 'nor is it the precondition for saying something intelligible about contemporary England'.[1] And so, say I, about Britishness, although to seek to explain why Britishness has suddenly sprung into political and academic prominence is, indeed, worthy of explanation—and I suspect that many contributors to this book will see this as the main object of the enterprise. But I will argue that it is political folly for politicians, or anyone else, to attempt to *define* or redefine such a protean concept which most of us take for granted rather than want to see explicated, particularly as a party matter—on which the parties can never and should never agree.

Britishness does not explain why the United Kingdom has held together, nor does it validate the recent and topical belief that by lack of clarity and intensity about Britishness the UK may fall apart. Aughey invokes Michael Oakeshott to suggest that Englishness (and the same goes for Britishness) is not so much a preface as a postscript: it is the exploration of the 'intimations' of a tradition that has many different intimations. He quotes Oakeshott that 'a tradition of behaviour is a tricky thing to get to know' because while everyone agrees it is there, it has diverse modulations and interpretations and each changes through time. Does it need saying that Britishness today is, for instance, very different from the stiff collar and tie kind of my youth in the late forties and early fifties? And I am grateful that Aughey quotes me as saying in 1991, before the present fervour and fashion for Britishness, Englishness and identity studies got under way, 'that the identity of the English is almost as difficult to specify as the name of the state'.[2] I am no late convert to some aspects of Oakeshott's thinking: long ago I described myself as a 'left-wing Oakeshottian', perhaps echoing Edward Thompson's *The Making of the English Working Class* or Raymond Williams's *The Long Revolution*.[3] Aughey also quotes Garton Ash reflecting that 'the very nature of Identity Studies' means that rarely is a definite, clear finding ever arrived at'.[4] However, Bhikhu Parekh has wisely said: 'While the concept of national character is problematic in a culturally diverse society, that of national

Published by Blackwell Publishing Ltd, 9600 Garsington Road, Oxford OX4 2DQ, UK and 350 Main Street, Malden, MA 02148, USA 149

identity is not. Immigrants can be expected to share national identity but not national character. Ethnic nationalism equates the two: civic nationalism keeps them apart.'[5]

Much ado about nothing?

So attempts to give definitions of Britishness, Englishness or indeed almost any other national identity are what Oakeshott meant by rationalism, or arbitrary 'arrests of experience'. Both concepts are sentiments, feelings drawn from an ever changing historical tradition. So it is surprising that these concepts, being sentiments, are taken so seriously politically in what has been basically (some say notoriously) a British (English and Scottish) empirical tradition of thought. Is not what holds us together mainly interest, practical judgement, utilitarian concerns on continuing advantages and the sheer convenience of a political or civic culture based on compromise and the avoidance of civil war? Of course, this only may explain why we hold together as one state; such a utilitarian view says nothing of the morality of political policies and individual behaviour within the state. But it is odd how much the sentiments of nineteenth century romanticism have recently infected pragmatic political thinking: the belief that systematised shared sentiments or definable common feelings are necessary. They are not. Have we forgotten in England Thomas Hobbes, Jeremy Bentham and John Stuart Mill; or in Scotland David Hume and Adam Smith? There is nothing ignoble or strange in between fifteen and twenty per cent of Catholics in Northern Ireland who vote for Sinn Fein but none the less say that they wish to retain the union. They probably prefer unity in their hearts, but in their heads as sensible family men and women they may first want to know what is in the unity package, how it might change their quality of life, life-chances or whatever. Some may simply favour *good government* and power-sharing where they are. They are not for 'unity above all else'. The same could be said of Scotland and Scottishness.

In the outburst of serious scholarly writing in Scotland on the three-hundredth anniversary of the Act or Treaty of Union, opinion has swung away far away from Robert Burns's eloquent, much quoted but silly 'bought and sold by English gold', to seeing that the votes in the last Scottish Parliament were predominantly swayed by calculation as to what was in Scotland's best interest: the opportunities of a relatively poor country getting inside the English imperial trade barriers; the seeming guarantee against a Stuart Catholic restoration and civil war; and all this in a hard-bargained agreement that left Scotland with its own ecclesiastical, legal, local government laws and establishment, the seeds of a famous educational system, and entry into the English now British imperial trade system.[6]

Much has been made of Linda Colley's *Britons: Forging the Nation 1707–1807*. She set out vividly and conclusively the evidence for the deliberate and well orchestrated Hanoverian campaign to merge Englishness and Scottishness into Britishness: henceforth neither Scotland nor England but Great Britain and later the United Kingdom. However, while it succeeded at the level of political institutions (more or less, for Scotland was largely left to govern itself, and the Argylls and the Dundas who managed government business would have been no use to Whitehall and Westminster had they lost their standing in Scotland by becoming Anglicised or only British), at a popular level Britishness does not seem to have caught on. I can find no folk songs in the last great age of folk songs that hail Britain or Britannia (*Rule Britannia* and *Hearts of Oak* were government sponsored theatre songs): it is ever 'old England' or 'auld Scotland'. Scottishness was the popular culture just as Englishness, albeit until recently in a lower register of explicitness, predominated over Britishness. Britishness was a common, primary identity in the white settler colonies of the nineteenth century. Today it is strong as a dual self-description of most immigrants: British Muslim, say, or 'British Asian'. 'English British' is not used in common parlance but could characterise those English who feel a wider attachment to 'Great Britain' or to the 'United Kingdom'. However, many English still confuse Britishness with Englishness. While very few Scots express their primary identity as British, a majority are 'Scottish British', with the emotional weight on the former but legal allegiance still on the latter. Consider that from the beginning of the British military need to recruit Scots in the American War of Independence and the Napoleonic Wars, the prohibitions following the 1745 rebellion, and right through the two World Wars to today, no one in Whitehall was foolish enough to try to integrate Scottish soldiers into British or English line regiments rather than specifically Scottish regiments. Even FIFA still recognises, perhaps surprisingly, four national football teams from the one United Kingdom rather than one British team. Finally, who ever talks about 'British novels' or poetry, rather than four distinctive national modes? Britishness political and legal institutions are real, but there are four recognisable cultures. Yes, each influenced by and interacting with the others, but in distinctive national ways.

Concluding a summary their series of opinion surveys on perceptions of national identity in England and Scotland, Frank Bechhover and David McCrone say: 'Englishness, Scottishness and Britishness may be more cultural than political.' Their figures show a relatively weak association between identity and party political support, suggesting that 'it is difficult to mobilise national identity in a straightforwardly political way', even for independence. 'The material we have presented thus suggests strongly that these matters are by no means as clear cut as the political rhetoric would have people believe, and that any or all of these arguments could backfire.'[7]

Mr Brown of London town

Britishness has figured greatly in recent speeches by Gordon Brown. Simon Lee, with deadly scholarly precision, found that in these speeches the only examples he gives of our glorious liberties etc. were *all* from English history![8] There was nary a mention of the Declaration of Arbroath or the signing of the Covenant, nor of course of Bannockburn, these as firm in Scots mythology as Magna Carta in English. Plainly Brown has either become Anglicised through long weeks in London reacting each morning to placate the Scotophobic London press; or his target was the almost equally mythical 'Middle England'; so an almost fatuous attempt to impress that he wore his obvious Scottishness very lightly: 'British Scottish' not 'Scottish British'.

Brown's banging on about Britishness is both mistaken and irrelevant.[9] In his 2007 speech to the TUC annual conference, according to the *Guardian*, he used the term 34 times and in his speech to the Labour party conference the BBC counted about 80 strikes—not all to define it, of course, but 'our British' attached to this and that almost promiscuously (including the unfortunate and notorious populist 'British jobs for British workers').

This is a profoundly mistaken rhetorical tactic if it is aimed at the SNP, for while nearly all Scots are strongly nationalistic a majority are not separatist (even a quarter of SNP voters favour the Union). There is nationalism and Nationalism. But the trouble is that Gordon Brown really does seem to believe that unity of the United Kingdom is in danger if there is not a strong and common sense of Britishness. Consider the mission statement or *sloaghan* he had drafted for a conference hosted by HM Treasury back in November 2005:

How 'British' do we feel? What do we mean by 'Britishness'? These questions are increasingly important in defining a shared purpose across all of our society. The strength of our communities, the way we understand diversity, the vigour of our public services and our commercial competitiveness all rest on a sense of what 'Britishness' is and how it sets shared goals.

Not only the global economy makes these assertions in the last sentence, in Bentham's phrase, nonsense on stilts. And must Britishness express a 'shared purpose' and shared 'goals'? Do states really have 'purposes' and 'goals'? Such teleological language is a pale rhetorical echo of the old destructive nationalism of central Europe and the Balkans. Is this really how states hold together, especially in the modern world, whether we like it or not, of a global economy and of all notions of national sovereignty needing to be so qualified as to be almost useless in understanding actual politics whether national and international? This idea of national purpose is what Goethe called 'a blue rose'. And the search for it has proved damaging already as well as frustrating. Both Thatcher and Blair openly spoke of restoring our sense of national importance, to put the 'Great' back into Great Britain. This was a hangover from the old days of Empire and the Second World War—which, of course, we won, albeit with a little help from the USA and the USSR. And this search has meant the American alliance, with—considering the Iraq war—too few questions asked or reservations made.

We do not need a heightened sense of Britishness and clear national purpose to hold us together. Perhaps we just need good government and social justice. National leaders should be careful when they invoke 'our common values'. Perhaps our main common value has been to respect, on the whole, the values of others. In July 2004 Brown gave the British Council Annual lecture on Britishness and invoked *values*, our British values:

The values and qualities I describe are of course to be found in many other cultures and countries. But when taken together, and as they shape the institutions of our country these values and qualities—being creative, adaptable and outward looking, our belief in liberty, duty and fair play—add up to a distinctive Britishness that has been manifest throughout our history, and shaped it.

'Liberty, duty and fair play'—well, some Scots are beginning to play cricket, of a kind, even if 'fair play' is still a wee bit marginal in the Old Firm encounters. I think Mr Brown plants both feet firmly in mid-air.

For citizenship education

Brown told readers of the *Daily Telegraph* that 'I am certain that the teaching of British history should be at the heart of the modern school curriculum, and the current review of the curriculum should root the teaching of citizenship more closely in British history.'[10] His first point is a good one. History was in both Key Stages 3 and 4 in the first national Baker curriculum for England, but Baker's successor Kenneth Clarke took it out of KS 4 *ipse dixit*; so there is no compulsory history after the age of 14. But Brown's second point was either a misunderstanding or a repudiation of the thrust of the citizenship curriculum. For that was based on the knowledge and skills needed to be active citizens, not just good citizens; what was enjoined was *learning* by discussion of real issues and by participation in school and community affairs, not just *teaching* from the front about institutions. David Blunkett backed that from the beginning, even under the eyes of a nervous and traditionalist Blair. We said (I was chair of the advisory group): 'We aim at no less than a change in the political culture of this country both nationally and locally: for people to think of themselves, willing able and equipped to have influence in public and with critical capacity to weigh evidence before speaking and acting.'[11] (I did not feel the need to tell the group that this was civic republican theory, but they liked the language and the aspirations.)

We wanted to leave teachers as much flexibility as possible to adjust to local conditions, so the prescriptions are both short and general. On Britishness and diversity the national curriculum simply said: 'Pupils should be taught about . . . the origins and implications of the diverse national, regional, religious and ethic identities in the United Kingdom and the need for mutual respect and understanding.' But that was written before the London bombings, and some ministers began to think that a revised citizenship curriculum could help greatly against recruitment to terrorist organisations. I thought that most unlikely. But Brown's *obiter dictum* on citizenship did lead to a review[12]— fortunately in the sensible hands of a retired headteacher of a successful multi-ethnic school, Sir Keith Ajegbo, assisted by Dr Dina Kiwan.[13] In 1998 there had seemed less need to elaborate on diversity than in 2007. But now they proposed adding a fourth leg to the citizenship stool, previously: *social and moral responsibility, community involvement* and *political literacy* (what you need to know to get some done usually working with others). This fourth leg was called *Identity and Diversity: Living Together in the UK*: that all pupils in England, would be taught about 'shared values and life in the UK. This will be informed by an understanding of contemporary issues and relevant historical context which gave rise to them.' But the emphasis in guidance papers is on *discussion* of what are or may be shared values and also *discussion* of what is Britishness. Few teachers would have any confidence about teaching *the* values of Britishness, whether from their common sense or from a book; so in practice discussion is in the spirit of the rest of the citizenship order. Early in the report they noted from their wide consultations: 'The term "British" means different things to different people. In addition, identities are typically constructed as multiple and plural. Throughout our consultations, concerns were expressed, however, about defining "Britishness", about the term's divisiveness and how it can be used to exclude others.' So one does not have to be Aughey, Crick, Oakeshott or Popper to believe that definitions do not settle arguments.

For new citizens

The 'Living in the United Kingdom' advisory group set up by David Blunkett in 2002 (which I chaired—fifty–fifty old Brits and new Brits) reported the following year as *The New and the Old*.[14] Its remit was to propose what 'sufficient' should mean following the Naturalisation, Immigration and Asylum Act 2002 that required United Kingdom residents seeking citizenship to show 'a sufficient knowledge of English, Welsh or Scottish-Gaelic' and 'a sufficient knowledge about life in the United Kingdom'. For once, officials were wise enough not to try themselves to tease out in statutory terms what was 'sufficient'. The Home Secretary accepted most of our recommendations, even if sufficient funding for fully effective implementation was not forthcoming from the Treasury.

Those who thought they had sufficient English[15] could take a machine readable test based on a handbook *Life in the United Kingdom: A Journey to Citizenship*,[16] and the others had to attend classes given by professional ESOL (English as a second language) teachers and make progress by one standard level. However, the media, led by the BBC, insisted in calling these two tests—as if they were one—'the Britishness test'. They were no such thing. The *Journey to Citizenship* (now in a second edition), written mainly for ESOL teachers and those preparing for machine readable test,[17] contains useful information about settling in and integration. There was and still is no element of testing for Britishness. Certainly there was a short history, 'The Making of the United Kingdom', at the beginning as background for teachers and others, but specifically not to be part either of the test or the ESOL programme of studies.

The BBC instantly called it 'the Britishness report', possibly in haste and error (trying as so often to anticipate a report, rather than waiting to read it or even the official press release); but the popular press followed suit either by false expectation or malign design. Many newspapers had asked their readers what they wanted in a test, with responses—the date of Magna Carta and Nelson's last words etc.—that would have failed nearly all applicants and most of the native population. I put the matter more cautiously in a Foreword to ABNI's 2005–06 annual report:

There were some [sic] press comments that the programme of studies was not historical and too little concerned with Britishness, but we were unanimous that people become British by learning about the laws, institutions and customs of our country, essential for settling in with mutual understanding.

For the report had taken the view that a sense of Britishness, however perceived, felt or defined, would grow on immigrants through time by their becoming citizens and living in a civic culture and being decently treated. On platforms I would say that we assumed the oldest and most basic contract: that immigrants give their loyalty to a country in return for the protection of its laws.

Well, we did feel the need—and pressure—to say something about Britishness in the report, even if it did not (and has not) carried forward into either the ESOL certification for naturalisation or the machine test. Here is exactly what we said, carefully (in both senses of that word):

Para. 2.6 Who are we British? For a long time the United Kingdom has been a multinational state composed of England, Northern Ireland, Scotland and Wales, and also a multicultural society. What do we mean by a multicultural society? We see a multicultural society as one made up of a diverse range of cultures and identities, and one that emphasises the need for a continuous process of mutual engagement and learning about each other with respect, understanding and tolerance . . . Such societies, under a framework of common civic values and common legal and political institutions, not only understand and tolerate diversities of identity but should also respect and take pride in them—Australia, Canada, India, South Africa and the United States of America are examples of multicultural societies.

And we pointed out that identities are never fixed in every respect, they are always changing, and that many people in the UK have a sense of dual identities. Then in para. 2.7 we took John Bull by the horns as we finessed the problem gently:

To be British seems to us to mean that we respect the laws, the elected parliamentary and legal structures, traditional values of mutual tolerance, and that we give our allegiance to the state (as commonly symbolised by the Crown) in return for its protection. To be British is to respect those over-arching specific institutions, values, beliefs and traditions that bind us all, the different nations and cultures, together in peace and in a legal order. For we are all subject to the laws of the land including

Human Rights and Equal Rights legislation, and so our diversities of practice must adhere to these legal frameworks.

Even the even more cautious revised version of the *Journey to Citizenship*: *Life in the United Kingdom* said: 'The UK has been a multinational and multi-cultural society for long time, without it being a threat to its British identity, or its English, Scottish, Welsh or Irish cultural and national identities.'

Interestingly, in the traditional oath still to be sworn at the new citizenship ceremonies ('I swear by Almighty God / do solemnly and sincerely affirm that, on becoming a British citizen, I will be faithful and bear true allegiance to Her Majesty Queen Elizabeth the Second, her heirs and successors according to law') and immediately afterwards a new Pledge ('I will give my loyalty to the United Kingdom and respect its rights and freedoms. I will uphold its democratic values. I will observe its laws faithfully and fulfil my duties and obligations as a British citizen'),[18] the only mention of 'British' is in that purely legal context—in which even Mr Alex Salmond is undoubtedly a British citizen, at least for a guid while yet. Any mention of 'Britishness' as a traditional bundle of values, beliefs and traditions was realised as provocative to much Scottish and Welsh sentiment, and very difficult to define; it could run the risk (I naughtily suggested) of being overwhelmed by undiluted enthusiasm in Unionist Northern Ireland. All this was, I think, a wiser approach to 'Britishness' than some ministerial speeches and many editorials.

A note on Scottishness

Paradoxically, to consider 'Scottishness' might set to rest some fears that without an explicit strong Britishness the United Kingdom implodes. As many surveys show, the awareness and sense of being Scottish has been stronger than that of being British or English, though now the salience of Englishness in England is growing, as Aughey has charted and flags of St George testify. Scottish nationalism is strong and almost universal. But we need to distinguish carefully nationalism and Nationalism. The one is a strong national consciousness, just as Englishman may have it without wishing to break up the United Kingdom; but Nationalism implies separatism, even though now Alex Salmond's New SNP speaks of 'independence in Europe'; and he reassuringly says that 'independence is a political not a social matter'.[19] And certainly the SNP has been remarkably successful in attracting immigrant votes and even members. The old ethnic party of twenty-five years ago now sees itself as a multicultural national party professing a common civic culture. 'Muslim Pakistanis identify strongly with Scotland rather than Britain—and do regardless of whether they were born in Scotland or not.'[20] But surveys suggest that only three out of ten Scots support independence (a figure that has altered very little since before devolution) and that in the 2007 elections to the Parliament of Scotland only 63 per cent of those who intended to vote SNP supported its core policy of independence.[21] There were other reasons to vote SNP. And Bechhofer and McCrone's surveys[22] also show conclusively that intensity of national feeling and even dislike of 'Britishness' does not, for a majority, lead to a desire for independence. Britishness hardly enters into it.

Presumably, to end where I began, a tacit but strong pragmatic loyalty to the United Kingdom based on habit, tradition and interest, underlies strong feelings of national identity and even immigrant identities. We don't need a Britishness campaign to ensure holding the United Kingdom together, just good government. If there are changes they will come through political events, misgovernment and economic mistakes, not through heightened Scottishness or Englishness.[23]

Notes

1 Arthur Aughey, *The Politics of Englishness*, Manchester, Manchester University Press, p. 6.
2 Aughey, ibid., p. 6, quoting Bernard Crick, 'The English and the British' in Crick, ed., *National Identities: The Constitution of the United Kingdom*, Oxford, Blackwell and The Political Quarterly, 1991.
3 Bernard Crick , 'The world of Michael Oakeshott', in his essays *Political Theory and Practice*, London, Allen Lane / The Penguin Press, 1972, pp. 120–34.
4 Timothy Garton Ash, 'Is Britain European?', *International Affairs*, vol. 77, no. 1, pp. 1–13.
5 Bhikhu Parekh, *A New Politics of Identity*, Basingstoke, Palgrave Macmillan, 2008, p. 284.
6 See T. M. Devine, 'Three hundred years of the Anglo-Scottish union', in Devine, ed., *Scotland and the Union: 1707–2007*, Edinburgh, Edinburgh University Press, 2008, pp. 1–19; also Christopher A. Whatley, 'The making of the union of 1707: history with a history', in Devine, *Scotland and the* Union, ibid., pp. 23–38.
7 Frank Bechhofer and David McCrone, 'Being British: A crisis of identity?', *The Political Quarterly*, vol. 78, no. 2, pp. 251–60.
8 Simon Lee, 'Gordon Brown and the "British Way",' *Political Quarterly*, vol. 77, no. 3, pp. 369–78.
9 The paragraphs to the end of this section are taken from my Mackintosh Memorial lecture, 'The Four Nations: interrelations', as printed in *The Political Quarterly*, vol. 79, no. 1, 2008, pp. 71–9.
10 Gordon Brown 'We need a United Kingdom', *Daily Telegraph*, 13 January 2007, p. 23.
11 *Education for Citizenship and the Teaching of Democracy in Schools*, London, QCA, 1998, para. 1.5, p. 7.
12 *Curriculum Review: Diversity and Citizenship* (DES, 2007).
13 Sir Keith Ajegbo was Headteacher of Deptford Green School, a multi-ethnic school with an outstanding reputation for citizenship education. Dina Kiwan is lecturer in citizenship education at Birkbeck College. Previously she was seconded to the Home Office as the Head of Secretariat to the Advisory Board for Naturalisation and Integration (ABNI), on the implementation of the recommendations of the 'Life in the UK' advisory group.

14 Home Office, 2003.
15 Technically ESOL Entry level 3, which is the ability to talk comprehensibly on an unexpected subject (that is, not just one's trade or job) and to read instructions. Writing is not tested.
16 Produced by ABNI in cooperation with the Citizenship Foundation, published by The Stationery Office.
17 *Journey to Citizenship* is now, after I left ABNI, somewhat watered down from the more realistic tone of 'how it is' rather than 'how we'd like you to think it is'. See Patricia White, 'Immigrants into Citizens', *The Political Quarterly*, vol. 79, no. 2, 2008, pp. 221–31.
18 Brought in, I was told, when the Queen and Tony Blair refused to alter the Oath to mention such things. Some existing citizens object to others taking the Oath at all, by no means all writers in the *Guardian;* but surveys have shown that immigrants like the feeling of being associated with the Queen as head of state.
19 Quoted in Crick, 'The Four Nations', *ibid*.
20 W. L. Miller, 'The death of Unionism', in Devine, ed., *Scotland and the Union*, pp. 186–9. But his title implies the death of an ideology not of the Union.
21 Devine, *op. cit*, p. 18.
22 Ibid., pp. 258–60.

Churchill's Dover Speech (1946)

PETER HENNESSY

FOR A child of the early postwar (I was born in 1947) what Britain stood for was powerfully felt but rarely spoken of for pretty well the first thirty years of my life. The concept of 'national identity' was a still uninvented stranger to 'my age'. But we knew what it was—a kaleidoscopic mixture of particles, some vivid and recent like the afterglow of the great, shared collective experience of the Second World War in which the German bombers, the V1s and V2s had brought the front line to our very streets.

Other granules resulted from the extension of wartime solidarity in the shape, for example, of the Health Service, the nearest thing to institutionalised altruism the country had seen and a shining talisman of national intent. In a funny (in both senses) way, the Ealing Comedies of the late forties and early fifties played into the sense of who we were with their mild, understated, self-ironic sending-up of the Brits, their class structures and their peculiar customs and habits.

Then there was Winston Churchill and his singular word-power—the rhetoric, between 1940 and 1945, of nationhood under fire. That, too, glowed on long after VE Day. And one of its finest early postwar manifestations I only came across recently thanks to my friend, Sir Peter Ramsbotham, the former diplomat, who had a copy of Churchill's Dover Speech of 14 August 1946 in his personal archive.

Churchill delivered it as Lord Warden of the Cinque Ports. It should be remembered, when you read it, that he was both Prime Minister *and* Minister of Defence during the Second World War. It is for individual readers to make of it what they will. But, for me, its powerful echo of John of Gaunt's famous speech ('This precious stone set in the silver sea / Which serves it in the office of a wall / Or as a moat defensive to a house / Against the envy of less happier lands') in Shakespeare's *King Richard the Second* does not sound contrived. Nor does its celebration of our 'tolerances and decencies' and what we regarded then as our distinctive way of life.

Thinking back to my early years, I would have reckoned Churchill's words to be an exceptionally vividly crafted encapsulation of what we Brits felt we were and really were. He was, albeit in incomparable language, simply analysing the shared compost that had made us and plucking out of the air the assumptions we daily breathed. The idea of a British government seeking to draft a formal statement of national values would, I suspect, have struck him as risible, redundant and absurd. To some of us children of the early postwar it certainly does.

© 2009 The Author. Editorial organisation © 2009 The Political Quarterly Publishing Co. Ltd
Published by Blackwell Publishing Ltd, 9600 Garsington Road, Oxford OX4 2DQ, UK and 350 Main Street, Malden, MA 02148, USA 159

Herewith the text as he shaped it, and abbreviated it, in his idiosyncratic way on the page. Let us, as it were, lean over the white cliffs of Dover 62 years ago and eavesdrop on the grand old man.

Original speaking notes of speech made by Winston Churchill in Dover, 14 August 1946

Five years hv passed
   since I accepted the office
      of Lord Warden
         at His Majesty's gracious desire,

and I hv felt it a high honour
   to take my place
      in the line of eminent men
         who hv preceded me.

In time of peace
   the duties of the Lord Warden
      are mainly social.

However, it fell to my lot
   to have to guard the Cinque ports
      at a time
         when they were all in the front line

when,
   as we now know,

two and possibly three German armies
   were gathered along the opposite coasts

which, on a fair day,
   we can so plainly see
      fm Dover castle.

The invasion menace lay upon us
   as it had not done
      since Napoleon waited at Boulogne

before his plans were blown to pieces
   by the Battle of Trafalgar.

I took a keen interest in my duties
   wh were by no means purely ceremonial.

They did not in any way clash
   w the tasks of the Minister of Defence.

In fact,
    it was probably a convenience
        tt the two offices
            were blended into one.

In this way
    no dispute ever arose
        betw the Lord Warden of the Cinque Ports
            and the Minister of Defence,

and even if any unfortunate division of interest
    or opinion
        had occurred,

we shd hv appealed together
    to the P.M.,

who was vy much on our side.

I cd always feel sure
    he wd see us through.

I had gt confidence in him
    and in the National Govt
        over wh he presided.

In fact,
    I may say tt in my long political experience
        I hv never known a Govt
            wh commanded
                my whole-hearted allegiance and support
                    to anything like the same degree

either before or since.

=

Nowadays much is lapped in controversy
    and many voices are heard.

Some say this and some say that.

But one this is indisputable—

    The Cinque Ports remain unconquered
        and hv a right to claim
            tt they are unconquerable.

We can still say
    tt nearly a thousand years hv passed
        since a foreign invader
            has set his foot upon English soil.

In the Wars of the Roses
  Red and White claimants
    several times returned with foreign aid
      at the head of their factions.

King William III
  was invited fm Holland
    by the majority of the British nation.

but since 1066—

and all that—

we hv never seen
  the camp fires of an invader
    fm a hostile and foreign power
      burning in our island home.

We hv thus bn able,
  in a manner not open to Continental states

to develop
  our own English and British way of life.

We hv a certain standard
  of tolerances and decencies
    wh are treasured by us
      and envied or admired by others.

In Party politics
  The rule is 'tit for tat'

For the rest
  our plan is freedom and fair play.

When English people cannot forgive
  they usually forget.

Long immunity
  fm foreign ravage or oppression
    has made us what we are,

w all our weaknesses and peculiarities
  and all our reserves
    of virtue and strength

It is here on the cliffs of Dover
  tt Britannia shd be seated.

  'The nations not so blest as thee
  Must in their turn to tyrants fall
  While thou shalt flourish great and free.
  The dread'—

Or perhaps we may say the hope—
   'and envy of them all'.

We trust indeed
   tt prophecy will continue to be made good
     in the future
       as it has bn in the past.

=

In these recent war years
   hard times fell upon the Cinque Ports.

Dover lay

Not only under the bombs and the rockets
   of the enemy,

but under his cannon-fire.

Our big guns were ready first.

Under peace conditions
   the War Office take about three years
     to mount a 14 or 15-inch gun.

Ours were ready in ten weeks.

I often brought foreign statesmen,
   envoys and generals

   to visit these batteries
     and peer across the Channel
       at what was then Hitler's Germany
         but now is once again
           our beloved France.

They all went away w the feeling
   'thus far and no farther'.

And so it turned out in the end.

=

I remember being in Margate
   when a bomb hit a small restaurant,

   and being poignantly affected
     by seeing all the crockery
       and stock-in-trade
         of these poor people
           smashed to bits.

When I got back to London
   I said to the Chanc. of the Exch.,

my valued friend, Sir Kingsley Wood,

'All these losses much be shared equally.

Let all parts of the country contribute
    by insurance or taxes
        to pay compensation for war damage.'

Fm this came
    the gt War Damage Compensation scheme

by wh enormous funds hv bn gathered
    and will, I suppose, be paid out
        to those entitled to the relief
            in what our ever-growing bureaucracy
                will describe as 'due course'.

I remember also, near St Margaret's Bay,
    one day in July, 1940,
        meeting on one of the beaches
            a Brigadier who asked me my advice.

On his front he had two anti-tank guns,

    but they had only seven rounds of ammunition apiece

    instead of hundreds.

Only seven shots to fire!

The Brigadier asked me
    whether it would be right
        to fire one round in practice,

        to let the men understand
            the weapon they handled—

        to let them see it shot off.

That gives one an idea
    of the plight we were in.

This was the kind of question
    that had to be answered
        in those grim days.

In this case the answer was obvious.

Not a round cd be spared fm the crisis.

We must make up for past neglects
    by getting as close as possible
        to the hostile tank.

After all, that is the traditional British method.

We make up by sacrifices and sufferings
  for lack of foresight
    and continuity of policy.

    and then,
      when by God's mercy,
        we have come safely through,

    it has too often been our practice
      to cast it all away and start again.

=

. . .

We must not presume too much
  upon our Fortune.

The flotillas of the Navy
  guarded the narrow seas w ceaseless vigilance.

The R.A.F guarded the flotillas
  And the Kent and Sussex airfields
    w superb ascendancy.

The Battle of Britain was won,
  and w it our right to live.

The strip of salt water,

  on wh we hv looked today,

  reinforced this time
    by the command of the air above it,

  saved us once again.

It saved much more.

During the year
  when we stood alone,

  it saved the freedom of the world.

It gave our gt allies
  time to prepare.

It gave Hitler the time to make his fatal mistake.

Here,
  along these harassed and bombarded coasts,

  you bore,
    I will not say the brunt,
      but a full share of the brunt

of the gigantic world struggle which
  in the end
    was carried to the unconditional surrender

    of all our foes.

We hv moved into a new age.

Secrets hv bn wrested fm Nature
  wh ought to awe and prevent
    the quarrels of mankind,

  even if they cannot assuage
    their rivalries and suspicions.

We can no longer guarantee
  tt this strip of salt water
    will once again save the liberties of Europe,

    As it did against Napoleon,

    or tt it will save the freedom of mankind,
    as it did against Hitler.

Far larger forces must be made to play their part.

Far wider combinations
  than the defence of the English Channel
    will be needed.

But one thing at least we will promise.

In our own place
  and in our own way

  this glorious Foreland of England,

  the shrine of its Christianity,
    the cradle of its institutions,
      the bulwark of its defence,

  will still do its best for all.

And we will still strive forward,

  weary, it may be, but undaunted,

  towards that fair future
    for all the men in all the lands,

  wh we thought we had won
    but of wh we will never despair.

Index

ABNI (Advisory Board on
   Naturalisation and Integration)
   154–6, 157, 158
Act of Union 1707 1, 21, 34, 43, 57,
   138–9, 150
Afghanistan 108–9
Africa 12
Ajegbo, Keith 154, 157
Alexander, Douglas 91, 98, 99
Alexander, Wendy 102, 104
Alfred, King 57
All-Wales Convention 120
Anderson, Benedict 25, 30, 45, 76
A New Politics of Identity 40
Anglosphere 60–1
Angus, Ian 20
Arnold, Matthew 11, 12
Ascherson, Neal 85
Atlanticism 96
Aughey, Arthur 147, 148, 149, 154, 156,
   157
Australia 15, 46, 60, 67, 68–70, 117, 155

Baker, Lord 30
Baldwin, Stanley 11
Ballard, J. G. 74
Barker, Ernest 55, 138, 139, 147
Barker, Rodney 142, 147
Barnes, Julian 128, 134
Barnett, Anthony 99
Barnett formula 107, 118
Barrett Brown, Michael 88, 98
BBC 25, 63, 64, 76, 78–85, 90, 104,
   113–14, 152, 154, 155
   classical music 81–2
   Coast 25
   distribution of resources 79–80
   news gathering 79–80
   Radio Four 82
   Reith lectures 83
   Whatever Happened to the Likely Lads?
   75
   World Service 82
Bechhofer, F. 51, 52, 147, 151, 157

Beiner, Ronald 52
Belgium 117
Benn, Tony 86, 94, 97, 99
Bentham, Jeremy 150, 152
Bevin, Ernest 13, 16
Bill of Rights 43, 50, 108–10
Birtwhistle, Harrison 81
Blackstone, William 55, 57
Blair, Tony 12, 18, 35–6, 86, 94, 98, 104,
   108, 152, 153
Blake, William 13
Blondel, Jean 137, 146
Blunkett, David 125, 134, 153, 154
Bogdanor, Vernon 135
Bourassa, Henri 50
Bower, Tom 87, 98
Bragg, Billy 126, 134
British Council 90, 104, 153
British Election Studies 48
British Empire 2, 13–14, 15, 22, 28, 36,
   63, 95, 125, 126–7
British Library 27, 30
Britishness
   common culture 36–7, 45–50
   concepts of 32–3, 41–3, 62–5
   exceptionalism 11–14, 75, 77–8
   identity 33–4, 36–7, 42–3, 57
   institutions 104
   national debate 10–11, 14–20
   national identity 47–50, 76–84
   opinion surveys 62–71
   pride in 65–7
   re-branding 76–7
   role of the state 44–5
   self-definition 34–6
   shared interests 105
British Social Attitudes Surveys 18, 48,
   52, 112–13, 114
Britons: Forging the Nation 1707–1837
   7–8, 21, 29, 31, 40, 52, 58, 76, 85,
   135, 150–1
Brown, Alice 52
Brown, Gordon 8, 10, 14, 19, 23, 41, 58,
   86–100, 125